Criminal Justice Policy and Planning

Criminal Justice Policy and Planning

4th edition

Wayne N. Welsh

Philip W. Harris

AMSTERDAM • BOSTON • HEIDELBERG • LONDON
NEW YORK • OXFORD • PARIS • SAN DIEGO
SAN FRANCISCO • SINGAPORE • SYDNEY • TOKYO

Anderson Publishing is an imprint of Elsevier

ELSEVIER

Acquiring Editor: Pam Chester
Development Editor: Ellen S. Boyne
Project Manager: André Cuello
Designer: Joanne Blank

Anderson Publishing is an imprint of Elsevier
225 Wyman Street, Waltham, MA 02451, USA

Notices
Knowledge and best practice in this field are constantly changing. As new research and experience broaden our understanding, changes in research methods or professional practices may become necessary. Practitioners and researchers must always rely on their own experience and knowledge in evaluating and using any information or methods described herein. In using such information or methods they should be mindful of their own safety and the safety of others, including parties for whom they have a professional responsibility.

To the fullest extent of the law, neither the Publisher nor the authors, contributors, or editors assume any liability for any injury and/or damage to persons or property as a matter of products liability, negligence or otherwise, or from any use or operation of any methods, products, instructions, or ideas contained in the material herein.

Library of Congress Cataloging-in-Publication Data
Application submitted

British Library Cataloguing-in-Publication Data
A catalogue record for this book is available from the British Library.

ISBN: 978-1-4377-3500-0

Printed in the United States of America
12 13 14 15   10 9 8 7 6 5 4 3 2 1

Working together to grow
libraries in developing countries

www.elsevier.com | www.bookaid.org | www.sabre.org

ELSEVIER   BOOK AID International   Sabre Foundation

For information on all Anderson publications visit our website at
www.andersonpublishing.com

Contents

Preface

The purpose of this book, broadly speaking, is to acquaint students, practitioners, and policy-makers with scientific techniques for analyzing criminal justice problems and developing solutions. We not only offer guidelines for developing new programs and policies, but we also analyze existing criminal justice interventions, asking to what degree such efforts were guided by logic and planning, rather than partisan politics and untested hunches.

Change, some of which is planned, touches every aspect of our lives. In criminal justice, new interventions aimed at reducing crime constantly seem to spring up. Some notable interventions of recent years have included mandatory sentencing, "three strikes and you're out" laws (aimed at incapacitating repeat felony offenders), the Brady Act (requiring waiting periods and background checks for prospective firearm purchasers), drug courts, boot camps, "Weed and Seed," prisoner reentry initiatives, and others. But to what degree are such interventions guided by a rational planning approach? What problems do they attempt to address, and what causal theory about crime do they assume? What difficulties could have been anticipated (e.g., a shortage of prison space; criticisms that programs or policies are inconsistent, unfair, or even unconstitutional)?

Our point is this: what we call "planned change" encompasses a multitude of criminal justice policies, programs, and projects that are developed, implemented, revised, torn down, and recreated every year. We are interested in how such policies, programs, and projects are currently developed and in how they should be developed. Poor planning and faulty problem analysis, we argue, are the primary reasons that so many criminal justice interventions fail to live up to their promises.

Consider the example of three-strikes laws. Evidence suggests that the laws are unfair, expensive, and ineffective. As Dickey (1997) argued, "When the law's hidden costs and unintended consequences are assessed, its simple goal is obscured by effects that are alarming in their scope" (p. 62). We illustrate some of the pitfalls of poor planning in Case Study I–1, using the seven-stage framework that guides our work (see "Introduction").

Where the costs of unsuccessful intervention are high, in terms of human suffering as well as finances, we can and must do better in devising solutions to criminal justice problems. One should be skeptical, even critical, but not cynical. In spite of the pitfalls of poor planning, it is possible to address and reduce even the most pressing problems in criminal justice. We invite students, practitioners, politicians, academics, and planners to subject their own assumptions, decisions, and plans to scrutiny.

In this newly revised fourth edition, we discuss both successful and unsuccessful programs and policies. We include new case studies and examples that examine recently identified problems (e.g., illegal immigration, terrorism) and innovations (e.g., a model domestic violence law enforcement policy, a model mentoring program, a DNA backlog reduction program, hot spots policing, Operation Ceasefire, restorative justice, and specialized problem-solving courts). We have also updated all research findings and statistics relevant to numerous other programs and policies (e.g., Disproportionate Minority Confinement, three-strikes laws, the Brady Act). Highlights of changes to the fourth edition include the following:

- Updated research and statistics on diverse criminal justice problems (school violence, domestic violence, AIDS, drug abuse) and interventions;
- Updated examples and case studies, including more currently relevant topics, an enhanced policy focus, and coverage of all branches of the criminal justice system;
- Five new case studies: Case Study 1–2: *Idaho SAC Helps State Police Solve Personnel Allocation Problem*; Case Study 3–2: *Model Domestic Violence Law Enforcement Policy*; Case Study 4–1: *A Sample Grant Application to the National Institute of Justice (DNA Backlog Reduction Program)*; Case Study 5–2: *Hot Spots Policing— Implementation Issues*; and Case Study 6–1: *Evaluation of an Illegal Immigration Enforcement Policy.*
- Updated material on the Bureau of Justice Assistance (BJA) monitoring requirements for grantees and the Office of Justice Programs (OJP) Standards for Financial Management Systems;
- Updated discussion of evidence-based programs, logic modeling, and propensity score analysis;
- New citations and Web links to relevant articles and reports to illustrate key concepts;
- New student exercises and assignments to provide more in-depth examinations of case studies and concepts;
- Newly developed online resources for students, including links to articles, reports, and videos; detailed PowerPoint chapter outlines; and additional case studies;
- Newly developed online resources for instructors, including tests, quizzes, exercises, discussion topics, assignments, group projects, answer keys, and PowerPoint presentations for class lectures.

Two other overarching changes deserve mention. First, the introductory chapter is no longer numbered as a chapter. Instead, each of the seven chapters has been renumbered to reflect the corresponding stage in the seven-stage model of planned change (e.g., Chapter 1 now covers Stage 1: Analyzing the Problem; Chapter 2 covers Stage 2: Setting Goals and Objectives; and so on). This change will make it easier for instructors (and students!) to match up each stage with its corresponding chapter. Second, we continue to make a clear distinction between two different uses of the seven-stage model: (1) for developing new interventions and (2) for analyzing existing interventions. Two tables in the Introduction (Tables I-1 and I-2) summarize major steps of the seven-stage model separately for each of these two purposes. This distinction is maintained throughout the book, noting differences between the two uses where appropriate.

As authors, the challenge we face is to present and communicate the methods of analyzing criminal justice problems and interventions in a clear, concise manner. We have found no existing book adequate to the task. Some are simply far too jargonistic or technical; others are idiosyncratic, abstract, or unfocused. And to make life even more difficult for us, none presents a systematic model for either analyzing or planning criminal justice programs and policies. This book attempts to meet these challenges. No doubt, even in its fourth edition, it is still less than perfect, and we welcome all comments and suggestions for improvements. Could advocates of planned change do any less?

Reference

Dickey, Walter J. (1997). "The Impact of 'Three Strikes and You're Out' Laws: What Have We Learned?" *Corrections Management Quarterly, 1*, 55–64.

Acknowledgments

The authors are grateful to their families for all their love and patience, especially during those times when we sequestered ourselves to do the research and writing for this book. Thank you, Dea, Ilana, and Ellen.

We appreciate the thoughtful guidance provided by Michael Braswell, Acquisitions Editor for Anderson Publishing, and the helpful comments of Victor Kappeler at Eastern Kentucky University during the developmental stages of the first edition. Comments by Professor Frank Cullen at the University of Cincinnati on an earlier version were most valuable in shaping this work and bringing it to fruition. We also thank Ellen Boyne at Anderson Publishing for her careful and thoughtful editing on all four editions. Of course, any errors or omissions are the responsibility of the authors alone.

We express great appreciation to the many students who have served as "clients" for this book in our university classes and who gave us extremely helpful comments and feedback each step along the way.

Last but not least, we thank the many fine men and women in criminal justice agencies; community programs; the private sector; and local, state, and federal government whom we have had the good fortune to work with and learn from in our criminal justice research.

About the Authors

Wayne N. Welsh is a Professor of Criminal Justice at Temple University. He received his Ph.D. in Social Ecology from the University of California, Irvine, in 1990 and his M.A. in Applied Social Psychology from the University of Saskatchewan (Canada) in 1986. Undergraduate courses he has taught include Introduction to Criminal Justice; Violence, Crime, and Justice; Environmental Criminology; and Planned Change in Criminal Justice. Graduate courses include Violence, Crime, and Aggression; Criminal Justice Organizations: Structure, Process, and Change; and Rehabilitation, Re-entry, and Recidivism. He is the author of *Counties in Court: Jail Overcrowding and Court-Ordered Reform* (1995) and *Criminal Violence: Patterns, Causes and Prevention*, 3rd ed., with Marc Riedel (2011). He has published more than 50 peer-reviewed articles in journals such as *Criminal Justice and Behavior, Drug and Alcohol Dependence, Crime & Delinquency,* and *Criminology*. Welsh served as Deputy Editor of *The Prison Journal* from 1993 to 2000. He has conducted research in two broad areas: (1) applications of organizational theory to criminal justice and examinations of organizational change and (2) theories of violent behavior and intervention/prevention programs. Welsh has been Principal Investigator or Co-Principal Investigator on numerous federal and state-funded research grants. He is currently working on a project called CJDATS (Criminal Justice Drug Abuse Treatment Systems), which is a national collaborative research project funded by the National Institute on Drug Abuse (NIDA), which is part of the National Institutes of Health. It includes ten Research Centers (including Temple University in Philadelphia) and a Coordinating Center (CC). Key research questions address the need to develop a better understanding of the organizational and systems issues that can facilitate or hinder implementation of effective drug treatment and other services. Based upon a collaborative research partnership between the Pennsylvania Department of Corrections (DOC) and Temple University that began in 1998, a series of projects examined critical interactions between inmate characteristics, treatment program characteristics, responsiveness to treatment, and postrelease outcomes such as recidivism, relapse, and employment. This ongoing research relationship has increased the capacity of both agencies to produce useful knowledge. Other research projects have included a school violence study titled "Building a Culture and Climate of Safety in Public Schools: School-Based Management and Violence Reduction in Philadelphia," and a 3-year study funded by the Pennsylvania Commission on Crime and Delinquency, "Reducing Over-Representation of Minorities in the Juvenile Justice System."

Phil Harris is an Associate Professor in the Department of Criminal Justice at Temple University. He received his Ph.D. in Criminal Justice from the State University of New York at Albany in 1979. His teaching and research have focused primarily on the areas of juvenile justice, juvenile correctional strategies, and organizational and system development. He serves as the strategic planning adviser to the Council of Juvenile Correctional Administrators, which he cofounded in 1994, and is a member of Pennsylvania's Juvenile Justice and Delinquency Prevention Committee. Prior to arriving at Temple in 1980, he served as a professional services administrator for a private juvenile correctional agency in Montreal, where he was responsible for assessment services and staff training. Beginning in 1992, he and Peter

Jones designed and implemented an outcome-based information system, ProDES, that for 10 years provided a continuous flow of outcome information on all programs that receive youths from Philadelphia's Family Court. Output from this system has included multiple evaluations of more than 90 programs. In 1999, ProDES was a finalist in the Innovations in American Government competition sponsored by Harvard University and the Ford Foundation. His publications include articles such as "The role of crime specialization, neighborhood social disorganization, and spatial contagion in determinants of juvenile recidivism" in the *Journal of Adolescence* (2011); "Effects of neighborhood context on juvenile recidivism rates: Does recidivism offense type matter?" in *Journal of Youth and Adolescence* (2010); "Identifying chronic juvenile offenders," in *Justice Quarterly* (2001); "A century of juvenile justice," in NIJ's volume, *The Nature of Crime: Continuity and Change* (2000); "Substance abuse and race in a delinquent population" in *The System in Black and White,* edited by Michael W. Markowitz and Delores D. Jones-Brown (2000); and "Differentiating delinquent youths for program planning and evaluation" in *Criminal Justice and Behavior* (1999). He recently completed an evaluation of a juvenile sex offender program and is currently working on a book on matching delinquent youths to programs. Harris is the 2001 recipient of the Alva and Gunnar Myrdal Government Service Award, given annually by the American Evaluation Association, and the 2005 Marguerite Warren and Ted Palmer Award from the Sentencing and Corrections Division of the American Society of Criminology.

Introduction

CHAPTER OUTLINE

- **Examples of criminal justice interventions** include gun control and regulation (e.g., the Brady Act), "three strikes and you're out" laws, juvenile waiver laws, and specialized problem-solving courts (community courts, drug courts, and domestic violence courts).

- **Planned change versus unplanned change.** Any project, program, or policy, new or revised, is intended to produce a change in some specific problem. It is limited in scope, it is aimed at improving quality of life for its clients, it includes a role for consumers, and a "change agent" guides it.

- **There are three approaches to planned change.** They include policy, program, and project.

- **The need for planned change has been sharpened by three trends.** They are: declining resources, accountability, and expansion of knowledge and technology.

- **The perils of planned change.** Any change to existing procedures and conditions is likely to be resisted. Two broad approaches to change should be carefully considered: *collaborative strategies* versus *conflict strategies*.

- **A seven-stage model for planned change** specifies the sequence of steps required for analyzing a problem, determining its causes, and planning and carrying out some intervention. The seven stages consist of (1) analyzing the problem, (2) setting goals and objectives, (3) designing the program or policy, (4) developing an action plan, (5) developing a plan for monitoring program/policy implementation, (6) developing a plan for evaluating outcomes, and (7) reassessment and review.

There are many different types of "programs," "policies," and "projects" in criminal justice: different interventions within government (federal, state, and local), community, and private agencies. In fact, one could argue that these many interventions comprise a majority of what criminal justice really is all about: a series of constant innovations and experiments attempting to discover what works to meet the goals of criminal justice (e.g., to reduce criminal behavior, to protect public safety). These numerous innovations attempt to change *individuals, groups, organizations, communities*, and even *societal and cultural norms* in some cases, to improve the achievement of criminal justice goals. Criminal justice, then, is much more than just the daily business of police, courts, and corrections that forms the grist for many university courses and professional training in criminal justice. Here are just a few examples of criminal justice interventions (Figure I–1).

The problem is that many criminal justice interventions fall short of their goals because of poor planning, poor implementation, and poor evaluation. It is fair to say that we have not yet discovered "what works" to reduce crime. What we truly need, though, is not more programs, or new programs, *per se*; we need *better* programs. We need a better understanding of planned change, and the methods and processes through which policies and programs are developed, implemented, evaluated, and managed, in order to improve

- Prisoner reentry policies and programs, including the Second Chance Act (P.L. 110-199), prison-based drug treatment and community aftercare, vocational and basic education, post-release employment assistance, and reintegration assistance.
- Specialized problem-solving courts (community courts that seek to improve the quality of life in high-crime neighborhoods, drug courts that combine criminal sanctions with treatment for addicted offenders, and domestic violence courts that emphasize victim safety and defendant accountability).
- Operation "Weed and Seed" (a federal initiative that "weeds" illegal drug sales out of communities through intensive law enforcement and prosecution efforts, then "seeds" the communities with protective, economic, and social resources).
- Mandatory arrest policies for domestic violence offenders.
- "Three strikes and you're out" laws that aim to put away repeat offenders for long periods of time.
- Juvenile waiver laws (serious juvenile offenses may be transferred to adult courts, or automatically tried as adult offenses).
- Megan's Law (federal law mandating that every state develop a procedure for notifying residents of the location of convicted sex offenders residing in their communities). Convicted sex offenders are required to notify authorities of their current address at all times, and states are required to make this information available to the public.

FIGURE I–1 Examples of criminal justice interventions.

the effectiveness of such interventions. Such change is ubiquitous in governmental, community, private, and nonprofit agencies. This book provides a systematic framework for analyzing and improving existing interventions, but also for planning new ones so as to maximize chances of success.

Planned Change versus Unplanned Change

Planned change involves planning. Planning means that some person or group of persons has explicitly thought about a problem and developed a specific solution. However, solutions (interventions) vary considerably in the degree to which thorough, explicit, or deliberate planning has been undertaken (Figure I–2).

■ ■ Planned Change ■

Any project, program, or policy, new or revised, intended to produce a change in some specific problem. The intended change may occur within individuals, groups, organizations, systems of organizations, communities, cities, regions, states, or, much more rarely, within entire cultures or societies.

As the examples and case studies in this book will illustrate, interventions are often poorly planned or even unplanned. *Unplanned change* means that little explicit or proactive planning has been undertaken at all. Instead, unplanned change often comes about as a reaction to a crisis, a dramatic incident publicized by the media, a political opportunity, a lawsuit against criminal justice officials, or an untested set of assumptions about a specific

1. A nonprofit organization working with juveniles in poor neighborhoods applies for state funding after reading a solicitation for proposals to develop after-school delinquency prevention programs.
2. Following several tragic school shootings during the 1990s, hundreds of school districts across the United States announced that they were revising their disciplinary policies and installing tougher security measures.
3. A parolee shoots and kills a police officer after a routine traffic stop. Intensive scrutiny and revision of state parole policies immediately follows.
4. A local police agency adopts a crime-mapping approach to detect crime "hot spots" and reallocates police resources to address specific problems in specific neighborhoods.
5. Following the 9/11 terrorist attacks, the U.S. Federal Government passed the USA PATRIOT (Uniting and Strengthening America by Providing Appropriate Tools to Intercept and Obstruct Terrorism) Act, P.L. 107-56, on October 26, 2001, granting federal officials widespread investigative powers into suspected terrorist activities. Provisions included expanded electronic surveillance capabilities, nationwide search warrants issued in one jurisdiction but valid in any jurisdiction where evidence may be found, seizure of suspected terrorist assets, and detention of noncitizens for at least seven days without filing any charges.

How much planning do you think guided the development of these interventions?

1	2	3
Completely Unplanned	Some Planning	Very Thorough Planning

FIGURE I–2 The birth of a program or policy: Examples.

problem. Unplanned change, even if it is motivated by sincere intentions, is more likely to be ineffective *and* wasteful of valuable public resources.

Planned change improves the likelihood of successful intervention, but it cannot guarantee it. Even when planned change is successful, it may not be permanent. Planned change is *dynamic,* like the problems it seeks to address. People who play critical leadership roles come and go over time, initial shock about a problem and enthusiasm about an intervention abates, the political environment changes, other problems demand greater attention, and the impact of the intervention may be unknown. Good planning, however, increases the odds of success by explicitly considering such factors.

In general, planned change differs from unplanned change in at least three ways (Kettner, Daley, & Nichols, 1985):

1. *Planned change is limited in scope, and specific.* It is confined to specific goals and achievable objectives; it seeks to develop clear, precise definitions of problems before developing solutions.
2. *It includes a role for consumers.* Programs and policies must consider the unique perspectives and needs of the people affected by the intervention. In addition to the "targets" of the intervention (ex-offenders in a halfway house, for example), "consumers" include those within a specific area likely to be affected by an intervention. Neighbors, local schools, and crime victims are examples of consumers who may be affected by a halfway house program. Cooperative planning of the intervention is an important part of program planning, monitoring, and evaluation.
3. *A "change agent" guides planned change.* Some individual must be responsible for coordinating the planning and development of a new program, or the revision of an old one. Such an individual will guide the analysis of the problem to be solved, search for causes of the problem, review similar interventions in use elsewhere, and

facilitate the collaboration of clients, staff, and consumers involved in the planning process. This individual may come from various backgrounds: she may be a program director appointed by a specific agency such as county probation, a university professor with a research grant, a director of a nonprofit agency such as an ex-offender program, a consultant hired by a criminal justice agency to formulate a plan, or perhaps even a state representative who introduces new legislation authorizing alternatives to incarceration.

Three Approaches to Planned Change: Policy, Program, and Project

There are three general approaches to planned change, which differ in terms of their specificity and complexity. The most specific type of intervention is a *project,* the next most specific is a *program,* and the most complex and comprehensive is a *policy.*

Policies vary on the *complexity* of the rule or guidelines (simple to complex), and the amount of discretion afforded to those who apply policies (constrained to flexible). How an instructor calculates grades in a course is a matter of policy, and students are typically informed of this policy at the start of a course. The existence of a grading policy helps to ensure that all students are treated fairly. Similarly, police officers are required to read *Miranda* warnings to people they have arrested, before beginning to ask questions that might be used in court against the defendant. Both of these examples pertain to relatively simple rules designed to protect the interests of individuals. Discretion is relatively constrained, although the Supreme Court has formulated specific exceptions. Sometimes policies are much more complex: the federal government may construct a "social" policy, such as President Lyndon Johnson's War on Poverty in the 1960s, designed to address large-scale social and economic problems. Organizations, too, create policies specifying how they are going to expend their resources: the U.S. Health Department's emphasis on juvenile violence prevention was tied to its budget in such a way that specific resources were set aside to deal with this problem. The policy was relatively complex (different rules and guidelines applied to different situations, and guidelines were quite broad) and flexible (the policy allowed decisionmakers to use discretion to develop or fund specific programs). Complexity and flexibility do not always correspond: for example, state sentencing guidelines are generally complex (different rules apply to different offenders and offenses) but vary considerably in the amount of discretion afforded to the sentencing judge. We address these issues in more depth in Chapter 3.

■ ■ Policy ■

A rule or set of rules or guidelines for how to make a decision.

An example of a *program* would be a local Boys and Girls Club that offers an after-school program for minority juveniles residing in a high-risk community. Another example is a boot camp correctional program that is intended to reduce the amount of time that offenders spend in custody. Offenders are sentenced to an intensive, short pro-gram of rigorous physical and academic services that is followed by probation rather than a term in prison. Theoretically, such programs may reduce the cost of corrections, increase the rehabilitative impact of corrections, and satisfy the aim of retributive punishment. Programs, then, consist of services that are linked together by a single set of goals and an organization.

■ ■ Program ■

A set of services aimed at achieving specific goals and objectives within specified individuals, groups, organizations, or communities.

Projects are usually intensive efforts by groups within an organization, a system of orga-nizations, or a community to achieve a short-term objective. Evaluating a community cor-rections program, instituting a crackdown on drunk driving, or conducting an assessment of needs for a computerized information system are examples of projects.

■ ■ Project ■

A time-limited set of services provided to particular individuals, groups, organizations, or com-munities, usually focused on a single need, problem, or issue.

While the distinction between programs and projects is sometimes ambiguous, depending on whether the intervention is permanent or short-term, the distinction between programs and policies deserves more careful attention. Two examples illustrate the differences between a program and a policy, the two most common types of change (Figure I–3). In each of the two cases below, a program is but one small component of a much larger policy formulated at the local, state, or federal level. In each case, a *policy* (legislation in these two examples) authorized or mandated the use of specific *programs* for certain populations.

Boot camps, rigid military-style drill camps intended as an alternative to incarceration for certain offenders, were mandated and funded by the Violent Crime Control and Law Enforcement Act of 1994. The federal government allocated $24.5 million in competitive funds available for boot camps in 1995, and authorized $7.9 billion in the time period 1996–2000.

Operation "Weed and Seed," a U.S. Department of Justice initiative launched in 1992 as part of President Bush's continuing "War on Drugs" campaign, is a two-pronged community

Problem	Program	Policy
• Jail overcrowding	Boot camps	Federal Crime Bill
• Drug abuse	Operation "Weed and Seed"	The federal "War on Drugs"

FIGURE I –3 The relationship between programs and policies.

intervention. First, law enforcement agencies and prosecutors cooperate in "weeding out" criminals who participate in violent crime and drug abuse and attempt to prevent their return to the targeted area. Second, "seeding" involves the development of community services including prevention, intervention, treatment, and neighborhood revitalization. In each case, federal policy led to the formulation and funding of specific programs.

Policies, therefore, often contain the authorization or impetus for many specific programs, but policies often provide only very general prescriptions for what kind of approach should be used to solve specific problems. We can begin to see that the development of many programs and policies arises out of a political process that determines not only which problems will receive attention and priority in the first place, but also what kind of intervention approach (e.g., changing individuals versus changing specified conditions in a community) will be used to address those problems.

The Need for Planned Change

The quest to find "what works" to achieve the goals of criminal justice has not yet been fulfilled and will not likely be fulfilled anytime soon. In fact, many people (policymakers, academics, politicians, and citizens) disagree profoundly about the desirability of certain intervention approaches (e.g., drug treatment for convicted offenders versus tougher criminal sanctions to reduce drug abuse). Even if there were not such strong disagreement in values, it would still be difficult to find widespread agreement about how effective specific interventions have been (e.g., school-based delinquency prevention programs).

Several factors fuel debates over program effectiveness. For one thing, it is usually difficult to evaluate the long-term effects of social interventions. There are many different social variables to measure and control for, and this complexity often defies measurement. In addition, the objectives themselves may be poorly defined. Or, the problem may be poorly defined. Or, both the problem and the goals may be well defined, but the intervention was not implemented correctly, and thus we cannot have faith in any outcome results obtained by evaluation, whether they point to program success or failure. Indeed, evaluation results that do not address implementation problems should be treated with suspicion.

We will address these issues in more detail in subsequent chapters, but our point is that there is currently little consensus about "what works" in criminal justice. A major reason for this lack of consensus, we argue, is a lack of sufficient attention to principles of planned change. Three ongoing trends continue to sharpen our needs for planned change (Kettner, Daley, & Nichols, 1985): (1) declining resources; (2) accountability; and (3) the expansion of knowledge and technology.

Declining Resources

Since 1980, there have been huge cuts in social services spending, especially programs affecting the poor and minorities (e.g., subsidized health care, welfare, daycare for working parents, school lunches, and after-school programs) (Gans, 1996). Since 2000, these cuts have continued (APSA Task Force on Inequality and American Democracy, 2004; Jacobs & Skocpol, 2005). Part of the explanation for these changes lies in public concern over high taxes. However, it is obvious that taxes are the basis for the provision of public services, and cuts in taxes mean cuts in services (somewhere). Cuts in social services may have increased inequalities and magnified social problems that already existed (Piven, 2006). For example, the problem of homelessness was exacerbated by cuts in funding available for mental health care, substance abuse treatment, and health care (Rossi, 1991).

Partly as a consequence of declining resources, many groups have organized to promote change, both legally (through lawsuits) and politically (by advocating for changes in laws and government programs). Advocacy efforts have often succeeded in raising awareness about a particular problem and stimulating change. A good example is provided by the problem of domestic violence. In the early 1900s, women's groups organized and protested for numerous changes, including the rights to vote and to work. Advocacy by women's groups in the 1970s and 1980s led to changes in police and court policies for dealing with sexual harassment, rape, and domestic violence. Such advocacy contributed greatly to the perception that existing programs and policies were not working, and that some kind of change was needed (Buzawa & Buzawa, 2003). One can find numerous examples of groups that have campaigned for change in existing policies and programs (e.g., groups protesting welfare reforms that restrict eligibility and benefits; groups advocating for programs and policies to address problems of homelessness, AIDS, etc.).

Accountability

As public resources have dwindled, agencies have increasingly been called upon to demonstrate their effectiveness and efficiency in meeting their goals. There has been suspicion by many that public money has not always been well spent. A dialogue has resurfaced over the past decade about how to make public institutions more effective and accountable, although the means for achieving this goal are subject to debate (Welsh & Zajac, 2004a). This is especially the case within the public sectors of education, human services, and welfare, where there is considerable public expenditure, conflicting values and goals, and high stakes (Zajac, 1997). Annual budget hearings at the state and federal level are tense events for directors of publicly funded agencies, who are increasingly called upon to justify their funding requests with evidence of improved outcomes and cost-effectiveness (Cohen, 2000; Welsh & Farrington, 2000). There is currently a furor in criminal justice research and practice over the need for "evidence-based" programming, but much disagreement as to what the standards of "evidence" entail (Gandhi, Murphy-Graham, Petrosino, Schwartz Chrismer, & Weiss, 2007).

According to a report to the U.S. Congress, the effectiveness of most crime prevention strategies will remain unknown until the nation invests more in evaluating them (Sherman et al., 1998). Using rigorous, scientifically recognized standards and methodologies, a review of more than 500 impact evaluations revealed only a handful of definitive conclusions. Congress can solve this problem, the authors suggested, by limiting the scope of required evaluations but requiring that evaluations that are funded receive sufficient funding to answer questions about effectiveness. In order for this approach to be effective, Congress should match the funding earmarked for program spending with corresponding funding to pay for the evaluations.

Expansion of Knowledge and Technology

We have greater technological abilities than ever before, and these changes have created both new opportunities and new problems. Improvements in computing technology have dramatically increased our information collection, storage, and retrieval capabilities. We now have ready access to many types of criminal justice data, including information about reported crimes, police arrests, convictions, sentencing, prison time served, parole, and recidivism. Improved data collection and access mean that our ability to analyze specific needs and problems has improved.

For example, improved justice information systems have contributed to our understanding of problems such as racial disparities in sentencing (Tonry, 1995). High-powered computers and statistical packages make it possible to collect and compare data on the processing of thousands of defendants in different regions over time, and statistically control for various legal (e.g., previous criminal record) and nonlegal factors (e.g., race, socioeconomic status) that influence sentencing. There are no longer disputes about whether sentencing disparities exist or not, but rather where, why, and how much. Computers have also increased the ability of researchers to discover what works. The effects of juvenile and adult correctional programs are increasingly the subjects of sophisticated outcome evaluations and meta-analyses (see Chapter 6).

Other technological changes have improved our ability to detect crime and monitor offenders. Computerized DNA and fingerprint identification systems have greatly reduced the amount of time required to scan and match potential suspects with forensic samples, and both regional and national data banks of criminal information are now available to criminal justice agencies for investigation. DNA testing and analysis technologies have become increasingly sophisticated, and forensic DNA evidence has been used with increasing frequency both to convict the guilty and to exonerate the innocent (Lovrich, Pratt, Gaffney, & Johnson, 2003). Many previously unsolvable cases became solvable because viable suspects could be identified and arrested or removed from suspect lists.

Electronic monitoring equipment has made it possible for probation and parole agencies to more cost effectively supervise certain offenders in a community rather than a prison setting, at least as part of their sentence. However, increasingly sophisticated drug-testing equipment has also made it possible to detect minute amounts of prohibited drugs in an individual's body, leading to huge increases in the number of parolees who fail to complete their parole terms successfully and return to jail or prison (Petersilia, 2003).

As computerized information systems have grown, a whole new field of crime dubbed "computer crime" has evolved, in which perpetrators attempt to break into secure computer systems of individuals and corporations, usually for the purpose of illegally obtaining classified information, money, or both (i.e., "identity theft"). Needless to say, methods of detecting, investigating, and prosecuting this whole new category of crime are evolving rapidly, but seemingly slower than the rate of growth in the crime itself (D'Ovidio, 2007; Stambaugh et al., 2000).

The Perils of Planned Change

Any change to existing procedures and existing conditions carries a certain amount of risk. The proposed change is likely to be resisted by someone, perhaps even its intended beneficiaries (e.g., a city successfully lobbies for state funds to build a new prison, but then faces vigorous protests from communities being considered for the location of the new prison). Regardless of the specific change proposed, universal consensus is rare; resistance is the norm.

In many cases, people fear and resist change because it may threaten their job security or bring about unwanted scrutiny (e.g., citizen review boards of complaints against police). There is often a fear that the change might only make things worse. For example, critics argued that tough new government powers granted under the USA PATRIOT Act, passed in October of 2001, led to the unwarranted harassment and detention of large numbers of citizens and legal immigrants (Babington, 2006). Regardless of the many varied reasons for which resistance emerges in any specific case, those who propose change must be prepared for disagreement and resistance. Again, *planned* change, rather than unplanned change or poorly planned change, can go a long way toward minimizing resistance, especially if the "change agent" (the person or agency that has introduced the proposed intervention) has involved different constituents in the planning process from the beginning.

Even prior to beginning work on planning a specific intervention, the change agent should have identified potential sources of resistance, and considered the potential costs and benefits of two very different approaches to handling resistance: (1) *collaborative* strategies; or (2) *conflict* strategies (Babington, 2006). While the actual outcomes of either strategy are impossible to predict without knowing detailed circumstances of the case in question, there are several serious costs associated with conflict strategies that generally make them unattractive options:

- They create greater resistance;
- They require greater resources;
- They create more unexpected effects; and
- Change tends to be temporary (compliance) rather than long-term.

Collaborative strategies seek involvement from all parties concerned. For example, a police commissioner might ask police officers about their views on community policing before it is adopted as a department policy and imposed on them. State sentencing commissions might ask judges about perceived difficulties in sentencing before drafting, adopting, or revising sentencing guidelines.

■ ■ Collaborative Strategies ■

Collaborative strategies emphasize participation from those affected by change. Individuals, groups, or organizations known to oppose the intervention in part or *in toto* are included in the design and planning of the intervention.

Conflict strategies are more likely to come into play where opposing parties have a strong history of disagreement; leaders favor a dictatorial, authoritarian style of management; resources are scarce and there is much disagreement over allocation; the stakes of the proposed change are high (i.e., large benefits to certain parties and perhaps large costs to others); time pressures are great; and the likelihood of successfully suppressing the opposition is perceived (correctly or incorrectly) as high. A good example is provided by brutality lawsuits launched against local police departments. Because citizens perceived the existing system of reviewing complaints as ineffective and heavily biased in favor of police, legal reform in complaint review procedures has evolved. Another example is provided by lawsuits against local, state, and federal prisons for overcrowding and other conditions of confinement. Such lawsuits, some lasting as long as 13 years, usually followed a period of unsuccessful and rancorous discussion and negotiation (Welsh, 1995). Changes eventually resulted, but at considerable cost to human and fiscal resources.

■ ■ Conflict Strategies ■

Conflict strategies approach resistance in an adversarial manner. Those who resist the proposed change are seen as opponents who must either be persuaded or coerced to change their views.

A Seven-Stage Model for Planned Change

A "model" specifies the sequence of steps required for (1) analyzing a problem, (2) determining its causes, and (3) analyzing (or planning and carrying out) a specific intervention. The model presented in this book may be used to plan new interventions, analyze existing interventions, or both (e.g., revising a current program or policy) (Figure I–4).

Planning a New Intervention	Analyzing an Existing Intervention
• Critical activities can be enacted (or avoided) so as to increase the likelihood that a proposed intervention will be implemented with fidelity (as planned) and effectively produce a desired change in a specific problem.	• Critical activities and decisions that informed the planning process can be identified and analyzed so as to help understand why a particular intervention did or did not produce a desired change in a specific problem.

FIGURE I–4 Two different uses of the seven-stage model.

Our model of planned change is based on a problem-solving approach: the goal is to develop solutions to specific problems through a rational process of planning. The 1968 President's Commission report, *The Challenge of Crime in a Free Society* (President's Commission on Law Enforcement and Administration of Justice, 1968), was extremely influential in shaping current conceptions of criminal justice as a "system," (Walker, 1992) and it stimulated attempts to improve criminal justice programs and policies through *comprehensive, coordinated* planning. As Moore (1998) suggests, "The Crime Commission had two big things in mind: (1) how to produce an effective, decent criminal justice system and (2) how to deal with crime. ... They also had a *managerial or implementation vision* [emphasis added], which was a theory about how the processes and institutions of the criminal justice system needed to be developed..." (167-168). This vision was to be guided by data and knowledge rather than ideology and passion.

The Commission's Report was the major impetus for passage of the Omnibus Crime Control and Safe Streets Act of 1968 and the creation of the federal Law Enforcement Assistance Administration (LEAA). The Commission's goals of rational criminal justice planning and social justice remain as relevant today as then. Reflecting on the positive contributions of the President's Commission report, Moore notes that "The authorization to experiment has been spread widely, and that turns out to be a very good thing for society" (176-177). At the same time, the goals of rationality and social justice have proven far more difficult to achieve than originally expected (U.S. Department of Justice, 1998).

We present our seven-stage model here with the assumption that either a *new* program or policy is being developed or an *existing* program or policy is being analyzed. Because procedures differ slightly depending on whether a new intervention is being planned or an existing intervention is being analyzed, we summarize the stages separately for each (Tables I–1 and I–2).[1] The seven stages are only briefly described in this chapter; each is described in detail in subsequent chapters.

Stage 1. Analyzing the Problem

The first step is to analyze the problem, carefully collecting information about dimensions of the problem, the history of the problem, who is affected by the problem, and potential causes of the problem. For example, we ask the following questions: What and where is the problem? How big is it? How long has the problem existed? Do different groups of people have different definitions of the problem? Who is affected by the problem? What causes the problem? What theories do we have about causes of the problem? What kinds of interventions have been tried elsewhere? Who is likely to support a certain course of action, and who is likely to resist it?

The pitfalls of faulty problem analysis are enormous, and can completely subvert effective intervention. Many interventions fail not necessarily because the intervention itself is

[1]Because projects differ from programs and policies mainly in terms of their shorter duration and more focused intervention approach, the seven-stage model can be easily applied to projects as well.

Table I-1   New Interventions: A Systematic Approach to Program and Policy Development

Stage 1. Analyzing the Problem	Stage 2. Goals and Objectives	Stage 3. Program or Policy Design Stage	Stage 4. Action Planning	Stage 5. Program or Policy Implementation	Stage 6. Evaluating Outcomes	Stage 7. Reassessment and Review
Document the need for change.	Write goal statements.	Choose from different intervention options.	Identify resources needed.	Design instruments to collect monitoring data.	Develop outcome measures based on objectives.	Planning for Failure: Avoid exaggerated claims.
Describe the history of the problem.	Write specific outcome objectives for each goal.	Program Design: • Define the target population.	Plan to acquire or reallocate resources.	Designate responsibility to collect, store, and analyze data.	Specify the research design to be used.	Planning for Success: Ongoing reassessment, learning, and revision are crucial.
Examine potential causes.	Seek participation in goal setting.	• Define target selection procedures.	Specify dates to complete implementation tasks.	Develop information system capacities.	Identify potential confounding factors.	Learning and Adapting: Successful interventions must adapt to change.
Examine previous interventions.	Specify an impact model.	• Define program components and activities.	Develop mechanisms of self-regulation.	Develop mechanisms to provide feedback to stakeholders.	Identify users and uses of evaluation results.	Initiate the Program or Policy Design from Stage 3.
Identify relevant stakeholders.	Identify compatible and incompatible goals in the larger system.	• Write job descriptions of staff and specify skills required.	Specify a plan to build support.		Reassess the entire program/policy plan.	Initiate the Action Plan from Stage 4.
Conduct a systems analysis.	Identify needs for interagency collaboration.	Policy Design: • Define the target population of the policy.				Initiate Monitoring of Program/Policy (Stage 5 plan).
Identify barriers to change and supports for change.		• Identify the responsible authority.				Collect and analyze evaluation data; provide feedback to stakeholders (Stage 6 plan).
		• Define the provisions and procedures of the policy.				Reassess the entire program/policy plan and make necessary modifications to increase fit with environment.

Program/Policy Revision

Table 1.1 Existing Interventions: A Systematic Approach to Program and Policy Analysis

Stage 1. Analyzing the Problem	Stage 2. Goals and Objectives	Stage 3. Program or Policy Design Stage	Stage 4. Action Planning	Stage 5. Program or Policy Implementation	Stage 6. Evaluating Outcomes	Stage 7. Reassessment and Review
How was the need for change documented?	Describe goals of the program or policy.	How was the intervention approach chosen?	What resources were needed (what type, how much)?	Describe instruments used to monitor implementation. What gaps were detected?	Describe outcome measures used to assess objectives.	Were goals and objectives realistic and measurable?
Describe the history of the problem.	Describe the outcome objectives for each goal.	Program Design: • Define the target population.	How were resources acquired?	Who was responsible for collecting, storing, and analyzing data?	Specify the research design used.	To what degree is ongoing reassessment, learning, and revision continuing?
Which potential causes were examined?	Who participated in goal setting?	• Define target selection procedures.	Were implementation tasks specified and completed on time?	What information systems were developed? Were they adequate?	Were potential confounding factors identified and addressed?	What adaptations have been made, or are still needed?
Were previous interventions examined? How?	Specify assumptions about the impact model.	• Define program components and activities.	What mechanisms of self-regulation were developed?	What mechanisms were developed (if any) to provide feedback to stakeholders?	How were evaluation results used, and by whom?	Specify any intended changes to program or policy design (Stage 3).
Were relevant stakeholders identified? If so, how?	How were compatible and incompatible goals in the larger system addressed?	• Give job descriptions of staff and specify skills.	How was support for the program or policy built?		What are the implications of the results for further program or policy revision?	Specify any intended changes in action planning (Stage 4).
Was a systems analysis conducted? If so, how?	How were needs for interagency collaboration identified and addressed?	Policy Design: • Define the target population of the policy. • Identify the responsible authority.				Specify any intended changes in procedures used to monitor program or policy implementation (Stage 5). Specify any intended changes in evaluation procedures (Stage 6).
How were barriers and supports for change identified and addressed?		• Describe the provisions and procedures of the policy.				Specify procedures and time frame for reassessment.

Program/Policy Revision

flawed, but because it addresses the wrong problem (or an inadequately defined prob-lem). Major activities at this stage include the following:

- Document the need for change: collect and analyze data about the problem.
- Describe the history of the problem.
- Examine potential causes of the problem.
- Examine previous interventions that have tried to change this problem.
- Identify relevant stakeholders (those who have a legitimate interest in the problem and/or the intervention).
- Identify barriers to change and supports for change.
- Conduct a systems analysis.

This last step, a systems analysis, involves conducting research on the system within which the problem exists. Most problems are produced by more than one source, and most solutions affect more than one part of a system. It is important, then, to learn as much as possible about how different conditions interact to produce the problem. For example, prison crowding is not simply the result of more crime, or even judges sending more people to prison. Changes in laws and penalties specified by law also contribute to increasing prison populations (Blumstein & Beck, 1999). Unless we understand *how* these changes affect the prison population, we stand little chance of developing effective solutions.

Example I–1   Prostitution as a Problem

After a series of well-publicized police sweeps and arrests, a community identifies prostitution as a serious *problem*. The presumed *cause*, determined by intuition rather than careful analysis, is that police have simply not taken the problem seriously enough. The proposed *intervention*, then, is a police crackdown, with intensive law enforcement targeted in areas frequented by prostitutes and their customers. However, what if these causal assumptions were wrong, or left out something important? What if it turns out that the problem is mainly limited to the summer months, and the majority of prostitutes are teenage runaways or drug addicts trying to make money to survive? Such information might lead to very different types of interventions: perhaps shelters, crisis counseling, drug treatment, or job training and assistance.

Stage 2. Goals and Objectives

Every intervention attempts to achieve some kind of outcome (i.e., some change in the problem), but sometimes it is difficult to figure out what it is. *Goals* are broad aims of the intervention (e.g., reduce drug abuse); *objectives* specify explicit and measurable out-comes. It is amazing how many expensive and otherwise well-designed interventions fail to define the desired outcomes of the intervention adequately. Without specific, agreed-upon criteria for success, it is impossible to determine whether any intervention works. If you don't know where you are going, as the saying goes, don't be surprised when you don't get there. Major activities at this stage include the following:

- Seek participation from different individuals and agencies in goal setting.
- Write goal statements specifying the general outcome to be obtained.
- Write specific outcome objectives for each goal: these should include a time frame for measuring impact, and a specific measure of impact.
- Specify an impact model: this is a description of how the intervention will act upon a specific cause so as to bring about a change in the problem.
- Identify compatible and incompatible goals in the larger system: Where do values of different stakeholders overlap or conflict?
- Identify needs and opportunities for interagency collaboration. For example, police and prosecutors may need to collaborate to make a new drunk driving law work. Prosecutors could clarify the evidence needed to obtain convictions; police officers could strategize about the likelihood of obtaining different kinds of evidence.

Example I–2   The Goals of Drunk Driving Laws

A new state law is passed that provides tougher sentences for drunk drivers. A mandatory 48-h jail sentence is imposed on second-time offenders; a mandatory 3-month jail term is imposed on third-time offenders. The goal is obvious: to reduce drunk driving. Six months after the law is passed, there is widespread disagreement about whether the law is working. Advocates of the law point to a 10% reduction in drunk driving arrests. Critics point to insurance statistics that indicate an increase in traffic accidents involving alcohol. Who is right? Does the law work or not? After much discussion, both sides realize that they lack an agreed-upon criterion for judging the outcome of the intervention. Eventually, they agree that a desirable outcome (change in the problem) is that 1 year after the law was passed, there should be a 30% reduction in auto fatalities due to drunk driving. The difficulty, it turns out, is that no specific objective was defined before the law was passed, and without such an objective, multiple and conflicting criteria for judging "outcomes" could be debated endlessly.

Stage 3. Program or Policy Design

This is one of the most crucial and time-consuming stages in the planning process. It often requires considerable review of information collected during the first two stages of planning. It involves specifying, in as much detail as possible, who does what to whom, in what order, and how much. It is the "guts" of the program or policy, including its staff, its services, and its clients. While the steps for analyzing programs and policies are similar, at the design stage we find it best to distinguish activities for programs and policies separately. Major activities for program design include:

- *Define the target population:* Who is to be served, or changed? This often involves specifying some level of need (e.g., level of drug involvement) and characteristics of intended clients (e.g., age, gender, geographic residence).
- *Define client selection and intake procedures:* How are clients selected and recruited for the intervention? For example, drug court programs are often intended for first-time,

nonviolent offenders. A list of eligible clients might be obtained from court records; an application from the client may be required; an interview and screening process may be required to determine the client's suitability for the program.

- *Define program components:* Specify the precise nature, amount, and sequence of services provided. Who does what to whom, in what order, and how much? Boot camp programs, for example, might contain several components: military-style drills and physical training, academic or vocational education, life skills or problem-solving training, drug awareness education, social skills training, and so on.
- *Write job descriptions of staff, and define the skills and training required.* How many and what kind of staff are required to operate the program? What specific duties will they carry out? What kind of qualifications do they need, and what further training will be necessary? How much money is needed for staff salaries and training?

Major activities for policy design include:

- *Define the target population of the policy.* Which persons or groups are included, and which are not? For example, legislators in various states had to write specific requirements for inclusion and exclusion under new three-strikes laws. Which offenders (e.g., felony vs. misdemeanor) and offenses (e.g., violent vs. property) should be included?
- *Identify the responsible authority.* Who will carry out the policy, and what will their responsibilities be? For example, what roles will judges, prosecutors, defense attorneys, and others play in any case, and how can we ensure that each understands three-strikes policy correctly? Will each party understand their individual responsibilities and options? Will they need special training or orientation? Are additional court or prison resources required?
- *Define the provisions of the policy.* A policy should identify the sanctions, services, opportunities, or interventions that will be delivered, and the conditions that must be met in order for the policy to be carried out. Under one three-strikes policy, for example, state legislators had to write specific rules for how case processing and sentencing decisions were to be made: when and how would the district attorney's office make charging decisions under the new law? How would pretrial motions be handled? Would trials be conducted in private or in public? What are the appropriate terms of incarceration?
- *Delineate the procedures that must be followed.* Individuals responsible for implementing a specific set of rules must clearly understand the specific actions to be taken to ensure that the policy is carried out consistently. For example, three-strikes laws specify decisions regarding the charging, processing, and sentencing of repeat offenders. These might include the court's procedures for notifying a suspect and his or her attorney that the suspect is about to be charged under three-strikes laws, including delivery of written notice and clearly specifying the suspect's legal rights and options under the new law. Procedures may also specify who signs such forms, other individuals or agencies that need to be notified, and records that must be maintained.

Example I–3   The Design of a Model Mentoring Program (Center for the Study and Prevention of Violence, Institute of Behavioral Science, University of Colorado at Boulder, 2011)

Big Brothers Big Sisters of America (BBBSA) has been recognized as a "model" violence prevention program, partly because of its well-specified design and replicability across numerous jurisdictions. More than 70,000 youths are supported and mentored in more than 500 agencies across the United States. BBBSA distinguishes itself from many other mentoring programs via clear and rigorous procedures.

Client selection and intake:

- BBBSA typically targets youths (aged 6-18) from single parent homes.
- Youth *Assessment* involves a written application, interviews with the child and the parent, and a home assessment; it is designed to help the caseworker learn about the child in order to make the best possible match, and also to secure parental permission.

Program components:

- Volunteers interact regularly with a youth in a one-to-one relationship.
- Agencies use a *case management* approach, following through on each case from initial inquiry through closure.
- *Orientation* is required for all volunteers.
- *Volunteer* Screening includes a written application, a background check, an extensive interview, and a home assessment; it is designed to screen out those who may inflict psychological or physical harm, lack the capacity to form a caring bond with the child, or are unlikely to honor their time commitments.
- *Matches* are carefully considered and based upon the needs of the youths, abilities of volunteers, preferences of the parent, and the capacity of program staff.
- *Supervision* is accomplished via an initial contact with the parent, youth, and volunteer within two weeks of the match; monthly telephone contact with the volunteer, parent and/or youth during the first year; and quarterly contact with all parties during the duration of the match.

Staff job descriptions, skills, and training:

- The case manager screens applicants, makes and supervises the matches, and closes the matches when eligibility requirements are no longer met or either party decides they can no longer participate fully in the relationship.

Stage 4. Action Planning

Once the design is complete, the next stage is to develop an "action plan" that specifies the sequence of tasks that need to be completed in order to successfully launch, or "implement," the program or policy. These include technical and interpersonal tasks (e.g., identifying and acquiring the necessary resources for the program; locating office space and/or meeting space; hiring and training staff; designing client intake and reporting forms;

purchasing equipment and supplies; setting dates and assigning responsibility for the completion of specific tasks). Major activities at this stage include the following:

- Identify resources needed and make cost projections: How much funding is needed?
- Plan to acquire or reallocate resources: How will funding be acquired?
- Specify dates by which implementation tasks will be accomplished, and assign responsibilities to staff members for carrying out tasks.
- Develop mechanisms of self-regulation (create mechanisms to monitor staff performance and enhance communication).
- Specify a plan to maintain and build support.
- Anticipate sources of resistance and develop responses.

Example I–4   Action Planning for a Delinquency Prevention Program

Major program components of a community-based delinquency prevention program included a 7-day challenge course in which juveniles were encouraged to examine their lives and set goals; one-to-one mentoring of youths by adult partners; and weekly follow-through meetings of all mentors and clients (Welsh, Harris, & Jenkins, 1996). The program's funding proposal spelled out in necessary detail a myriad of tasks, responsibilities, and costs required in order to launch the program. For the mentoring component, adult mentors (volunteers) were trained to support youths to participate fully in the 7-day course and the follow-through program (1 workshop leader × 3 days × $350 per day = $1,050).

Stage 5. Program or Policy Implementation

At this stage, we attempt to find out if the program or policy *was* implemented properly. *Monitoring* refers to the collection of information to determine to what degree the program/policy design (Stage 3) is being carried out as planned. Data are collected to find out what is actually being delivered to clients (e.g., observations, surveys, interviews). The purpose is to identify gaps between the "program on paper" (design) and the "program in action." Adjustments then need to be made to revise either the design of the program or policy (e.g., program components) or its implementation. We ask the following types of questions at this stage: Are program/policy activities actually being carried out as planned? Is the intended target population being reached? Are staff carrying out their assigned responsibilities? Major activities at this stage include the following:

- Design monitoring instruments to collect data.
- Designate responsibility for data collection, storage, and analysis.
- Develop information system capacities.
- Identify any gaps in implementation.
- Develop mechanisms to provide feedback to staff, clients, and stakeholders.

> ### Example I–5   Monitoring Implementation of Prison-Based Therapeutic Community (TC) Drug Treatment Programs
>
> In recent years, modified therapeutic community (TC) drug treatment programs have been widely implemented in prison settings. The aim of the TC is total lifestyle change, including abstinence from drugs, elimination of antisocial behavior, and development of prosocial attitudes and values. Individual and group counseling, encounter groups, peer pressure, role models, and a system of incentives and sanctions form the core of these programs. In spite of the pervasiveness of the prison TC model, surprisingly little information is available about the implementation of prison-based drug treatment programs in local and state correctional systems (Welsh & Zajac, 2004b).
>
> Taxman and Bouffard developed a monitoring technique to examine the degree to which certain treatment components typically associated with the TC model were present. Techniques included structured observations conducted by well-trained researchers, in addition to structured interviews, examination of official program documents, and collection of client-based data (e.g., drug testing, infractions, disciplinary actions) (Taxman & Bouffard, 2002). Researchers examined six TC programs in short-term jails. Overall, monitoring illustrated a lack of correspondence between the prototypical TC model and the implementation of these six programs:
>
> - *Program emphasis:* Few of the programs implemented the overall TC philosophy. Interviews with staff members indicated that they did not use a particular program model, formal curriculum, or structured treatment phases.
> - *Treatment process:* Researchers observed a focus on awareness training, emotional growth training, and peer encounter techniques. The most commonly used activities, however, emphasized individual rather than group work, underutilizing activities intended to facilitate community cohesion.
> - *Treatment style:* In contrast to the TC model, informal (unscheduled and client-initiated) meetings were relatively rare, as indicated by observational data and interviews with both counselors and group members.

Stage 6. Evaluating Outcomes

The goal of this stage is to develop a research design for measuring program or policy outcome (a specific, intended change in the problem, as defined by objectives). Did the program or policy achieve its intended objectives? Why or why not? For a new program or policy, note that all planning, up to and including the formulation of an evaluation plan, should precede the actual start-up of the intervention (Stage 7). Major activities at this stage include the following:

- Develop and analyze outcome measures based on objectives.
- Specify the research design to be used.
- Identify potential confounding factors (factors other than the program that may have influenced measured outcomes).
- Identify users and uses of evaluation results.
- Reassess the entire program or policy plan.

Example I–6   Evaluation of a Model Mentoring Program (Center for Study and Prevention of Violence, 2011)

An evaluation of the Big Brothers Big Sisters of America (BBBSA) program compared children who participated in BBBSA to similar, nonparticipating peers. After an 18-month period, BBBSA youths

- were 46% less likely than control youths to initiate drug use during the study period.
- were 27% less likely to initiate alcohol use than control youths.
- were almost one-third less likely than control youths to hit someone.
- were better than control youths in academic behavior, attitudes, and performance.
- were more likely to have higher-quality relationships with their parents or guardians than control youths.
- were more likely to have higher-quality relationships with their peers at the end of the study period than did control youths.

Stage 7. Reassessment and Review

For a new program or policy, all six stages of planning should ideally be completed prior to the initial start date. If a review of the planning process uncovers any discrepancies at any of the six prior stages, these gaps should be carefully addressed before proceeding. Stage 7, then, involves putting into motion the program or policy *design* and *action plan* (Stages 3 and 4), *monitoring* program or policy implementation (Stage 5), and, if appropriate, *evaluating* outcomes (Stage 6). Once evaluation data are analyzed, feedback is provided to all stakeholders, and the program or policy design should be thoroughly reassessed to determine where revisions are necessary. At the end of the process, the change agent asks whether further adjustments are necessary to meet objectives. What are the strengths and weaknesses of the intervention? Decisions may have to be made about whether an intervention should be launched or continued, and whether it should receive funding or not. Major activities at this stage include the following:

- Initiate the program/policy design and action plan.
- Begin monitoring program/policy implementation.
- Make adjustments to design or implementation as gaps are found.
- Decide whether the program/policy is ready to be evaluated.
- Collect and analyze evaluation data.
- Provide feedback to users and stakeholders.
- Review and reassess the entire program/policy plan and make modifications where needed.

This last point is extremely important. Lots of changes are made in the criminal justice system, but few stick. Several writers have commented on the importance of mutual adaptation: both the intervention and the environment must change if the new program or policy is going to work (Berman, 1981; Harris & Smith, 1996; McLaughlin, 1976).

In New York City, for example, staff at the Center for Alternative Sentencing and Employment Services (CASES) wanted to make sure that their clients fit the target population: jail-bound—not probation-bound—offenders (Clear, Cadora, Byer, & Swartz, 2003; Schall & Neises, 1998). The program was designed to provide intensive community services that would enable offenders to stay in the community. A systems analysis showed, however, that judges in the different boroughs of New York used different criteria for placing offenders in jail. In Queens, for example, judges required fewer jail sentences for offenders than did judges in Manhattan. In order to prevent the CASES program from being used for probation-bound cases, staff adjusted the criteria for accepting clients to the sentencing patterns in each borough. Adaptation of the program increased its chances of achieving its objective (keeping offenders in the community).

Conclusion

We need a systematic *plan* for any change effort. Good intentions are rarely sufficient to bring about successful change. We must beware of the "activist bias" (Sieber, 1981), by which well-intentioned advocates of change assume that they already know what the problem is and what is needed. Such advocates may insist that we desist all this prolonged planning and simply "get on with it." The perils of unplanned or poorly planned change should by now be obvious: expensive, poorly articulated, poorly implemented, ineffective programs and policies that are unable to successfully compete for scarce funds. There are four key points to remember about this seven-stage, systematic model of planned change that you are about to explore:

1. *Program and policy planning is an interactive and ongoing process.* It is crucial to review and modify planning (where needed) at each stage of the analysis. This takes time, but it is time well spent.
2. *A rational planning approach provides a framework for developing logical and effective programs and policies.* The default (too often) is to use unarticulated and untested assumptions to guide planning.
3. *Keys to success are participation and communication with all stakeholders* (e.g., program staff, clients, individuals or agencies whose cooperation is needed, funding sources, citizens affected by the intervention, elected representatives) throughout the change process.
4. *Rarely does planning go smoothly.* We strongly believe that the advantages of systematically attending to the elements of planning discussed in this book can greatly improve the chances of developing effective policies and programs. We also recognize that the environments in which this planning occurs are messy and unpredictable. It takes willpower, a clear vision of what you want to accomplish, and lots of communication to remain rooted in the planning process. Planned change increases the likelihood of successful intervention; it cannot guarantee it.

■ ■ What's to Come? ■

Chapter 1: This chapter discusses one of the most critical and most overlooked stages of planning—defining and understanding the problem or issue that is driving the planning process.
Chapter 2: Once we have an understanding of the problem or issue, then we can identify what we want to achieve. Chapter 2 discusses the ways in which goals and objectives are framed so that we can communicate around the direction in which we want our change effort to move and know when we are heading in the right direction.
Chapter 3: In this chapter, we focus on how to design effective policies and programs. Design involves a number of critical decisions, such as who specifically will benefit from the intervention, which will affect greatly our ability to achieve our goals.
Chapter 4: Next we will learn about some of the more pragmatic aspects of planning that are essential to the real world of planning, including budgeting and cost projections, orienting staff, and assigning responsibility for completion of specific implementation tasks.
Chapter 5: This chapter gets us into the area of accountability. We decided what we wanted to do and who would do what. Now we need to make sure that we do it. We need to monitor our activities and learn about when and why we drift away from what we set out to do.
Chapter 6: How can we learn about what's working and what's not? How can we improve upon our past performance? These are questions that we discuss in the context of evaluation. The methods of evaluation are important to understand in order to draw valid conclusions.
Chapter 7: Finally, Chapter 7 brings us into the arena of experience. As we carry out our plans, new information is created that requires a response. A program or policy may have looked good on paper, but it must adapt to the real world of people, organizations, and competing goals. The results of evaluation data should be used to guide a continuous process of reassessment and improvement.

In the next seven chapters, we provide detailed discussions of the seven stages of planning and the major concepts and terms associated with each stage. We have placed a great deal of emphasis on providing case studies that illustrate these concepts and help the reader to discover how these concepts can be applied in a variety of criminal justice contexts.

Discussion Questions

1. Describe three trends that have increased the need for planned change.
2. Define "planned change," and give an example.
3. Define "unplanned change," and give an example.
4. Define and describe an example of each of the following: (1) policy, (2) program, and (3) project.
5. Why are collaborative strategies of change preferable to conflict strategies? Explain.
6. Briefly describe the first six stages of planned change (analyzing the problem, setting goals and objectives, designing the program, developing an action plan, monitoring program implementation, and evaluating outcomes). What are the major questions we need to ask at each stage?

7. How did the 1968 President's Commission Report influence thinking about criminal justice planning?
8. Give an example of "mutual adaptation."

EXERCISE I–1

Describe briefly, in three paragraphs: (a) some *problem* in criminal justice. Why is it a problem? What makes it a problem? (b) What is one possible *cause* of this problem? (c) What is one possible *intervention* (a program or policy, as defined earlier in this chapter) that might change this problem?

■ ■ ■ ▬▬▬▬▬▬▬▬▬▬▬▬▬▬▬▬▬▬▬▬▬▬▬▬▬▬▬▬▬▬▬▬▬▬

Case Study I–1 The Pitfalls of Poor Planning: Three-Strikes Legislation

Stage 1: Problem Analysis

The proper starting point for program or policy planning is to ask what problem needs to be addressed. How does a specific issue become targeted for change, and why? How big is the problem, where is it, who is affected by it, and so on? What evidence has been used to demonstrate a need for change?

There is a widespread misconception that crime rates have been steadily rising in recent years and that a larger and larger portion of serious crimes is committed by recidivating felons. In fact, crime rates decreased steadily since the early 1990s, while recidivism rates remained remarkably stable. While California's three-strikes law became one of the harshest sentencing laws in the nation, it is doubtful that any coherent problem analysis guided policy development in this arena.

Assumptions speak faster and louder than facts, and politicians may too eagerly cater to the perceived public will rather than documented problems. Three-strikes laws were a rapid and visible response to public outcries following heinous or well-publicized crimes (Parent, Dunworth, McDonald, & Rhodes, 1997). "We have a serious crime problem in this country," according to Walter Dickey, a University of Wisconsin law professor. "We are sold this as a solution. It gets all kinds of energy and attention, and yet it is relatively ineffectual" (Cannon, 1996).

The California Legislature overwhelmingly approved three-strikes a year after repeat felon Richard Allen Davis broke into a Petaluma home and abducted 12-year-old Polly Klaas at knifepoint in 1993 (Lagos, 2011). The body of Klaas was found 9 weeks later in a shallow grave. Davis, it turned out, had a long criminal history and had been wanted on a parole violation at the time of the crime.

Stage 2: Setting Goals and Objectives

Before designing programs or policies, we must be clear about the specific outcomes they are expected to achieve, and what specific values guide choices to select one course of action over another. The intent of three-strikes is to incapacitate violent offenders for long prison terms—25 years to life. If the law successfully increases the imprisonment rate, according to this logic, fewer offenders will be free to victimize the population. The laws have no specific deterrent effect if those confined will never be released, but their general deterrent effect could, at least in theory, be substantial. Legislators convey the message that certain crimes are deemed especially grave and that people who commit them deserve harsh sanctions.

Such laws may compromise values such as equity (fairness). A California study (Greenwood et al., 1994) found that blacks were sent to prison under the "three-strikes" law 13 times more often than whites. Forty-three percent of the third-strike inmates in California were African-American, although they made up only 7% of the state's population and 20% of its felony arrests. Controversy still ensues over exactly what outcomes three-strikes laws were expected to achieve and whether numerous unintended consequences, including racial disparity, could have been avoided.

Stage 3: Program or Policy Design

For any program or policy to have a chance at being effective, it is absolutely essential that the target population and all provisions, procedures, and services be clearly spelled out ahead of time. In other words, there should be absolutely no doubt about who does what to whom—in what order, how much, or how often. This was clearly not the case with three-strikes laws.

One might expect some consistency between three-strikes laws in different states and between state and federal three-strikes laws. In reality, laws vary widely across states in terms of the definition of a "strike," the conditions under which the law is triggered, and the severity of the sanctions. Some state laws call for third-time offenders to receive life without parole. In others, prisoners are eligible for parole after 30 or 40 years (Greenwood et al., 1998).

Target populations for three-strikes laws seem particularly poorly defined. During the first few years of the law's implementation in California, about 1,300 offenders were imprisoned on third-strike felonies and more than 14,000 criminals for second-strike felonies. California's law calls for a doubling of the prison sentence for a second felony and for a sentence of 25 years to life for a third conviction. The California law was written to cover 500 felonies, including many nonviolent offenses. Some of the felonies include petty theft, attempted assault, and burglary. Thus, about 85% of all those sentenced under the three-strikes laws were involved in nonviolent crimes. For instance, 192 marijuana possessors were sentenced for second and third strikes, compared with 40 murderers, 25 rapists, and 24 kidnappers (Greenwood et al., 1998).

To critics, Shane Taylor provides a tragic example. At age 27, Taylor was drinking beer with friends in a car parked at a rural lookout spot when police pulled up to investigate. One of the officers noticed a small bag poking out of Taylor's wallet that contained methamphetamine. Combined with two prior convictions for burglaries he had committed at age 19, Taylor received the most severe punishment possible under California's three-strikes law: 25 years to life. Fifteen years later, both the prosecuting attorney and the sentencing judge have acknowledged that the punishment was too harsh. An appeal of Taylor's sentence is pending with the California Supreme Court, and Taylor's lawyers say that the law has led to numerous other troubling cases (Greenwood et al., 1998).

Stage 4: Action Planning

Prior to implementing a new policy such as three-strikes, a systematic plan is needed that assigns responsibilities for communication, coordination, and completion of specific tasks required to enact the new law. Everyone involved must clearly understand his or her roles and responsibilities. Possible obstacles and sources of resistance should be anticipated and sought out. By the time the new three-strikes laws were implemented, everyone should have understood and accepted their roles. Evidence suggests the opposite.

State prosecutors avoided the three-strikes laws because they saw little need for them with existing sentencing laws (Greenwood et al., 1998). Another reason is that the laws were narrowly written, making them difficult to apply. Plea bargaining and charge bargaining became increasingly common methods for circumventing three-strikes laws.

The criminal courts typically rely on a high rate of guilty pleas to speed case processing and avoid logjams. Three-strikes laws disrupt established plea-bargaining patterns by preventing a prosecutor from offering a short prison term (less than the minimum) in exchange for a guilty plea. However, prosecutors can shift strategies and bargain on charges rather than on sentences. The findings of research on the impact of mandatory sentencing laws are instructive (Tonry, 1987). Officials make earlier and more selective arrest, charging, and diversion decisions; they also tend to bargain less and to bring more cases to trial (Tonry, 1987).

Stage 5: Monitoring

Following implementation of a policy such as three-strikes, it is essential to monitor, that is, collect data to determine to what degree the actual provisions, procedures, or services are actually being implemented as designed. Adjustments may be needed, but absolutely no valid evaluation can be conducted if the laws are not being properly implemented. That would be tantamount to arguing that "x caused y," when we have no idea what "x" (the policy) was. Three-strikes laws fare badly on this criterion also.

At the federal level, where three-strikes legislation was included in the 1994 crime bill, the law had been used on only nine occasions 2 years later. Twenty-four other federal cases were pending (Tonry, 1987). At the federal level, the long-term impact was minimal because less than 2% of violent felonies are resolved in federal courts.

A May 2010 report by the California State Auditor concluded that those now in prison serving three-strikes sentences will cost the state a total of $19.2 billion. The report found that about 53% of those inmates are serving a sentence for a nonserious, nonviolent crime (Tonry, 1987).

Three-strikes statutes simply weren't being used in many of the 25 states that passed similar laws (Tonry, 1987). Some states have not used them at all; others have applied their laws infrequently and inconsistently. Even within a single state such as California, there was considerable variability in how state laws were interpreted and used across different counties.

Stage 6: Evaluation

We need measurable evidence that any policy, particularly an expensive one such as three-strikes, effectively and efficiently achieves what it was intended to do (i.e., reduce crime, protect public safety). Three-strikes laws were intended to reduce serious crime by incapacitating repeat offenders, and by deterring others from becoming repeat offenders.

A 1994 report by the RAND Corporation predicted a 28% decrease in crime over the 25 years following passage of the law. RAND also predicted tremendous increases in criminal justice costs, mainly through the construction and operation of additional prison cells necessitated by three-strikes laws. Three-strikes laws, researchers expected, would also result in defendants mounting more rigorous defenses to avoid severe sanctions, leading to fewer guilty pleas and more trials, greater court workloads and backlogs, and increased jail overcrowding. The existing evidence, so far, is mixed (Tonry, 1987):

- States with three-strikes laws did not experience greater declines in crime than states without such laws.
- Three-strikes states did not experience greater increases in statewide incarceration rates (e.g., number of adults incarcerated per 10,000 population), although the likelihood of incarceration per conviction (e.g., number of adults incarcerated per 10,000 convictions) has increased substantially.
- The California prison population certainly increased in terms of total numbers, but at a rate no faster than before the implementation of three-strikes laws. California already had one of the highest incarceration rates in the country, and three-strikes laws did not significantly change this rate of incarceration.
- No consistent effects in terms of dramatic workload increases or court backlogs were found in California. Counties varied dramatically in how the law was implemented. For example, some district attorneys followed the letter of the law more strictly than others. Strikes were dismissed in one-quarter to one-half of all strike-eligible cases in some counties.

In a more recent evaluation, researchers examined UCR data from 188 large cities for the time period 1980–2000. They found that cities in the 25 three-strikes states showed no significant reduction in crime rates, and surprisingly, the laws were associated with higher homicide rates in cities in the 25 three-strikes states (Kovandzic, Sloan, & Vieraitis, 2004).

RAND researchers cautioned that the full effects of the laws will remain unknown until offenders imprisoned under three-strikes laws have been incarcerated longer than they would have been under previous laws. It is also difficult (in any research study) to control for the many other social, political, and economic factors (besides three-strikes laws) that may affect crime rates (Stolzenberg & D'Alessio, 1997; Zimring, Kamin, & Hawkins, 1999).

Stage 7: Reassessment and Review

Better planning in each of the areas discussed above could have reduced widespread inconsistency and failures in implementation and could have helped reduce the number of unknown or unintended consequences of the laws (e.g., impacts on court workloads and backlogs, impacts on jail and prison crowding). Auerhahn (2001) illustrates how sentencing reforms such as three-strikes laws and California's Proposition 36 (intended to provide treatment to California's incarcerated drug offender population) result in impacts that are often far less (or far different) than what political pundits claim (Auerhahn, 2001).

Critics argue it's time to change the law, as California faces crushing budget deficits and a court order to reduce its prison population by 33,000 over the next 2 years. However, previous attempts to change the law have failed, including voters' rejection in 2004 of Proposition 66, which would have limited three-strikes convictions to violent or serious felonies (Auerhahn, 2001).

Questions

1. Briefly explain how the seven-stage model of planned change can be used to analyze an existing policy such as three-strikes laws.
2. Using Table I–2 as a guide, briefly describe one example of each of the seven stages for three-strikes laws.

References

APSA Task Force on Inequality and American Democracy (2004). *American democracy in an age of rising inequality: Report of the American political science association task force on inequality and American democracy.* Washington, DC: American Political Science Association. Retrieved March 2, 2008, from the APSA web site at: http://www.apsanet.org/imgtest/taskforcereport.pdf.

Auerhahn, K. (2001). *Incapacitation, dangerous offenders, and sentencing reform.* Albany: State University of New York Press.

Babington, C. (2006). Congress votes to renew patriot act, with changes. *The Washington Post*, A03 (March 8).

Berman, P. (1981). Thinking about programmed and adaptive implementation: matching strategies to situations. In H. Ingram & D. Mann (Eds.), *Why policies succeed or fail.* Beverly Hills, CA: Sage.

Blumstein, A., & Beck, A. J. (1999). Population growth in U.S. Prisons, 1980-1996. In M. Tonry & J. Petersilia (Eds.), *Prisons: Crime and justice v. 26,* (pp. 17–61). Chicago: University of Chicago Press.

Buzawa, E. S., & Buzawa, C. G. (2003). *Domestic violence: The criminal justice response* (3rd ed.). Newbury Park, CA: Sage.

Cannon, A. (1996). Survey: "Three-strikes" laws aren't affecting crime. The federal government and states aren't hastening to use them. California is the notable exception. *The Philadelphia Inquirer.* Tuesday, September 10, 1996.

Center for the Study and Prevention of Violence, Institute of Behavioral Science, University of Colorado at Boulder. (2011). *Blueprints for violence prevention: Big brothers big sisters of America (BBBSA).* Retrieved August 5, 2011, from: http://www.colorado.edu/cspv/blueprints/modelprograms/BBBS.html.

Clear, T. R., Cadora, E., Byer, S., & Swartz, C. (2003). *Community justice.* Belmont, CA: Wadsworth.

Cohen, M. A. (2000). Measuring the costs and benefits of crime and justice. In D. Duffee (Ed.), *Criminal justice 2000. v. 4* (pp. 263–314). Washington, DC: U.S. Department of Justice, National Institute of Justice (NCJ-182411).

D'Ovidio, R. (2007). The evolution of computers and crime: Complicating security practice. *Security Journal, 20,* 45–49.

Gandhi, A. G., Murphy-Graham, E., Petrosino, A., Schwartz Chrismer, S., & Weiss, C. H. (2007). The devil is in the details: Examining the evidence for "proven" school-based drug abuse prevention programs. *Evaluation Review, 31,* 43–74.

Gans, H. (1996). *The war against the poor: The underclass and antipoverty policy.* New York: Basic Books.

Greenwood, P. W., Everingham, S. S., Chen, E., Abrahamse, A. F., Merritt, N., & Chiesa, J. (1998). *Three strikes revisited: An early assessment of implementation and effects (NCJ 194106).* Washington, DC: U.S. Department of Justice, Office of Justice Programs, National Institute of Justice.

Greenwood, P. W., Rydell, C. P., Abrahamse, A. F., Caulkins, J. P., Chiesa, J., Model, K. E., & Klein, S. P. (1994). *Three strikes and you're out: Estimated benefits and costs of California's new mandatory-sentencing law.* Santa Monica, CA: RAND. Retrieved March 6, 2004, from the RAND web site at: http://www.rand.org/publications/MR/MR509/.

Harris, P., & Smith, S. (1996). Developing community corrections: An implementation perspective. In A. T. Harland (Ed.), *Choosing correctional options that work: Defining the demand and evaluating the supply.* Thousand Oaks, CA: Sage.

Jacobs, L., & Skocpol, T. (Eds.), (2005). *Inequality and American democracy: What we know and what we need to learn.* New York: Russell Sage Foundation.

Kettner, P. M., Daley, J. M., & Nichols, A. W. (1985). *Initiating change in organizations and communities.* Monterey, CA: Brooks/Cole.

Kovandzic, T. V., Sloan, J. J., III, & Vieraitis, L. M. (2004). "Striking out" as crime reduction policy: The impact of "three strikes" laws on crime rates in U.S. cities. *Justice Quarterly, 21*, 207–239.

Lagos, M. (2011). *Rethinking California's "three-strikes" law: Stanford project appeals sentences seen as too harsh.* Retrieved August 4, 2011 from the *San Francisco Chronicle* web site: http://articles.sfgate.com/2011-07-03/news/29732356_1_three-strikes-law-three-strikes-three-strikes-cases.

Lovrich, N. P., Pratt, T. C., Gaffney, M. J., & Johnson, C. J. (2003). *National forensic DNA study report (NCJ 203970).* Washington, DC: U.S. Department of Justice, National Institute of Justice. Available at: http://www.ncjrs.org/pdffiles1/nij/grants/203970.pdf.

McLaughlin, M. (1976). Implementation as mutual adaptation: Change in classroom organization. In W. Williams & R. F. Elmore (Eds.), *Social program implementation.* San Diego: Academic Press.

Moore, M. (1998). Synthesis of symposium. In: *U.S. Department of Justice, The challenge of crime in a free society: Looking back, looking forward* (pp. 167–178). *Symposium on the 30th Anniversary of the President's Commission on Law Enforcement and Administration of Justice (NCJ 170029).* Washington, DC: U.S. Department of Justice, Office of Justice Programs. Retrieved January 16, 2008, from the U.S. Department of Justice web site at: http://www.ojp.usdoj.gov/reports/98Guides/lblf/lblf.pdf.

Parent, D., Dunworth, T., McDonald, D., & Rhodes, W. (1997). *Key legislative issues in criminal justice: Mandatory sentencing (NCJ 161839).* Washington, DC: U.S. Department of Justice, Office of Justice Programs, National Institute of Justice.

Petersilia, J. (2003). *When prisoners come home: Parole and prisoner reentry.* New York: Oxford University Press.

Piven, F. F. (2006). Response to "American democracy in an age of inequality." *Political Science and Politics, 39*, 43–46.

President's Commission on Law Enforcement and Administration of Justice. (1968). *The challenge of crime in a free society.* New York: Avon Books.

Rossi, P. (1991). *Down and out in America: The origins of homelessness* (2nd ed.). Chicago: University of Chicago Press.

Schall, E., & Neises, E. (1998). Managing the risk of innovation: Strategies for leadership. *Corrections Management Quarterly, 2*, 46–55.

Sherman, L. W., Gottfredson, D., MacKenzie, D., Eck, J., Reuter, P., & Bushway, S. (Eds.), (1998). *Preventing crime: What works, what doesn't, what's promising.* Washington, DC: U.S. Department of Justice, National Institute of Justice.

Sieber, S. D. (1981). *Fatal remedies.* New York: Plenum.

Stambaugh, H., Beaupre, D., Icove, D. J., Baker, R., Cassaday, W., & Williams, W. P. (2000). *State and local law enforcement needs to combat electronic crime (NCJ 183451).* Washington, DC: U.S. Department of Justice, Office of Justice Programs. Retrieved January 16, 2008, from: http://www.ncjrs.org/pdffiles1/nij/183451.pdf.

Stolzenberg, L., & D'Alessio, S. J. (1997). "Three strikes and you're out": The impact of California's new mandatory sentencing law on serious crime rates. *Crime & Delinquency, 43*, 457–469.

Taxman, F., & Bouffard, J. A. (2002). Assessing therapeutic integrity in modified therapeutic communities for drug-involved offenders. *The Prison Journal, 82*, 189–212.

Tonry, M. (1987). *Sentencing reform impacts.* Washington, DC: U.S. Department of Justice, National Institute of Justice.

Tonry, M. (1995). *Malign neglect: Race, crime, and punishment in America.* New York: Oxford University Press.

U.S. Department of Justice. (1998). *The challenge of crime in a free society: Looking back, looking forward. Symposium on the 30th Anniversary of the President's Commission on Law Enforcement and Administration of Justice (NCJ 170029).* Washington, DC: U.S. Department of Justice, Office of Justice Programs.

Retrieved January 16, 2008, from the U.S. Department of Justice web site at: http://www.ojp.usdoj.gov/reports/98Guides/lblf/lblf.pdf.

Walker, S. (1992). Origins of the contemporary criminal justice paradigm: The American Bar foundation survey, 1953–1969. *Justice Quarterly, 9,* 47–76 (see also Chapter 1 of this book).

Welsh, W. N. (1995). *Counties in court: Jail overcrowding and court-ordered reform.* Philadelphia: Temple University Press.

Welsh, B. C., & Farrington, D. P. (2000). Monetary costs and benefits of crime prevention programs. In M. Tonry (Ed.), *Crime and Justice. v. 27* (pp. 305–361). Chicago: University of Chicago Press.

Welsh, W. N., Harris, P., & Jenkins, P. (1996). Reducing overrepresentation of minorities in juvenile justice: Development of community-based programs in Pennsylvania. *Crime & Delinquency, 42,* 76–98.

Welsh, W. N., & Zajac, G. (2004a). Building an effective research partnership between a university and a state correctional agency: Assessment of drug treatment in Pennsylvania prisons. *The Prison Journal, 84,* 143–170.

Welsh, W. N., & Zajac, G. (2004b). A census of prison-based drug treatment programs: Implications for programming, policy, and evaluation. *Crime & Delinquency, 50,* 108–133.

Zajac, G. (1997). Reinventing government and reaffirming ethics: Implications for organizational development in the public sector. *Public Administration Quarterly, 20,* 385–404.

Zimring, F. E., Kamin, S., & Hawkins, G. (1999). *Crime & punishment in California: The effect of three strikes and you're out.* Berkeley, CA: Institute of Governmental Studies Press.

1

Analyzing the Problem

Some preliminary analysis is needed to identify the issues involved with trying to change a particular problem. This important analysis sets the stage for all subsequent planning activities. Beware of the *activist bias:* the notion that we already know what to do, so let's get on with it. In almost all cases, the person who expresses such a view has a vague definition of the problem and its causes, and little knowledge of successful interventions. Without intending it, he or she is advocating a process of unplanned change that maximizes the likelihood of a poorly planned, poorly implemented, and ineffective intervention. The many hours of hard work and the motivation that must surely guide any successful change effort should not be wasted on unplanned change. How we analyze the problem guides what kind of interventions we come up with. If problem analysis is flawed, subsequent program or policy planning is also likely to be faulty.

Document the Need for Change

We begin analysis of a problem by examining information about the problem. We are interested in questions like the following: How do we define the problem? How big is it, and where is it? Is there a potential for change? We especially want to provide evidence for the existence of a need or problem.

We need to be very careful here. The media, politicians, or even criminal justice offi-cials socially construct many problems. By *social constructions,* we mean that certain problems are perceived, and decisions are made to focus attention and resources on a particular problem (Spector & Kitsuse, 2001; Walker, 2005). However, *perceptions* of a problem and *reactions* to it may be quite different than the actual size or distribution of a problem. We need methods to document, describe, and analyze problems. At min-imum, we need to be sure that a problem actually exists before taking any specific action, but we also need to know about the size and distribution of a problem in order to plan effective solutions.

Although the distinction is somewhat arbitrary, it is often worthwhile to differentiate a *need* from a *problem.* Students often point out that many "conditions" could be stated either way: for example, if victims of domestic violence lack access to shelters, then is there not only a need but also a problem, such as repeat incidents of abuse of this population? However arbitrary the distinction might appear at first glance, it might make a large dif-ference in the problem analysis (what kind of information we collect), analysis of causes (explanations of why certain conditions are lacking, versus why other conditions are pres-ent), and identification of relevant interventions (do we attempt to provide services that fill an important gap, or do we attempt to apply some intervention to change a problem?). Needs and problems are clearly related, but not identical.

■ ■ Need ■

A *lack* of something that contributes to the discomfort or suffering of a particular group of peo-ple. For example, we might argue that there is a need for drug treatment programs for convicted offenders, or that there is a need for shelters for abused women. In each case, an existing lack of services perpetuates the difficulties experienced by the target population.

Example 1–1   School Violence: A Problem Out of Control?

Shootings in and around schools have fueled a national debate about school violence. Following tragic incidents such as the Columbine High School massacre in 1999, the Virginia Tech shootings in 2007, and other widely publicized shootings on school properties, many school districts and campuses have scrambled to improve their security measures and disciplinary policies. While dramatic incidents fuel perceptions that school violence is out of control, available data suggest a more modest interpretation. One primary source of national data about school crime and safety is the annual report, *Indicators of School Crime and Safety* (Robers, Zhang, & Truman, 2010). Using indicators from various sources, results showed that:

- Among youths ages 5–18, there were 38 school-associated violent deaths from July 1, 2008, to June 30, 2009. Of these, 24 were homicides, and 14 were suicides. School-associated violent death is defined as "a homicide, suicide, or legal intervention (involving a law

---

Example 1–1   School Violence—Cont'd

enforcement officer), in which the fatal injury occurred on the campus of a functioning elementary or secondary school in the United States" (*Indicator 1*).

- The rates for serious violent crimes were lower at school than away from school in 2008. In 2008, students ages 12–18 were victims of four serious violent crimes per 1,000 students at school and 8 serious violent crimes per 1,000 students away from school (*Indicator 2*).
- In 2007, 4% of students ages 12–18 reported being victimized at school during the previous 6 months: 3% reported theft, and 2% reported violent victimization (*Indicator 3*).

Fortunately, tragedies such as Columbine are rare. Based upon current evidence, it is neither clear that school violence is out of control, nor that revision of school security policies is the proper (or only) solution. Thorough, localized problem analysis should precede the revision or development of school policies in any district.

Next, we attempt to apply some *boundaries* to the problem. For example, we might begin by stating a concern with juvenile violence. However, we are quickly overwhelmed with information about the problem, different causal explanations, and different interventions (Riedel & Welsh, 2011). Are we really concerned with all types of juvenile violence, or with more specific settings? Are we really interested in specific types of violence, such as gang violence, school violence, gun-related violence, drug-related violence, interpersonal conflicts versus violence committed against strangers, or instrumental (goal-oriented) versus affective (emotional) violence? This is an important point. We need to do some research first to narrow our definition of the problem. It is entirely possible that we might decide to focus not only on a specific type of violence, but upon a specific age group (say, middle-school children), a specific jurisdiction (e.g., a community with a high rate of violence, or a specific city, county, or state), or a particular demographic group (e.g., poor children living in inner-city areas). Whatever our reasons for choosing to set boundaries in particular ways (personal, political, or theoretical interests), identifying boundaries involves making judgments about how widely or narrowly to define a problem.

■ ■ Problem ■

The *presence* of something that contributes to the discomfort or suffering of a specific group. For example, we might argue that a specific community experiences a high rate of robberies committed by addicts to buy drugs, or that there is a high rate of repeat incidents of abused women applying to courts for protection orders. In each case, there is a clearly defined condition present that perpetuates the suffering of a particular group of people.

■ ■ Incidence ■

The number of *new* cases of a problem within a specific time period (e.g., the number of new cases of AIDS diagnosed in a specific calendar year). According to the Joint United Nations Programme on HIV/AIDS, an estimated 2.6 million people worldwide acquired the human immunodeficiency virus (HIV) in 2009, down from 3.1 million in 1999 (Joint United Nations Programme on HIV/AIDS (UNAIDS) and World Health Organization (WHO), 2010).

We first attempt to document the need for change through an analysis of existing conditions. Is there a problem? How big is it? What is the level of "need"? What is the evidence for a problem? One way of documenting a problem is to look at its incidence versus prevalence.

■ ■ Prevalence ■

The *existing* number of cases of a particular problem as of a specific date (e.g., the *total* number of people with AIDS as of a specific date). As of December 31, 2009, 33.3 million people worldwide were estimated to be living with HIV/AIDS, up from 26.2 million in 1999 (Joint United Nations Programme on HIV/AIDS (UNAIDS) and World Health Organization (WHO), 2010).

Where do we find this kind of statistical information, as well as more descriptive information about the problem? We usually need to look at some kind of data to estimate the degree and seriousness of a problem. There are several techniques available; we'll briefly review four of them for now (Figure 1–1). Wherever time and resources allow, it is always desirable to use as many techniques as possible to converge upon a specific problem.

- *Key informant approach:* We could conduct interviews with local "experts" to assess level of need or seriousness of a problem (e.g., community leaders, police officers, social service agents, clergy, etc.). One problem with this technique is that people to be interviewed need to be selected carefully for their expertise. We need to be aware that their views may be biased or inaccurate.
- *Community forum:* We could bring together a wide variety of people interested in a particular problem. Through discussion and exchange of ideas, we attempt to identify major problems or needs to be addressed. One common difficulty is that the most vocal groups may not necessarily be representative of a given community (e.g., special interest groups).
- *Community survey:* We may decide to conduct a survey by sampling part of a community or specific areas in a city. We might ask people, for example, "how serious would you rate the following problems in your community ...?" A common problem with this technique is that it requires skilled researchers, and it can be very expensive and time-consuming.
- *Social indicators:* Social indicators are statistics reflecting some set of social conditions in a particular area over time. For example, the U.S. Bureau of Census collects and reports extensive data on unemployment, housing, education, and crime. Common problems include difficulty in collecting data on certain questions (e.g., underreporting of illiteracy due to embarrassment), and samples that are unrepresentative of the population (e.g., the census undercounts transients and unregistered immigrants).

FIGURE 1–1 Data-collection techniques: Documenting the need for change.

Government documents and other public data sources provide valuable (but free) information resources on a multitude of criminal justice topics (for one valuable resource on social indicators for criminal justice, see the National Criminal Justice Reference Service (NCJRS) web site at: http://www.ncjrs.gov/). Here are two examples.

- *Drug use by high school seniors.* In 2010, in response to the question "On how many occasions, if any, have you used marihuana/hashish during the past 12 months?," 34.8% of high school seniors reported using these drugs at least once. This figure was up from 31.7% in 2007 (National Institute on Drug Abuse, 2011).
- *Domestic violence.* In 2009, a "nonstranger" (i.e., a friend, acquaintance, spouse, ex-spouse, parent, child, brother/sister, other relative, boyfriend/girlfriend) committed fully 68% of all nonfatal violent crimes against females (Truman & Rand, 2010).

FIGURE 1–2 Examples of social indicators for criminal justice problems.

Social indicators are perhaps the most accessible and widely used type of data for analyzing criminal justice problems (Figure 1–2). For example, the Uniform Crime Reports (UCR), collected by the FBI, consist of all crimes reported to the police, and all police arrests for specific crimes. Data are available for each state and for the nation as a whole. These figures are widely used to calculate changes in the homicide rate, for example, from year to year. Another widely used indicator is the National Crime Victimization Survey (NCVS), which is a survey administered to a national probability sample, asking respondents to report whether they have been a victim of specific crimes within a specific time period (e.g., the previous 6 months), as well as other information about any victimization, such as degree of injury suffered and characteristics of the offender (if known).

By examining social indicators, we can define a problem and attempt to change it. For example, as part of the Community Corrections Program Development Project funded by the National Institute of Corrections, Temple University researchers collaborated with the Los Angeles and Orange County Probation Departments. They found that a high-risk group of only 8% of juveniles account for the great majority of repeat referrals to juvenile court. Consequently, many agencies—probation, health, mental health, social services, school districts—cooperatively developed programming for an "8% solution" specifically targeting this high-risk group (Kurz & Schumacher, 2000).

Social indicators are extremely useful for identifying the seriousness of a problem, how it varies across groups (e.g., high vs. low income), and how it is changing over time (is it getting better or worse?). Such data are not without biases, however, and the potential user needs to be aware of these (Biderman & Lynch, 1991; Riedel & Welsh, 2008). For example, crime victimization measures may be biased by numerous factors (e.g., respondent misunderstanding of questions or crime definitions; faulty recall of incidents and time periods; deliberate underreporting due to fear, embarrassment, or the respondent's participation in illegal activities). Police-reported crime rates such as the UCR also carry potential biases, including police errors in recording and coding crime incidents. Many crimes are never even reported to the police for various reasons (e.g., victim or witness fear, embarrassment, or mistrust of the legal system). Social indicators, like the problems they measure, can be viewed as social constructions rather than objective indicators of reality. As Reiss and Roth noted: "Any set of crime statistics, therefore, is not based on some

---

Example 1–2 The New York Crime Story: Fact or Fiction?

The following example demonstrates some of the difficulties involved in analyzing problems and potential causes. How does this example illustrate the points discussed so far in this chapter?

Should we hesitate before praising public officials for decreases in crime (or blaming them for increases)? Former New York Mayor Rudolph Giuliani and former Police Commissioner William Bratton claimed that reductions in police-recorded crime rates from 1991 to 1996 (including a 55% decrease in homicide rates) were due to improved crime-fighting strategies and their "zero-tolerance" strategy toward crime. There were reasons to be skeptical (Blumstein, Wallman, & Farrington, 2000).

- The decline in the murder rate began in 1991, 3 years before either Giuliani or Bratton took office.
- Murder and violent crime rates dropped nationwide for the same time period; New York was not unique.
- Public officials often assume that police policies and resources are the major influences on crime statistics. Much criminological research over the past 50 years suggests otherwise.
- Many different factors influence crime rates, including changes in illegal drug markets, weapon availability, social and economic conditions, incarceration rates, age distribution of the population, and youth involvement in legitimate labor markets. It is extremely difficult to parcel out specific causes for crime decreases (or increases).

---

objectively observable universe of behavior. Rather, violent crime statistics are based on the events that are defined, captured, and processed as such by some institutional means of collecting and counting crimes . . ." (Reiss & Roth, 1993).

Describe the History of the Problem

As part of a problem analysis, we need to know something about the history of the problem: how long has a given problem existed, and how has it changed over time? Some of this information will have been gathered through research methods such as "key person" interviews, community forums, surveys, or examination of social indicators. Most likely, however, we will need to look further in published literature for specific, important historical events that shaped the definition of something as a social problem in need of attention, and how responses to the problem changed over time. What significant event or events helped shape the perception of certain conditions as a social problem in need of change? Such historical events often include lawsuits, legislation, dramatic public events, or specific social indicators such as crime statistics.

Lawsuits often fuel the perception of a problem, as they did with domestic violence. Liability issues led police to seriously consider calls for reform. The first of several major cases was *Thurman et al. v. City of Torrington* (Connecticut).[1] After the defense successfully

---

[1]*Thurman v. City of Torrington,* 595 F. Supp. 1521 (1984); *Thurman v. City of Torrington,* USDC. No. H-84120 (June 25, 1985).

demonstrated that police showed deliberate indifference to continued pleas for help from Ms. Thurman, the court awarded Ms. Thurman $2.3 million in damages. This case not only raised awareness of the problem of domestic violence, but led many police departments to favor a presumption of arrest.

Legislation may also create an important push for change. For example, changes in the federal Juvenile Justice and Delinquency Prevention (JJDP) Act led to ongoing state initiatives to reduce minority overrepresentation in juvenile justice (see Example 1–3 below).

Dramatic, violent, well-publicized events often raise awareness of a problem, as did riots at New York's Attica prison in September of 1971, which resulted in enormous damages and the deaths of 32 inmates and 11 guards. The Attica riots led to the most intensive investigation of prison violence in U.S. history to date, and drove prison management policies for years afterward (Riveland, 1999).

One useful technique for summarizing the history of responses to a problem is to construct a *"critical incidents" list:* a chronology of specific events explaining how a problem was recognized as such and how a specific type of intervention has developed. Once again, we caution readers that reactions to a problem are social constructions, not objective indicators of the problem. An example is given below.

Example 1–3   A Critical Incidents List: Reducing Disproportionate Minority Confinement (DMC) in Juvenile Justice

Here is a "critical incidents" list specifying major historical events and milestones in an important national policy initiative (Office of Juvenile Justice and Delinquency Prevention, 2008a).

1988	DMC was brought to national attention by the Coalition for Juvenile Justice in its annual report to Congress, *A Delicate Balance.*
1988	In the 1988 Amendments to the Juvenile Justice and Delinquency Prevention (JJDP) Act of 1974, Congress required that states address DMC in their state plans. Specifically, under the Formula Grants Program, each state must address efforts to reduce the proportion of youths detained or confined in secure detention facilities, secure correctional facilities, jails, and lockups who are members of minority groups if it exceeds the proportion of such groups in the general population.
1989	OJJDP developed a seven-point technical assistance strategy to help states fulfill the DMC requirements of the JJDP Act: (1) prepare instructions for the states; (2) conduct a national training workshop on the requirement for State Juvenile Justice Specialists and State Advisory Group members; (3) develop a work group to advise OJJDP and serve as training and technical assistance (TA) consultants; (4) prepare a TA manual; (5) provide training and TA to states upon request; (6) conduct training workshops at regional and national meetings; and (7) develop and distribute information concerning innovative approaches to address DMC.
1989	OJJDP issued instructions for the states on the statutory and regulatory requirements of the DMC core requirement.

Continued

Example 1–3 A Critical Incidents List—Cont'd	
1989 to present	OJJDP's Formula Grants Program training and technical assistance (TTA) contractor provided such services upon request on all aspects of this core requirement.
1990	OJJDP conducted a 4-day national training conference, "Implementing the Disproportionate Minority Confinement and Native American Pass-Through Amendments: A Workshop for State Planning Agencies and State Advisory Groups."
1990	OJJDP issued the *DMC Technical Assistance Manual* to guide State Juvenile Justice Specialists and State Advisory Groups to address DMC in three phases—identification, assessment, and intervention. Identification and assessment matrixes and the calculation of index values were provided as a measure of proportionality.
1991–1994	Through five competitively selected states (Arizona, Florida, Iowa, North Carolina, and Oregon), OJJDP established the DMC initiative to test various approaches to assessing DMC and experiment with approaches to reduce DMC.
1992	In the 1992 Amendments to the JJDP Act, DMC was elevated to a core requirement, with future funding eligibility (25% of the states' JJDP Formula Grants allocations) tied to state compliance. Each year, OJJDP reviews states' compliance with the DMC core requirement.
1993	A report, *The Status of the States: A Review of State Materials Regarding Overrepresentation of Minority Youths in the Juvenile Justice System,* was based on material submitted by the states to OJJDP through January 1993.
1993	Publication of an OJJDP Report, *Minorities and the Juvenile Justice System: Research Summary* (Pope & Feyerherm, 1995). This report concentrated on the official processing of minority youths. A comprehensive literature search on the processing of minority youths in the juvenile justice system from 1969 to early 1989 was conducted. The report identified existing programs and policies and examined methodological problems with previous work in this area.
1994	Publication of OJJDP Fact Sheet, *Disproportionate Minority Confinement* (Roscoe & Morton, 1994).
1995–1996	A national discretionary grants program was instituted to refine previous assessment findings, improve data systems, develop new interventions to reduce DMC, develop model DMC programs, and encourage multidisciplinary collaborations at the community level to reduce DMC. Eleven DMC discretionary grants were awarded.
1996–2006	Through a cooperative agreement with OJJDP, the Coalition for Juvenile Justice held the first National DMC Planning and Strategy Meeting, and has since made the DMC Conference an annual event with OJJDP financial support.
1997	Publication of *Disproportionate Confinement of Minority Juveniles in Secure Confinement: 1996 National Report* (Community Research Associates, 1996). This report was based on a review and analysis of states' 1994–1996 JJDP Act Formula Grants Comprehensive State Plans and the DMC Assessment Reports submitted by states to OJJDP. It provided a national summary of the nature and extent of DMC, the activities chosen to address it, and challenges experienced by the states.
1997–2004	OJJDP launched a National DMC Training, Technical Assistance, and Information Dissemination Initiative to foster development of effective strategies nationwide, using training, technical assistance, information

Example 1–3	A Critical Incidents List—Cont'd
	dissemination, and public education. Recent activities include: (1) conducting a DMC training of trainers, (2) reviewing data-collection instruments and identifying strengths and weakness, and (3) compiling a state-by-state status report on state DMC activities.
1998	An OJJDP Bulletin, *DMC: Lessons Learned From Five States* (Devine, Coolbaugh, & Jenkins, 1998), explained the DMC initiative and described how five pilot states (Arizona, Florida, Iowa, North Carolina, and Oregon) assessed DMC and implemented interventions to address identified problems.
1998	An OJJDP Bulletin, *DMC: 1997 Update* (Hsia & Hamparian, 1998), summarized the strategies promoted by OJJDP to reduce minority overrepresentation at all points of the juvenile justice system. Pennsylvania's multiyear, systematic, and data-driven effort to reduce DMC was examined.
1998–2002	The Building Blocks for Youth Initiative: This five-prong approach consists of: (1) conducting new research; (2) analyzing decision-making in the juvenile justice system; (3) directing advocacy for minority youths in the justice system; (4) building a constituency for change at the local, state, and national levels; and (5) developing communications, media, and public education strategies.
1999	An OJJDP Bulletin, *Minorities in the Juvenile Justice System* (Snyder & Sickmund, 1999), updated statistics on racial/ethnic makeup of juvenile offenders from arrest, court-processing, and confinement records.
1999–2002	The DMC Intensive Technical Assistance Project began with five states (Delaware, Kentucky, Massachusetts, New Mexico, and South Carolina) and expanded to include three more (Arkansas, California, and Tennessee).
2000	The *DMC Technical Assistance Manual* was published. This report summarized lessons learned over the preceding 10 years, and stressed the importance of ongoing DMC efforts to include ongoing evaluation of DMC strategies and monitoring of DMC trends.
2000	State DMC reports were compiled (Office of Juvenile Justice and Delinquency Prevention, 2008b), offering a central repository for historical records of DMC efforts and achievements in each state. This catalog is continually updated.
2000	OJJDP created a DMC web site (see http://www.ojjdp.gov/dmc/index.html) containing critical information, useful tools, and relevant publications. This web site is updated on an ongoing basis.
2000–2001	OJJDP expanded DMC training for state personnel from 1- to 2-h sessions to 1-day sessions at regional and national training, and also provided 1-day training at the OJJDP National Conference and the CJJ's National Pre-conferences.
2000 to date	OJJDP encouraged states to designate State DMC Coordinators to promote focused DMC efforts. The number of states with designated State DMC Coordinators increased from 10 in 1999 to 35 in 2006.
2000 to date	OJJDP's DMC Coordinator assisted OJJDP's State Representatives to develop individualized DMC compliance determination letters to states. The letters provide specific recognition of states' accomplishments and provide guidance for ongoing plans.

Continued

Example 1–3	A Critical Incidents List—Cont'd
2001	OJJDP provided a 1-day, in-depth DMC training to its state representatives to enable appropriate monitoring and the use of uniform methodology in determining DMC compliance.
2001	OJJDP's DMC Intensive Technical Assistance Project was expanded to include three additional states (Arkansas, California, and Tennessee).
2001	The Juvenile Justice Evaluation Center (JJEC) assists OJJDP in building evaluation capacity in the states, especially as those efforts relate to projects funded by the Formula Grants Program.
2002	A new OJJDP Bulletin, *Disproportionate Minority Confinement: A Review of Research Literature From 1989 Through 2001* (Pope, Lovell, & Hsia, 2002), provided an updated review and analysis of the literature.
2002	OJJDP sponsored a researchers' focus group to help the office develop a DMC research agenda.
2002	The JJDP Act of 2002, signed into law on November 2, 2002, modified the DMC requirement of the Act: "Addressing juvenile delinquency prevention efforts and system improvement efforts designed to reduce, without establishing or requiring numerical standards or quotas, the disproportionate number of juvenile members of minority groups who come into contact with the juvenile justice system." This change required an examination of possible disproportionate representation of minority youths at all decision points along the juvenile justice system continuum.
2003	OJJDP convened seven research consultants to consider a range of feasible methods to calculate disproportionality and to recommend an improved method to be recommended to OJJDP. The group recommended the DMC Relative Rate Index (RRI). Training on the new index was subsequently offered.
2004	As part of their FY 2004 Formula Grant applications, states submitted DMC Relative Rates Indexes with the most recently available data on various juvenile justice system contact points for the state and three counties with the largest minority concentration/localities with targeted DMC-reduction efforts.
2004	OJJDP published *Disproportionate Minority Confinement: 2002 Update* (Hsia, Bridges, & McHale, 2004).
2004	OJJDP awarded a 2-year grant to the Youth Law Center to develop new and accurate data-collection methods for Hispanic youths and implement activities to reduce DMC at critical points in the juvenile justice system at two sites.
2004	OJJDP provided two regional training sessions for state staff, entitled: *Diagnosis Determines Treatment: Interpreting and Using the DMC Index Numbers.*
2005	The Juvenile Justice Evaluation Center published *Seven Steps to Develop and Evaluate Strategies to Reduce Disproportionate Minority Contact* (DMC) (Nellis, 2005).
2006	OJJDP launched its web-based DMC Data Entry System, providing a central repository of state and local data across the country, and facilitating within-state or within-locality comparisons of DMC changes over time (see http://ojjdp.ncjrs.gov/ojstatbb/dmcdb/index.html).

Example 1–3	A Critical Incidents List—Cont'd
2006	OJJDP published online its *DMC Technical Assistance Manual, 3rd edition* (Office of Juvenile Justice and Delinquency Prevention, 2006), providing detailed guidance on DMC identification and monitoring, assessment, intervention, and evaluation.
2006	OJJDP awarded an 18-month grant to the Justice Research and Statistics Association to conduct an evaluation of the efficacy of DMC-reduction efforts of selected sites.
2007	In San Diego, CA, OJJDP conducted its first DMC Training of Trainers for 13 experienced, state-designated DMC coordinators. In October, at the annual DMC conference, OJJDP unveiled its DMC Reduction Best Practices Database.
2008	In January OJJDP conducted training for new and experienced DMC coordinators in New Orleans, Louisiana, and Phoenix. OJJDP updated the Summary of States' DMC-Reduction Activities.
2009	• OJJDP conducted two trainings for new DMC coordinators from 11 states in Washington, DC, and a web-based training on the Relative Rate Index (RRI).
	• OJJDP published the fourth edition of the *DMC Technical Assistance Manual*, which provides detailed guidance on DMC identification and monitoring, assessment, intervention, and evaluation, and two additional chapters on promising systems improvement strategies for Hispanic and Latino youths and the role of State DMC Coordinators.
	• OJJDP launched the Native American/Alaska Native Interagency Initiative to determine the extent of disproportionality with Native American/Alaska Native Youths.
	• OJJDP funded the DMC Analysis and Patterns Project under its Field Initiated Research and Evaluation (FIRE) solicitation. The purpose was to conduct a national analysis of Relative Rate Index (RRI) data to identify jurisdictions that have shown a consistent movement toward reduction in the RRI values over three consecutive years, to obtain detailed information on the approaches used by these jurisdictions, and to produce detailed case studies that can be replicated by other jurisdictions.
2010	• OJJDP conducted trainings in the following states: Massachusetts, Iowa, Nebraska, New Hampshire, New Jersey, and South Carolina.
	• OJJDP issued a proposal for the Community and Strategic Planning (CASP) Initiative. The purpose of the CASP is to provide effective strategies to facilitate state and local DMC initiatives to reduce and/or mitigate disproportionality throughout the juvenile justice system.
	• OJJDP hosted a 1-day training for DMC Coordinators and State Advisory Group (SAG) members October 22, 2010.
	• OJJDP continued to collaborate with the Department of Justice's Civil Rights Division to identify local jurisdictions to determine if high rates of DMC contribute to violations under the Civil Rights of Institutionalized Persons Act (CRIPA).

Examine Potential Causes of the Problem

This is a critical stage of the problem analysis. Different causes imply different solutions. If you choose a solution before you examine causes, it is likely that your intervention will be ineffective. Any intervention should be aimed at a specific cause or causes. By attempting to change one or more causes, the goal is to bring about a specific change in the problem. Causes mediate the effect of an intervention on a problem.

When we talk about examining causes, we are analyzing the *etiology* of a problem: the factors that cause or contribute significantly to a specific problem or need. A theory attempts to describe and explain relationships between cause and effect (e.g., a specific problem). A theory will describe causes of a specific problem, and it will outline proposed relationships between different causes. A theory may also suggest solutions to a problem: it provides a logical rationale for using one intervention over another.

Causes may be identified at different levels of analysis ranging from individual to social structural (see Example 1-4):

- *Individual:* Presumed causes lie within individuals (e.g., personality traits such as "aggressiveness").
- *Group:* Presumed causes lie within the dynamics of particular groups to which a person belongs (e.g., patterns of roles and relationships within a family).
- *Organizational:* Presumed causes lie within the particular culture and procedures of a specific organization, such as the police, courts, or prisons (e.g., how police are recruited, selected, or trained).
- *Community:* Presumed causes lie within the behavioral patterns and dynamics existing within a specific community (e.g., community "cohesiveness": degree of involvement in community organizations such as churches and community associations; attitudes toward deviance; supervision of juveniles) (Bursik & Grasmick, 1993)[2].
- *Social structural:* Presumed causes lie within the underlying social structure of society (e.g., the unequal distribution of wealth and power engendered by the economic system of capitalism) or its cultural attitudes regarding behaviors such as drug use, sexuality, education, crime, and so on. Factors commonly examined at this level of analysis include poverty, unemployment, and discrimination (LaFree, 1998; Messner & Rosenfeld, 2006).

---

[2]Definitions of "community" vary considerably. Should it refer to a small number of street blocks where regular, face-to-face interaction among residents occurs? Larger clusters of homes, businesses, and places that are still recognized by residents as distinct "communities"? City-designated wards or districts? Census tracts? Areas that are demarcated by physical boundaries such as busy streets, rivers, railroad tracks, parks? We do not attempt to resolve such debates here. The change agent should be explicit, however, about which definition of "community" he or she decides to adopt and why. For more detailed discussion, see: Bursik, R. J., Jr., & Grasmick, H. (1993). *Neighborhoods and crime: The dimensions of effective community control.* New York: Lexington Books. Reiss, A.J., Jr. & Tonry, M. (Eds.), *Communities and crime. Crime and justice.* Vol. 8. Chicago: University of Chicago Press. Sampson, R. J., Raudenbush, S. W., & Earls, F. (1993). Neighborhoods and violent crime: A multi-level study of collective efficacy. Science, 277, 918–924.

Example 1–4   Causes and Correlates of Domestic Violence

There are at least four general categories of causes (theories) or correlates of domestic violence (adapted from Buzawa & Buzawa, 2002).

- Individual
- Family structure
- Organizational
- Social structural

INDIVIDUAL-ORIENTED THEORIES

Researchers often examine characteristics of offenders and victims that increase the likelihood of domestic violence. Causes or contributing factors that lie within offenders may include poor self-control, low self-esteem, immaturity, depression, stress, poor communication skills, and substance abuse. Characteristics of victims contributing to domestic violence may include low self-esteem, psychological and financial dependence, and passivity.

FAMILY-ORIENTED THEORIES

Certain kinds of family structures or roles may create high potential for violence. For example, *social isolation* of families neutralizes potential support and increases risk of abuse. The best family-centered predictors of spouse abuse are: family conflict over male substance abuse, and conflicts over control in the relationship. Such conflicts tend to escalate over time. In addition, children who have been victimized themselves or who have witnessed domestic violence in the home are at higher risk for domestic violence (the "violence begets violence" thesis).

ORGANIZATIONAL THEORIES

Processes within criminal justice agencies may unintentionally contribute to domestic violence. In particular, reluctance by police to arrest suspected abusers received much criticism in the 1970s. Possible reasons for the "hands-off" response included:

- *Police culture and training:* Police are socialized into a "crime-fighting" culture; they dislike tasks that imply a "social worker" role.
- *Disincentives:* Police performance is often evaluated on the basis of numbers such as arrest rates and clearance rates, not "mediation skills."
- *Perceived futility:* Police perceive, often accurately, that few arrests for domestic violence actually result in successful prosecution (e.g., victims drop charges; prosecutors decline to proceed).

SOCIAL-STRUCTURAL PERSPECTIVES

Broad-based patterns of gender inequality in Western society are seen by many researchers as significant contributors to high rates of domestic violence. For example, patriarchal (male-dominated) religions have been said to affirm a family structure dominated by the authority and power of males. Economic patterns have also discriminated against women: women's traditional role as housewife was not as highly valued as men's "breadwinner" role, and women have historically been more economically dependent on men as a result. Other researchers point to the influence of a class-based social system: men have traditionally exerted domination over women in all areas of private and public life. According to this view, men retain more power and social advantage than women in a stratified society.

Any individual or agency who proposes any intervention always has some theory about what causes what, and at least a "hunch" about what kind of strategy would solve a specific problem and why (even if they haven't clearly thought about it or articulated it). In planned change, we very carefully think about theories and articulate them before we begin some intervention. We must explicitly tell the rest of the world what our causal assumptions about a specific problem are, and we must support these assumptions before proposing a specific type of change.

Where do we find causes and theories? By reading published material and doing library research on a problem. One should look at journal articles, books, and government and agency reports (e.g., U.S. Department of Justice, National Institutes of Health). There are many different theories of different kinds of social behavior, including criminal behavior. While some theories are very general, and most theories are constantly refined, we highly recommend that anyone proposing a criminal justice intervention acquire at least a basic knowledge of criminological and criminal justice theories, either through a course such as Criminological Theory, or by reading one of several excellent books on criminological theory (Akers & Sellers, 2008; Bernard, Snipes, & Gerould, 2009; Lilly, Cullen, & Ball, 2006). As we investigate causes, we should be guided by two major questions:

- What is the *evidence* for competing theories? No intervention should be aimed at causes that are not supported by empirical evidence of some sort.
- What kind of *intervention* is suggested by a particular causal theory? How can a specific cause be affected by an intervention?

Examine Previous Interventions

Some thorough research is needed to discover what types of interventions have previously been attempted to change a specific problem. Often, a single study will report both causal factors and the intervention that was designed to address those causes, but this is not always the case. The planner or analyst must attempt to find out what major interventions have addressed the problem of interest, and they should identify which specific causes the intervention was attempting to modify.

Excellent sources of information about interventions include key persons working in justice-related positions, criminal justice journals and books, and government reports. Numerous databases can be searched by key words and terms. Criminal justice literature searches can be conducted online, via university library systems and public web sites, including the National Criminal Justice Reference Service (NCJRS) sponsored by the U.S. Department of Justice (see http://www.ncjrs.gov). It is necessary to familiarize oneself with the various search instruments and techniques available.

Identify Relevant Stakeholders

Next, we identify the stakeholders in the change process. A *stakeholder* is any person, group, or agency who has a legitimate interest in the problem and/or the proposed intervention. We need to decide whose views should be considered in the planning process.

Some stakeholders will provide essential cooperation; others may provide potentially fatal opposition. If the intervention is to be successful, it is important that the right individuals, groups, and organizations are involved in the planning process. Otherwise, the intervention may run into insurmountable difficulties stemming from a lack of adequate information, resources, or cooperation. Who, then, should be included in the planning phase?

- Experts?
- Agency heads?
- Agency staff?
- Clients?
- Community groups?
- Business people in the neighborhood?
- Other community organizations (e.g., church, school)?

Before we can answer these questions, we need to review the information we have already collected, and answer some key questions. For example, what expectations do various individuals and groups have for change? What results are expected? Are there differences of opinion? We can think of potential stakeholders in terms of several key roles that participants may play in the change process (Kettner, Daley, & Nichols, 1985; Kettner, Moroney, & Martin, 2007). Major roles include the following.

■ ■ Change Agent System ■

Who begins the planning process to design an intervention? Who gets the ball rolling to address the problem? The change agent system usually includes the change agent and his or her sanctioning institution (e.g., the State Department of Corrections announces plans for developing offender reentry programs). Change agents come from many different backgrounds: legislators, criminal justice policymakers, professional planners, administrators, and service professionals.

■ ■ Initiator System ■

This includes those who bring the problem to the attention of the change agent. Initiators raise awareness about a specific problem (e.g., professional lobbyists, national groups such as the ACLU, National Organization of Women, the Urban League, etc.).

■ ■ Client System ■

This includes the specific individuals, groups, organizations, or communities that are expected to benefit from the change (e.g., juveniles, families, and their community might be expected to benefit from a delinquency prevention program that requires performance of community service).

■ ■ Target System ■

This includes the person, group, or organization that needs to be changed in order to reach objectives. For example, to reduce domestic violence, do we need to change abused women? Their spouses? The police response? The court response?

■ ■ Action System ■

This includes all those who, in some way, assist in carrying out the change plan, including program planning, implementation, monitoring, and evaluation. Particularly important is the agency responsible for providing programming or implementing a policy.

Sometimes, overlapping roles are possible. For example, the change agent may be part of both the target system and the action system: a Police Commissioner orders sweeping changes in police policy for dealing with domestic assault complaints. In such a case, the change agent, by virtue of overlapping roles, enjoys a degree of credibility or authority with both patrol officers (target system) and their supervisors who are responsible for implementing the new policies (action system). Overlapping roles may also enhance continuity: for example, the same person who initiates change (initiator system) carries it out (action system) with the cooperation of other participants. On the other hand, there are clearly instances in which overlapping roles are undesirable. For example, the person or agency actually carrying out the intervention should never be held responsible for program or policy monitoring and evaluation, due to their potential subjectivity or bias.

Conducting a Systems Analysis

Current thinking about criminal justice as a "system" was largely influenced by the 1967 President's Commission report (President's Commission on Law Enforcement and Administration of Justice, 1968; Rossum, 1978). Criminal justice problems and policies, the Commission concluded, are shaped by the *interactive* actions and decisions of various actors and agencies in any jurisdiction (e.g., a particular city, township, county, or state). At the same time, criminal justice projects, programs, and policies are shaped in a volatile political environment. Diverse interest groups and agencies compete for attention, and fragmented decision-making is common. Because criminal justice officials and agencies often act without consideration of how their decisions might affect those elsewhere in the system, the criminal justice system has often been called a "nonsystem." While the past 20 years have occasionally witnessed increased coordination among criminal justice units, there is still a long road to travel (Wellford, 1998).

A *system* can be defined as "all aspects of criminal justice case processing that relate to punishment or sanctions from the time of arrest—including decisions about pretrial custody—through the execution and completion of a sentence—whether that sentence is served in the community and/or in a correctional institution" (Burke, Cushman, & Ney, 1996). All individuals, groups, and organizations that play a role in such decisions in a specific jurisdiction are part of the relevant system.

The change agent, whether a consultant, a criminal justice or government official, or an academic, must identify relevant individuals and agencies in the policy environment: those whose decisions potentially have shaped the problem, and those whose decisions may potentially shape the development and implementation of change (i.e., new or modified policies, programs, or projects). Once identified, the change agent must consider how various officials and agencies have impacted the problem and solutions in the past, and how they might do so in the future. Many of the problems we seek to address in criminal justice are "systems" problems. Consider the following examples.

Example 1–5   Examples of "Systems" Problems

JAIL OVERCROWDING

Jails interact extensively with law enforcement agencies, courts, probation, and local government. Local police decide whether to arrest and book accused offenders, and thus control the major intake into the jails. Local courts influence jail populations through pretrial release decisions and sanctions for convicted offenders. Charging decisions by district attorneys influence the efficiency with which pretrial suspects are processed. Probation may administer both pretrial release programs, such as "ROR" (release on own recognizance), and intermediate sanctions for sentenced offenders, such as electronic surveillance, intensive supervision probation, and work release. County government is responsible for financial and personnel allocations to each of these agencies. In turn, county government decisions are affected by financial allocations and legislation determined at the state level (Welsh, 1995; Welsh & Pontell, 1991).

SENTENCING DISPARITIES

Concerns about disparities in sentencing (i.e., individuals committing similar offenses receive different penalties), the use of judicial discretion (wide variations in sentences across different judges and jurisdictions), and perceptions of excessive leniency or harshness have led to the development and revision of state and federal sentencing guidelines. But actual "sentencing" policy in any jurisdiction is an outcome resulting from the input of numerous individuals and agencies. Judges obviously impose criminal sanctions, but they must do so within the limits of state criminal statutes, set by the state legislature. Prosecutors make decisions about charging, which depend upon the strength and quality of evidence supplied by police, the ability and willingness of witnesses to testify, and so on. Prosecutors' charging decisions determine which criminal statutes apply to a case, and thus influence legal procedures and outcomes. Pretrial service providers make decisions about which defendants are eligible for

Continued

Example 1–5   Examples of "Systems" Problems—Cont'd

release pending trial, which in turn affect a defendant's ability to assist in the preparation of his or her defense. Defense attorneys participate in negotiations with prosecutors regarding admissible evidence, appropriate charges, potential plea bargains, and so on. Probation usually prepares a presentence report on convicted offenders, and their recommendations influence judicial options for sanctioning. At the time of sentencing, elected judges also consider the values of their constituents, their colleagues, and local justice officials. Judges must be at least to some degree aware of and responsive to their local political environment (Eisenstein, Flemming, & Nardulli, 1999).

Guidelines for Systems Analysis

A criminal justice system assessment involves gathering and analyzing information that may exist in the experiences of individual decision makers, in agency information systems and databases, and in agency reports and communications. In general, "a system assessment is a collaborative effort to synthesize individuals' experiences with the criminal justice system into a shared understanding of how things work now. This provides a common base upon which to evaluate the present, to shape a common vision for the future, and to make that vision a reality" (Eisenstein, Flemming, & Nardulli, 1999).

Based upon a model developed by the Center for Effective Public Policy (CEPP) (adapted from McGarry & Ney, 2006), this approach assumes the presence of two key elements: (1) a set of policymakers are committed to understanding and shaping their system to operate in a more collaborative manner (i.e., readiness to engage in a formal "systems" policy process); and (2) a team of outside consultants committed to working with the jurisdiction to complete the assessment. This approach requires the involvement of key decision makers who have the authority to make major decisions and who are willing to make a commitment to system-level policy analysis and development. No single individual can develop system policy, and absent system-level policy, criminal justice responses will continue to occur randomly and unpredictably. Five broad steps for criminal justice system assessment are described below; sources of information are summarized in Table 1–1. Restorative justice, an approach ripe for systems analysis, is presented in Case Study 1–3.

1. *Map the System.* How is the criminal justice system organized to carry out its mission? How do offenders flow through the system from time of arrest through sentencing? One effective strategy for gaining a shared understanding of the entire criminal justice system is to complete a map, or flowchart, of the criminal justice process. A policy team documents all of the decision points in the criminal justice process, the decision makers at each point, and the flow of offenders through the process. A general model of case flow through the criminal justice system is shown in Figure 1–3 (Bureau of Justice Statistics, 2004).

Table 1–1   Criminal Justice System Assessment: Steps and Information Sources

Category	What Is It?	Where Is It?	How Do We Get It?
Map the System	A visual depiction and description of how offenders flow through the criminal justice system and of each decision point in the process.	• Agency operating manuals. • State statutes. • Qualitative information to be collected through interviews and focus groups.	• As a team, discuss each decision point in the criminal justice system. Who are the decision-makers? Who has influence on that decision? • Consult with other practitioners and policymakers to gain a greater understanding of the informal decision-making process.
Document and Assess Current Policy and Practice	A summary report that describes the policies, procedures, and protocols of each of the agencies that impact the criminal justice system.	• Legislation. • Court decisions. • Agency descriptions. • Agency operating manuals. • Staff training curricula. • State statutes. • State sentencing policies. • Agency annual reports. • Audits. • Program evaluations.	• Make a list of all the agencies and statutes that guide sentencing policy and the use of sanctions. • Compile written documents from each. • Note all policies (both minor and major) that impact the system. • Note all agency descriptions and summarize. • Observe similarities and differences between agency goals and priorities, policies and procedures, guidance about use of sanctions.
Gather Information on the Offender Population	Statistical analyses, quantitative information, and profiles of the offender population. Population analyses could include trend analyses, recidivism studies, and/or population studies.	• Automated information systems: courts, probation, parole, corrections. • Manual records such as offender files, court records, police reports. • Manual data collection.	• Make a list of the questions and/or kinds of information desired about the offender population. • Develop a data-collection instrument and/or list of variables to be collected. • Determine a strategy for collecting and analyzing the data.
Identify Sanctions, Services, and Programs	A description of all of the options available for offenders and ex-offenders in a jurisdiction. These may be punitive, incapacitative, or rehabilitative in nature.	• Agency policy. • Statutes/sentencing laws. • Court policy. • Human services directories. • Bench books.	• Brainstorm a list of all of the sanctions available to respond to criminal offenses. • Determine what is known about each sanction, and develop a strategy for compiling this information. • Consider the development of a bench book and/or guide for supervising agents about each response that is available and for what kinds of offenses, or update an existing one.

Continued

Table 1–1   Criminal Justice System Assessment: Steps and Information Sources—Cont'd

Category	What Is It?	Where Is It?	How Do We Get It?
			• Observe the range of sanctions. Are there gaps? What are the per diem costs of each program? Is there a set of principles underlying the use of sanctions?
Identify Community Resources	A summary of the resources available in the community that can support the team's goals.	• Organizations' annual reports. • United Way reports. • "Health of the community" reports. • Chamber of Commerce reports.	• Make a list of all the human service agencies, businesses, charities, civic organizations, faith organizations, community leaders, and others that might have an interest in criminal justice. • Conduct a community survey or hold focus groups to learn more about the ways the community is interested in participating in criminal justice and the resources that exist in the community.

Source: Adapted from McGarry and Ney (2006). *Getting It Right: Collaborative Problem Solving for Criminal Justice.* Silver Spring, MD: Center for Effective Public Policy.

There is enormous variety in how justice functions are distributed across jurisdictions. At the state level, for example, typical actors and agencies include a Commissioner and Department of Corrections, the Attorney General, the Probation and Parole Department, officials in the State Planning Agency and/or the Governor's Office of Criminal Justice, a Senate Judiciary Committee, and so on. Often, a state Sentencing Commission or other state body sets policy and makes decisions about the distribution of justice funds. The actual structure and operation of policing, courts, and corrections vary substantially by state and locality. At the county level, various public and private agencies may provide pretrial assessment and services, prevention and treatment programs, halfway houses, and so on. We want to find out what agencies have responsibility for different elements of the sanctioning system, and how they relate to each other.

2. *Document and Assess Current Policy and Practice.* Sentencing and sanctioning policy in any jurisdiction is usually the result of formal and informal interactions between diverse policymakers. Here, we conduct an analysis of the formal policies in place in each agency that provide the framework for how those agencies operate. We want to develop a picture of how things work in a specific system: the steps in the process, how long the steps take, and the kinds of options available to decision makers.

What is the sequence of events in the criminal justice system?

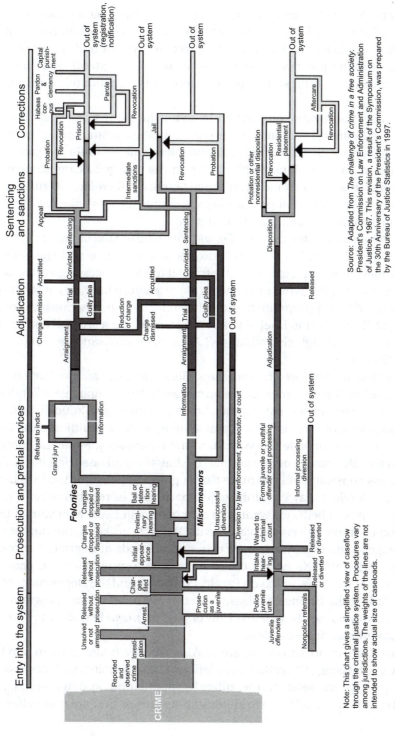

Note: This chart gives a simplified view of caseflow through the criminal justice system. Procedures vary among jurisdictions. The weights of the lines are not intended to show actual size of caseloads.

Source: Adapted from *The challenge of crime in a free society.* President's Commission on Law Enforcement and Administration of Justice, 1967. This revision, a result of the Symposium on the 30th Anniversary of the President's Commission, was prepared by the Bureau of Justice Statistics in 1997.

U. S. Bureau of Justice Statistics

FIGURE 1–3 Criminal justice system flowchart. *Source:* President's Commission on Law Enforcement and Administration of Justice (1967), *The Challenge of Crime in a Free Society* (Washington, DC: U.S. Government Printing Office). (The flowchart is available from the Bureau of Justice Statistics web site at: http://bjs.ojp.usdoj.gov/content/justsys.cfm)

Next, we want to develop an understanding of why things happen as they do. First, we complete a factual profile of each agency in the system. Second, we gather and summarize those agencies' policies as they affect the system and its process. Part of understanding why the process works as it does is to understand what each organization within the system brings to its work in terms of its mandate, its resources, and its policies.

However, formal policy often only begins to define the manner in which decisions are made and processes are carried out. In most communities, written policy guides only a small portion of activity. Inevitably, informal practices emerge to fill the gaps. Informal practices sometimes are developed with clear purpose and great care; sometimes they simply evolve over time. Understanding informal practice is therefore as critical as understanding current policy; informal practice both accounts for most of what occurs and is ultimately more readily changed than formal policy.

3. *Gather Information on the Offender Population.* Who are the offenders in the system and what do they look like? We need to know about the volume and characteristics of offenders that move through each stage of criminal justice processing and sanctioning. We need to understand what types of offenders are receiving what types of sanctions. Ideally, sanctions should be appropriate to individual offenders (e.g., seriousness of offense, past record, specific needs, and level of risk). For example, are scarce jail and prison beds being used for the most high-risk offenders? Are community sanctions being used for appropriate offenders?

4. *Identify Sanctions, Services, and Programs.* Here, we create an inventory of all of the community-based and governmental resources available to manage offenders or to respond to safety issues in the community. Some resources are "official" (that is, part of the criminal justice or local governmental system, such as health, mental health, or education). Others exist outside the system, in the community. Some are formal, such as nonprofit and faith-based organizations, businesses, and associations. Others are informal, perhaps consisting of little more than a group of neighborhood residents.

Sanctions and services may be punitive, incapacitative, or rehabilitative in nature. In addition to jail or prison beds, we want to record treatment beds, educational programming slots, and community service placements. We want to know the number of slots available, average length of stay, per-day costs, and methods of referral or access.

For example, what are the typical options available to prosecutors in charging and dismissal decisions? What discretion do Parole, Probation, and the Department of Corrections have regarding the timing of release, and the use of prerelease programs such as furlough and halfway house placements? How often does the judge follow the recommendations in a presentence investigation?

As we collect this information, we are looking for any major gaps in services and supports (either missing altogether, or deficient in capacity and accessibility to affected groups). As we look at the offender population and its needs, are any obvious needs not being met? Can we identify some groups that are more affected than others?

We also want to consider who pays for what in a specific jurisdiction. To what degree are agencies and programs funded by local, state, or federal funds? Private-sector funds? Nonprofit agencies? There is often tension between state and local governments over budget responsibility for public services such as criminal justice, education, and health. We need to understand, then, how funding is provided for various elements of sanctioning, the level of funding provided for each, whether the funding is likely to decrease or increase, and what conflicts or changes are likely in the near future.

5. *Identify Community Resources.* To what degree is the community involved in different aspects of criminal justice processing and sanctioning? What are community attitudes toward existing forms of sanctions? Who are active and vocal community leaders on criminal justice issues?

Jurisdictions vary in the degree to which community involvement has been invited or encouraged. For example, citizens may be involved in town-watch and similar community policing efforts. In some cases, citizens may be appointed to local criminal justice councils, police review boards, and other policy groups. Lack of community involvement can create suspicion and resistance; positive involvement can be an asset to planning and policy development.

Identify Barriers to Change and Supports for Change

We have talked only a bit so far about resistance to change. Even at this early stage, a decision must be made about whether to continue forward. Is the change attempt possible? Are the necessary resources and cooperation likely to be available? Before proceeding, we offer some techniques to identify potential barriers to change. These sources of resistance take many forms:

- *Physical* (e.g., the physical design of a jail prevents adequate supervision)
- *Social* (e.g., inequalities related to class, gender, race)
- *Economic* (e.g., inequalities related to income and employment)
- *Educational* (e.g., clients don't understand or know about services)
- *Legal* (e.g., criminal justice agencies are often legally obligated to do certain things and not do other things). For example, prison industry programs that could reduce the costs of incarceration are restricted by federal prohibitions regarding the movement and sale of prisoner-made goods.
- *Political* (e.g., some groups have more power than others to make their views heard; political processes can support or block a change).
- *Technological* (e.g., sophisticated information and communications systems may be required to implement a specific program or policy).

Consider the following example. Under permanent provisions of the Brady Act, effective November 1998, presale firearm inquiries are made through the National Instant Criminal Background Check System (NICS). State criminal history records are provided to the FBI through each state's central repository and the Inter-State Identification Index. The index points instantly to criminal records that states hold. Although the Brady Act required states to develop their criminal history record systems and improve their interface with the NICS, states complained bitterly that the federal government did not provide sufficient technical or financial resources to implement the informational requirements of the Brady Act (see Chapter 4).

Consider a second example. A county is under court order to reduce its jail population. Everyone agrees that a new jail is needed. However, when certain locations within the county are proposed as sites for the new jail, citizens with economic and/or political power organize community opposition to fight the construction of a jail in their own neighborhood. This "NIMBY" response ("not in my back yard") (Welsh, Leone, Kinkade, & Pontell, 1991) may take the form of protests or even lawsuits by powerful citizens to block construction. Is it fair that some can more effectively resist unwanted change than others?

One particularly useful technique for analyzing sources of support and resistance is called *force field analysis*. Remember that participation and communication are keys to change, and that collaborative strategies are preferred to conflict strategies. This technique requires us to consider diverse views and use collaborative strategies to reduce resistance and increase support for change.

The technique of force field analysis, developed by Lewin (1951), is based upon an analogy to physics: a body will remain at rest when the sum of forces operating on it is zero. When forces pushing or pulling in one direction exceed forces pushing or pulling in the opposite one, the body will move in the direction of the greater forces. The difference is that, in planned change, we are dealing with *social* forces rather than *physical* ones. To succeed in implementing any intervention, we want to try to reduce resistance to change (Figure 1–4).

Social change, like physical change, requires one of three options: (1) increasing forces in support of change; (2) decreasing forces against change (usually creates less tension and leads to fewer unanticipated consequences); or (3) doing both in some combination. There is always resistance to change. At best, there is inertia that the change agent must anticipate and overcome. Force field analysis is a valuable tool for doing this. Figure 1–5 illustrates potential driving forces and restraining forces associated with a city initiative to remove abandoned cars from the streets.

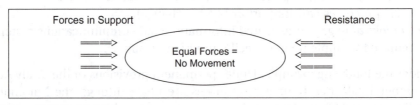

FIGURE 1–4 Force Field Analysis

Driving Forces (the pros)	Restraining Forces (the cons)
• Interest in the problem has recently been expressed by advocacy groups.	• The definition of "abandoned cars" is unclear to the public.
• The public service director supports the plan.	• Owners of older cars feel threatened.
• The City Council supports the plan.	• It is difficult to locate abandoned cars.
• Public climate favors cleaning up the city.	• The cost of transporting the abandoned cars once identified.
• Local auto salvage yards have agreed to take the cars at no cost.	• The expense involved in locating and disposing of abandoned cars.
• Health department cites old abandoned vehicles as potential health hazards.	• Need a procedure to verify vehicles declared "abandoned" and notify owners.

FIGURE 1–5 Objective: To remove abandoned cars from city streets by June 1.

Generally, we focus on reducing, rather than overcoming, resistance (see Figure 1–6). Case Studies 1–1 and 1–3 provide opportunities to apply these concepts. Three steps are involved in a force field analysis:

1. *Identify driving forces* (those supporting change) *and restraining forces* (those resisting change).
2. *Analyze the forces* identified in Step 1. Assess (for each):
   • *Amenability to change* (How likely is it that this force can be changed?)
   • *Potency* (How much impact would reducing this source of resistance have on moving the intervention forward?)
   • *Consistency* (Does this force remain stable or change over time?)
3. *Identify alternative strategies* for changing each force identified in Step 1. Focus on reducing sources of resistance.

In our travels to academic conferences, we often hear complaints by researchers that policymakers ignore the results of their research. In our consultations with policymakers, we often hear complaints that researchers use excessive jargon, research results are inconsistent, and research rarely provides the timely and specific information needed to base decisions upon. Clearly, researchers and policymakers need to interact more closely to facilitate *relevant* research and *informed* policy decisions (Blomberg, 2010; Petersilia, 1991; Rosenfeld, 2010; Wellford, 2010; Welsh & Zajac, 2004). Few social scientists took this task more seriously than Kurt Lewin, who asserted: "Research that produces nothing but books will not suffice" (Lewin, 1947).

Lewin coined the term *"action research"* to describe an intentional process of change whereby social science research intentionally and explicitly informs and shapes social action (including organizational and public policy decisions), and evaluates the results of that action. It involves fact-finding, planning, execution, and evaluation. Results from action research provide new information that gives planners a chance to learn and gather new insights about the strength and weaknesses of their decisions. Lewin emphasized that action research is a *dynamic* and *interactive* process. Successful action research requires attention to the "field" or system in which particular decisions are made, and identification of different "forces" (individuals, groups, or agencies) pushing for and against a particular type of change.

FIGURE 1–6 Kurt Lewin and "Action Research."

Discussion Questions

1. Define each of the following:
   (a) Change agent system
   (b) Initiator system
   (c) Client system
   (d) Target system
   (e) Action system
2. Define: (a) "need," and (b) "problem."
3. Define: (a) "incidence," and (b) "prevalence."
4. What techniques can we use to estimate the degree and seriousness of a problem? Describe each method of documenting the need for change: (a) key informant approach, (b) community forum, (c) community survey, and (d) social indicators.
5. What does it mean to say that a problem is "socially constructed"? Give an example.
6. (a) Define "etiology." (b) Describe the five levels of etiology, and give an example of each.
7. Define "theory."
8. What is a "systems analysis"? Describe the five steps in a criminal justice systems analysis. Use examples to illustrate your understanding of these concepts.
9. Discuss different types of barriers to change, and give an example of each: (a) physical, (b) social, (c) economic, (d) educational, (e) political, (f) legal, and (g) technological.
10. (a) Define "force field analysis." (b) Describe each of the three steps.
11. Define "action research."

■ ■ ■ ━━

Case Study 1–1 Domestic Violence

Instructions

Read the hypothetical case scenario on the next page. Then, break into groups (assigned by the instructor) and answer the questions below. Each group member should take some notes about the discussion, but the group will appoint a spokesperson to report the group's findings to the class. Plan on preparing a 5-min summary.

A headline in a local newspaper, the *Bigtown Chronicle,* read: "Woman killed by husband in domestic dispute." Bigtown Police said that Betty Benson, age 32, died of multiple stab wounds allegedly inflicted by her husband, Bill, age 34, following a violent argument in the couple's home. Police had been called to the home four times in the previous 6 months in response to complaints by neighbors that "there was a lot of yelling, and she was screaming like she was being beaten." Ms. Benson had declined to press charges in each instance.

The next day, there was a noisy protest in front of city hall by a local group called WASA (Women for Action against Spouse Abuse). WASA spokesperson Sarah Smith told reporters,

"This kind of nonsense has been going on far too long. The police were called to that house four times before she got murdered, and they didn't do anything to help her. The police should be arresting sick people like Bill Benson and putting them away for a long time, not just talking to them and letting them go right back to beating their wives."

Police Commissioner Frank Fine responded to the criticisms by pointing out that the police don't make the laws. "WASA can complain all they want," Fine said, "but the state legislature makes the laws regarding domestic assault, and right now, the law says that police can't make an arrest unless the victim swears out a complaint. We can't arrest people like Bill Benson just because they appear to be unsavory characters."

WASA began protesting in front of the state capitol, and 2 days later, Rep. Alan Atkinson introduced a new bill calling for sweeping changes in the laws regarding spouse abuse. The bill called for mandatory arrest and a mandatory 48-hr. detention period, pending investigation, for anyone suspected of spousal assault. According to the bill, the police would use "reasonable discretion" in enforcing the law. The local chapter of the ACLU (American Civil Liberties Union) expressed outrage, arguing that the new bill would deprive suspects of their constitutional rights of due process and give the police the power to be "judge, jury, and hangman."

Bob Bigheart, a spokesperson for the Bigtown Social Services Agency, said that tough new laws were not the answer. Instead, he suggested, the police should train officers in family crisis counseling so that they can mediate domestic disputes and refer couples to community agencies to help solve their problems. Police Commissioner Frank Fine says that is what the police do anyway: "We are a service-oriented police department," Fine said, "and our officers are among the best-trained in the nation." Claiming that the Commissioner was "arrogant and insensitive to the rights of victims," WASA called for Fine's immediate resignation.

Questions

The governor has asked you, as members of the State Planning Agency, to study the problem of domestic assault and make preliminary recommendations about what to do, if anything, to deal with the problem. Include the following in your answer:

1. Is there a problem here? If so, what is it? How can you tell?
2. Identify the participants and the role that each plays.
   * Change agent system
   * Initiator system
   * Client system
   * Target system
   * Action system
3. Identify the specific change being proposed, and conduct a force field analysis.
4. Who perceives the need for what kind of change? Are there differences of opinion? Whose views need to be considered, and how do you choose among competing views?
5. Do you need any additional information before you make your report to the governor? Should some kind of change proceed?

■ ■ ■ ▬▬▬▬▬▬▬▬▬▬▬▬▬▬▬▬▬▬▬▬▬▬▬▬▬▬▬▬

Case Study 1–2 Idaho's Statistical Analysis Center Helps State Police Solve Personnel Allocation Problem (Wing, 2008)

When the Idaho State Police needed to know how many troopers should patrol state roads, the Idaho Statistical Analysis Center (ISAC) used geographic mapping technologies and collaborative data to answer the question.

Statistical Analysis Centers (SAC) collect and distribute criminal justice data and research and evaluate statewide policy issues. The U.S. Bureau of Justice Statistics offers grant funds to encourage SACs to analyze topics of concern, such as human trafficking, cybercrime, domestic violence, and emerging drug trends. Many SACs also help maintain national data sets, including National Incident-Based Reporting System (NIBRS) data and state crime victimization research.

Currently, 53 states and territories have SACs. Each state's governor decides where to locate the SAC. The governor may choose to place the SAC in the governor's office, the state highway patrol, the state department of corrections, or a university.

The Idaho Statistical Analysis Center

Since its inception in 1978, the ISAC has been housed in the Idaho Department of Law Enforcement, which became the Idaho State Police in July 2000. ISAC provides statistical support, data analysis, program planning, evaluation research, and technical support to local, state, and national criminal justice agencies.

ISAC is currently working on several projects, including evaluations of B/JAG[1] and STOP[2] grant programs, a state victimization study, and projects that analyze NIBRS data to gain a better understanding of Idaho crime trends.

Patrolling Idaho's Interstates and Highways: How Many Troopers Are Needed?

The Idaho State Police wanted to determine how many troopers would be needed if a trooper were to pass every mile of the state's interstates and highways once a day. They also wanted to know the number of troopers needed to provide adequate coverage for calls for service and interagency assistance in each region of the state. To answer the Idaho State Police's questions, ISAC began a police allocation study in March 2007.

ISAC collected information on state and federal roadways in Idaho from a variety of sources, including the following:

- Idaho Department of Transportation data on crashes and average traffic for each milepost for 2004–2006.
- Idaho State Police computer-aided dispatch system information on calls for service for each milepost for 2004–2006.

ISAC used the information to categorize roads by frequency of traffic, crashes, and calls for service, using three tiers (high [1], medium [2], and low [3]). Data were analyzed using Statistical Package for the Social Sciences software, then plotted geographically using Geographic Information Systems software, as shown in Figures 1–7 and 1–8.

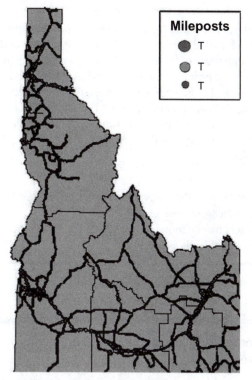

FIGURE 1–7 Tiered Mileposts on State and Federal Roads in Idaho.

$$N = \frac{HM \times HC}{7 \times PS \times SH \times PI}$$

N = Number of Troopers
HM = Highway Miles
HC = Hours of Coverage per Week
PS = Average Patrol Speed (includes stationary patrol)
SH = Shift Length
PI = Performance Objective Patrol Interval

FIGURE 1–8 Equation to determine the number of troopers needed per highway mile.

Conclusion

State SACs actively work to establish national and state networking relationships and research partnerships. The Idaho study was possible because of the collaborative opportunities available to ISAC. Combining criminal justice data sets with geographic mapping systems can provide meaningful research that effectively influences policy and practice.

Notes

1. The Edward Byrne Memorial Justice Assistance Grant (JAG) Program (42 U.S.C. 3751 (a)) is the primary provider of federal criminal justice funding to state and local jurisdictions. JAG funds support all components of the criminal justice system, including multijurisdictional drug and gang task forces; crime prevention and domestic violence programs; and courts, corrections, treatment, and justice information sharing initiatives.
2. The Services, Training, Officers and Prosecutors (STOP) Violence Against Women formula grant program provides federal financial assistance to states to develop and strengthen law enforcement activities, prosecution strategies, and victim services in cases involving violent crimes against women.

Questions

1. Describe the need for change. Why was this analysis conducted?
2. What types of social indicators were examined?
3. What are some practical implications of this analysis? For example, how might actual responses by state police to calls be affected?

Case Study 1–3 Incorporating Restorative and Community Justice into American Sentencing and Corrections

Instructions

Read the report below and answer the questions that follow (adapted from Kurki, 1999).

Restorative justice and community justice represent new ways of thinking about crime. The theories underlying restorative justice suggest that government should surrender its monopoly over responses to crime to those most directly affected—the victim, the offender, and the community. Community justice redefines the roles and goals of criminal justice agencies to include a broader mission—to prevent crime, address local social problems and conflicts, and involve neighborhood residents in planning and decision-making. Both restorative and community justice are based on the premise that communities will be strengthened if local citizens participate in responding to crime, and both envision responses tailored to the preferences and needs of victims, communities, and offenders.

In contrast to this bottom-up approach, recent changes in sentencing law are premised on retributive ideas about punishing wrongdoers and on the desirability of controlling risk, increasing public safety, and reducing sentencing disparities. Restorative and community justice goals of achieving appropriate, individualized dispositions often conflict with the retributive goal of imposing certain, consistent, proportionate sentences.

There are many ways to resolve this normative conflict. Restorative and community justice initiatives could continue to confine their efforts to juvenile offenders and people who commit minor crimes. This seems unlikely, as these approaches are expanding rapidly and winning many new supporters who want to extend their application. Alternatively, retributive sentencing laws could be revised or narrowed. But this too seems unlikely in the near term. How precisely the two divergent trends will be reconciled remains to be seen. Nevertheless, it seems likely that restorative and community justice values will to some extent become more institutionalized in criminal justice processes.[3]

What Is Restorative Justice?

Restorative justice has evolved from a little-known concept into a term used widely but in divergent ways. There is no doubt about its appeal, although the varied uses of the term cause some confusion. The umbrella term "restorative justice" has been applied to initiatives identified as restorative by some but not by others. Examples are sex-offender notification laws, victim impact statements, and murder victim survivors' "right" to be present at executions. Most advocates of restorative justice agree that it involves five basic principles:

- Crime consists of more than violation of the criminal law and defiance of government authority.
- Crime involves disruptions in a three-dimensional relationship of victim, community, and offender.
- Because crime harms the victim and the community, the primary goals should be to repair the harm and heal the victim and the community.
- The victim, the community, and the offender should all participate in determining the response to crime; government should surrender its monopoly over that process.
- Case disposition should be based primarily on the victim's and the community's needs—not solely on the offender's needs or culpability, the dangers he or she presents, or his or her criminal history.

The original goal of restorative justice was to restore harmony between victims and offenders. For victims, this meant restitution for tangible losses and emotional losses. For offenders, it meant taking responsibility, confronting shame, and regaining dignity.

This notion has evolved, with the major recent conceptual development being the incorporation of a role for the community. Many people still associate restorative justice primarily with victim-offender mediation or, more broadly (but mistakenly), with any victim-oriented services. The more recent conceptualization—that offenses occur within a three-dimensional relationship—may change the movement.

All three parties should be able to participate in rebuilding the relationship and in deciding on responses to the crime. The distinctive characteristic is direct, face-to-face dialogue among victim, offender, and increasingly, the community.

What Is Community Justice?

The concept of community justice is less clear. It can be portrayed as a set of new organizational strategies that change the focus of criminal justice from a narrow, case-processing orientation: operations are moved to neighborhood locations that offer flexible working hours and services,

---

[3]This paper is one of four in the first "round" of publications from the Executive Sessions on Sentencing and Corrections. Together the four constitute a framework for understanding the issues raised in the sessions. The other three are *Fragmentation of Sentencing and Corrections in America*, by M. Tonry (NCJ 175721); *Reconsidering Indeterminate and Structured Sentencing*, by M. Tonry (NCJ 175722); and *Reforming Sentencing and Corrections for Just Punishment and Public Safety*, by M.E. Smith and W.J. Dickey (NCJ 175724). All: *Research in Brief— Sentencing & Corrections: Issues for the 21st Century*, Washington, DC: U.S. Department of Justice, National Institute of Justice/Corrections Program Office, September 1999.

neighborhoods are assigned their own officers and are provided with more information than is standard practice, and residents may identify crime problems and define priorities for neighborhood revitalization. Most experience with community justice is in the context of community policing, but prosecutors, judges, and correctional officers are increasingly rethinking their roles and goals.

The most frequently cited standpoints for community justice are problem solving and community empowerment. Problem solving is understood broadly: first, as an effort to build partnerships between criminal justice and other government agencies and between government agencies and neighborhoods; and, second, as an attempt to address some of the complex social problems underlying crime.

Community justice proponents suggest that criminal justice agencies change the way they interact with the public, learn to listen to citizens, and work together with local people to prevent crime and solve crime-related problems (Barajas, 1996).

Advocates of community justice believe that to maximize public safety and optimize crime prevention, residents must work on an equal basis with government agency representatives and elected officials.

Dennis Maloney, Director of the Deschutes County, Oregon, Department of Community Justice has described the connection between citizen involvement and crime prevention: "In a community justice framework, the goal is to engage as many citizens as possible in building a better community. . . . People who share a strong sense of community are far less likely to violate the trust of others. Their stake in and bond with the community is the strongest force of guardianship to prevent crime from flourishing."

Should Restorative and Community Justice Be Incorporated into the Criminal Justice System?

Advocates of restorative justice and community justice often differ over the desirability of becoming part of the official criminal justice system. Restorative justice proponents believe in the efficacy of grassroots citizen efforts, and thus many want to keep restorative justice initiatives separate from the criminal justice system. Community justice advocates often support a total, systemwide transformation that would incorporate the new principles. Both groups are concerned about the role of government in these approaches and their growing popularity. They emphasize that restorative and community justice represent fundamental change: comprehensive philosophies or theories, not silver bullets or fads.

Proponents are also concerned that criminal justice agencies will add new community or restorative justice programs to appear "fashionable" or to solve a particular problem, but will do so without fundamentally rethinking their missions. Ronald Earle, District Attorney in Travis County, Texas, summarized this concern: "The question is how to focus the criminal justice system and fashion programs on a new way of thinking, not just another way of doing." Some advocates are skeptical about whether the new goals and principles can be meaningfully adopted by criminal justice agencies, which like many other government agencies tend to value passionless, specialized, professionalized, and routinized operations.

Another worry is that government agencies or experts will establish guidelines, standards, and requirements for programs reflecting these values, thereby bureaucratizing them and once again "stealing the conflicts" from communities. As Ronald Earle put it, the "unstructured lack of standardization is the genius of the movement," but, at the same time, he added, "there is a great temptation to create a national template for community justice programs." The challenge for government will be to encourage and support the new initiatives without stifling the spontaneity, creativity, and grassroots ties that are their strengths.

What Is Happening Now?

A fundamental difficulty in documenting or estimating the impact of restorative or community justice in the United States is the lack of systematic data. No one knows how many or what kinds of programs there are; how many offenders, victims, and volunteers participate; the amounts of restitution paid or community service performed; or the effects on victims, communities, and offenders. It is nearly impossible to monitor what is happening in different states or regions.

Little evaluation research is available, and there is no consensus on how to measure "success." Most advocates contend that recidivism is not the correct or only measure. Evaluations might also consider such measures as victim and offender satisfaction, amounts of restitution or community service, rates at which reparative agreements are fulfilled, levels of volunteer participation and community action, and victims' and offenders' quality of life.

Some advocates do not want to encourage rigorous evaluation because that might create pressure to standardize and "expertize" the movements. But because the varied programs and practices are what make restorative and community justice visible, concrete, and distinctive, it is important to document their types, analyze their characteristics, and evaluate outcomes.

The dearth of information affects the writings of practitioners and academics. There is, however, a sizable literature on the principles and goals of restorative justice, how it differs from traditional criminal justice approaches, and its processes and terminology (Braithwaite, 1999; Van Ness & Strong, 2006). Other works describe programs or present details of local projects (Galaway & Hudson, 1996; Messmer & Otto, 1992). Most of the literature on community justice focuses on community policing, with little information on community prosecution, courts, or corrections.

Restorative Justice Practices

Although something akin to restorative justice has long been observed in premodern and indigenous societies, restorative justice principles, in the form of victim-offender reconciliation programs, appeared in Western industrialized countries only in the 1970s. The first program was established in 1974 in Kitchener, Ontario. By the 1990s, such programs had spread to all Western countries—at least 700 in Europe and 300 in the United States.

Victim-Offender Mediation

Victim-offender mediation is the most widespread and evaluated type of restorative program. Offenders and victims meet with volunteer mediators to discuss the effects of the crime on their lives, express their concerns and feelings, and work out a restitution agreement. The agreement is often seen as secondary to emotional healing and growth. Victims consistently report that the most important element of mediation is being able to talk with the offender and express their feelings, and offenders also emphasize the importance of face-to-face communication. Advocates believe that developing an offender's empathy for the victim has preventive effects.

In many countries, victim-offender mediation is widely used. In Austria, for example, it became an official part of the juvenile justice system as early as 1989. Public prosecutors refer juveniles to mediation, probation officers coordinate cases, and social workers serve as mediators. If an agreement is reached and completed, the case is dismissed (Lösching-Gspandl & Kilchling, 1997). In the United States, most programs are operated by private, nonprofit organizations; handle largely juvenile cases; and function as diversion programs for minor, nonviolent crimes. However, there is a movement to develop programs established and operated (or at least initiated) by corrections departments, police, or prosecutors and used as a condition of either probation or dropping charges. Most studies of mediation programs report high rates of success (Umbreit, 1994).

Advocates are beginning to challenge the assumption that mediation is not suitable for violent or sexual crimes. Increasingly, in the United States and Canada, for example, victims and offenders meet in prisons. These meetings are not oriented to a tangible goal such as a restitution agreement, nor does the offender obtain benefits like early release or parole consideration. Usually the meetings are held because the victim wants to meet the offender and learn more about what happened to reach beyond fear and anger and facilitate healing. The results of a Canadian survey indicated that 89% of victims of serious, violent crimes wanted to meet the offender (Gustafson, 1997).

Serious violent crimes are usually mediated on a case-by-case basis, but the need for permanent programs is growing. Such programs are offered, for example, by the Correctional Service of Canada in British Columbia and the Yukon Territory and by the Texas Department of Criminal Justice.

Family Group Conferencing

Family group conferencing is based on the same rationales as victim-offender mediation, with two main differences. Conferencing involves a broader range of people (family, friends, coworkers, and teachers), and family members and other supporters tend to take collective responsibility for the offender and for carrying out his or her agreement. The other difference is that conferencing often relies on police, probation, or social service agencies for organization and facilitation.

Family group conferences originated in New Zealand, where they became part of the juvenile justice system in 1989. There, the new juvenile justice model, which incorporates Maori traditions of involving the family and the community in addressing wrongdoing, has four dispositional options:

- An immediate warning by the police.
- "Youth Aid Section" dispositions in which a special police unit may require, for example, an apology to the victim or community service.
- Family group conferencing.
- Traditional youth court sentencing.

About 60% of juvenile offenders receive a warning or go to the Youth Aid Section, 30% go to conferencing, and 10% go to youth court (Maxwell & Morris, 1993).

By the mid-1990s, family group conferencing had been adopted in every state and territory of Australia. In South Australia, it is used statewide as a component of the juvenile justice system and resembles the New Zealand approach. In Wagga Wagga, New South Wales, conferences (originally part of a police diversion program) were organized and facilitated by police officers who were often in uniform (Wundersitz & Hetzel, 1996). Responsibility was transferred to juvenile justice agencies in 1998, and trained community members now facilitate conferences. In Canberra, the Federal Police set up a program called the Reintegrative Shaming Experiment, which involved more than 100 trained police officers.

There is evidence that conferencing can be successful. An evaluation of the Bethlehem, Pennsylvania, Police Family Group Conferencing program revealed that typical police officers were able to conduct conferences in conformity with restorative justice and due process principles if adequately trained and supervised, and that very high percentages of offenders, victims, and other participants were pleased with the process (McCold & Wachtel, 1998). Evaluation of Canberra's Reintegrative Shaming Experiment showed similar results (Sherman et al., 1998).

Sentencing Circles

Sentencing circles originated in traditional Native Canadian and Native American peacemaking. They involve the victim and the offender, their supporters, and key community members, and they are open to everyone in the community. They attempt to address the underlying causes of crime, seek responses, and agree on offenders' responsibilities. The process is based on peacemaking, negotiation, and consensus, and each circle member must agree on the outcomes.

Sentencing circles are so named because participants sit in a circle, and a "talking piece" (a feather, for example) is passed from person to person. When participants take the talking piece, they explain their feelings about the crime and express support for the victim and the offender. Separate circles often are held for the offender and the victim before they join in a shared circle.

In Minnesota, sentencing circles are used not only in Native American communities but also in rural white, suburban, and inner-city black communities (see "Minnesota: A Pioneer in Restorative Justice"). Community Justice Committees, established by citizen volunteers, handle organizational and administrative tasks and provide "keepers" who lead the discussions. Judges refer cases, and the committees make the final decision on acceptance. The agreements reached are presented to the judge as sentencing recommendations. In some cases, the judge, prosecutor, and defense attorney participate in the circle, and then the agreement becomes the final sentence.

Reparative Probation and Other Citizen Boards

Reparative probation in Vermont involves a probation sentence ordered by a judge, followed by a meeting between the offender and volunteer citizen members of a Reparative Citizen Board. Together they draw up a contract, based on restorative principles, which the offender agrees to carry out. Fulfilling the contract is the only condition of probation (see "Vermont: Statewide Reparative Probation").

Vermont's program is different from most other restorative justice initiatives in the United States. Designed by the state's Department of Corrections, it operates statewide, handles adult cases, and involves a sizable number of citizen volunteers. Compared with family group conferencing or sentencing circles, the Reparative Citizen Boards work faster, require less preparation, and can process more cases; however, they involve fewer community members. For example, offenders' and victims' families and supporters usually are not present.

Citizen boards also may be established to adjudicate minor crimes. For example, a Merchant Accountability Board in Deschutes County, Oregon, consists of local business owners who adjudicate thefts of property valued at $50 or less, and some more serious cases involving property valued at between $51 and $750. Under an agreement with the district attorney, the police refer all minor shoplifting cases directly to the program. If offenders decide to participate, they are typically ordered by the board to pay fines, make restitution, or both.

Manitoba's Restorative Resolutions Project offers an alternative to custodial sentences for offenders who otherwise are likely to face a minimum prison sentence of 6 months. Offenders and project staff develop sentencing plans, and victims are encouraged to participate. The plans are presented to judges as nonbinding recommendations. Most plans require restitution, community service, and counseling or therapy. A recent evaluation revealed that offenders who participate have significantly fewer supervision violations and slightly fewer new convictions than those in comparison groups (Bonta, Rooney, & Wallace-Capretta, 1998).

Minnesota: A Pioneer in Restorative Justice

Minnesota has been a groundbreaker in restorative justice. Its Department of Corrections created the Restorative Justice Initiative in 1992, hiring Kay Pranis as a full-time Restorative Justice Planner in 1994—the first such position in the country. The initiative offers training in restorative justice principles and practices, provides technical assistance to communities in designing and implementing practices, and creates networks of professionals and activists to share knowledge and provide support.

Sentencing Circles

Besides promoting victim-offender mediation, family group conferencing, and neighborhood conferencing, the department has introduced sentencing circles. Citizen volunteers and criminal justice officials from Minnesota have participated in training in the Yukon Territory, where peacemaking circles have been held since the late 1980s. In Minnesota, the circle process is used by the Mille Lacs Indian Reservation and in other communities in several counties.

The Circle Process

The circle process usually has several phases. First, the Community Justice Committee conducts an intake interview with offenders who want to participate. Then, separate healing circles are held for the victim (and others who feel harmed) and the offender. The committee tries to cultivate a close personal relationship with victims and offenders and to create support networks for them. In the end, a sentencing circle, open to the community, meets to work out a sentencing plan. In the towns of Milaca and Princeton, follow-up circles monitor and discuss the offender's progress.

Vermont: Statewide Reparative Probation

A pilot reparative probation program began in Vermont in 1994, and the first cases were heard by a Reparative Citizen Board the following year. Three features distinguish this restorative justice initiative from most others in the United States: (1) The Department of Corrections, headed by John Gorczyk, designed the program; (2) it is implemented statewide; (3) and it involves a sizable number of volunteer citizens. In 1998, the program was named a winner in the prestigious Innovations in American Government competition.

The Process

The concept is straightforward. Following an adjudication of guilt, the judge sentences the offender to probation, with the sentence suspended and only two conditions imposed:

the offender will commit no more crimes and will complete the reparative program. The volunteer board members meet with the offender and the victim and together discuss the offense, its effects on victim and community, and the life situations of victim and offender. All participants must agree on a contract, which is to be fulfilled by the offender. It is based on five goals: (1) the victim is restored and healed, (2) the community is restored, (3) the offender understands the effects of the crime, (4) the offender learns ways to avoid reoffending, and (5) the community offers reintegration to the offender. Because reparative probation targets minor crimes, it is not meant as a prison diversion program.

The Numbers

In 1998, the 44 boards handled 1,200 cases, accounting for more than one-third of the probation caseload. More than 300 trained volunteers serve as board members. Ten coordinators handle case management and organization for the boards. The goal is to have the boards handle about 70% of the targeted probation cases. That only about 17% of offenders fail to complete their agreements or attend follow-up board meetings is a measure of the program's success. These offenders are referred back to court.

Related Initiatives

Other practices based on restorative justice are underway. More than 150 volunteers or Department of Corrections staff have been trained in family group conferencing. A Community Justice Center is operating in Burlington, and others are being developed elsewhere. The department is also looking into sentencing circles and ways to become more active in crime prevention and early intervention.

Community Justice Practices

People who have no personal experience with community justice are often preoccupied with what "community" means and who is involved. Explanations vary. Reginald Wilkinson, Director of Ohio's Department of Rehabilitation and Correction, says: "In a community, there would exist a sense of hope, belonging, and caring. … A sense of commitment, responsibility, and sacrifice would be basic tenets of a communitarian." For Minnesota Department of Corrections Restorative Justice Planner Kay Pranis, "Community self-defines around the issue that surfaces, so everybody who sees themselves as a stakeholder in a particular issue [makes up the community]." Vermont Department of Corrections Commissioner John Gorczyk says: "Beyond place, community is defined by relationships and the amount of interaction. In my community, the quality of those interactions, doing favors for one another, is what builds community."

Although in "practicing" community justice it is essential to identify the community and consider possible definitions, it is at least as important to think about the community's role. While many new approaches in criminal justice have improved access to and satisfaction with justice services, often they have not transformed the role of citizens from service recipient to participant and decision maker (Bazemore, 1997). For many community justice advocates, the ultimate goal is for communities to feel ownership of programs, but that can be achieved only if citizens participate. Even then the question remains whether government genuinely shares power or simply allows communities to supplement its power and exercise it only in certain types of cases.

Community Policing and Prosecution

Experiences with community policing show there is no shared understanding of the community's role, and that it is difficult to generate citizen participation. Priorities and routines vary; for example, some efforts rely on heavy street-level enforcement, while others emphasize citizen involvement, better-quality public services, delivery of community-based treatment, or diversionary policing that withholds enforcement as a way to build relationships with communities.

Few studies have attempted to measure the extent to which the rhetoric of community empowerment, involvement, and partnership building becomes reality, and the results are not particularly encouraging. Community input is often limited to assisting law enforcement. Many evaluations have not shown positive results, because implementation is often incomplete or partial (Skogan & Hartnett, 1997).

Many applications of community policing and prosecution are not fundamentally different from traditional approaches, although they may shift control to local levels and include the community in law enforcement efforts. They often promote tougher responses to crime than do traditional approaches because the emphasis is on a broader view of crime control that takes seriously minor, nuisance, and quality-of-life offenses. Some approaches, such as the one taken by the District Attorney of Travis County, Texas, however, clearly identify themselves as restorative (see "Travis County, Texas: Community Justice as the Prosecutorial Response").

Applications in Courts and Corrections

The first community court in the United States, New York City's Midtown Community Court, is based on the idea of partnership with the neighborhood and focuses on quality-of-life crimes. Several restorative elements are evident:

- Offenders are sentenced to work on projects in local neighborhoods.
- Court staff try to link offenders with drug treatment, health care, education, and other social services and thus combine punishment with help.
- The community is encouraged to participate in shaping restorative, community-based sanctions (Feinblatt & Berman, 1997).

Nearly 70% of those convicted are ordered to perform community work, and of these nearly 70% complete it without violations. By the Fall of 1996, almost 33,000 defendants had been arraigned (Midtown Community Court, 1997). The court houses health care and drug treatment providers, organizes education and job training, maintains mediation services for community-level conflicts, and provides counseling rooms and space to perform community service.

The Manhattan Court opened in 1993 and was followed by several others. The Portland (Oregon) Community Court began operations in 1998, and plans for community courts are underway in Baltimore, Hartford (Connecticut), Hempstead (New York), Indianapolis, Minneapolis, St. Louis, and no doubt elsewhere.

Deschutes County, Oregon, has made a comprehensive effort to implement community justice in corrections (as distinct from traditional community corrections), reinventing its Community Corrections Department as the Department of Community Justice. Committed to principles of both community and restorative justice, the department differs in this respect from most current community policing and prosecution initiatives.

The Deschutes approach is especially ambitious (see "Deschutes County, Oregon: Reinventing Community Corrections"). A true paradigm shift would combine operational strategies and the crime prevention and citizen involvement goals of community justice with the values and practices of restorative justice.

Travis County, Texas: Community Justice as the Prosecutorial Response

Ronald Earle, District Attorney of Travis County (Austin), Texas, is a strong advocate of restorative and community justice. Recognizing that people's natural reaction to crime is anger and fear, particularly if they lack power to influence responses, he believes this wasted energy can fuel positive change. This can be done if citizens are empowered and participate in planning and deciding on the response to crime.

To promote such participation, he drafted the Texas law that authorizes in each county a Community Justice Council and Community Justice Task Force. The task force includes representatives of criminal justice agencies, social and health services, and community organizations. With task force assistance, the council, consisting of elected officials, handles planning and policymaking and prepares a Community Justice Plan.

Many efforts are directed at juvenile offenses. In Austin, the Juvenile Probation Office offers victim-offender mediation for young people in trouble. For misdemeanors, juveniles may be diverted from court to Neighborhood Conference Committees. These consist of panels of trained adult citizens who meet with the juvenile offenders and their parents and together with them develop contracts tailored to the case.

The Travis County Children's Advocacy Center provides support and help to abused children through collaboration among social and criminal justice agencies, medical professionals, and private citizens. The Child Protection Team brings together police officers, social workers, and prosecutors to improve responses to child abuse and to reduce traumatization when cases are investigated and prosecuted.

Can the Justice System Incorporate Restorative Principles?

Although many activists would prefer that restorative justice remain an unofficial alternative to the criminal justice system, others contend that there are reasons for a systemwide shift to incorporate its values.

Why Not the Best?

If restorative justice is a significantly better way to deal with crime, proponents ask why not implement it systemwide? If it really is a better idea, why should it not become the governing principle of the whole criminal justice system rather than be confined to small-scale, grassroots activities? Minnesota Restorative Justice Planner Kay Pranis emphasized the need to focus on community when she said, "It is very important for us to recognize that our current criminal justice interventions actually destroy community. So even to get neutral would be a huge step for this system."

No Significant or Lasting Effects on Values and Practices

Advocates contend that restorative justice is unlikely to have significant or lasting effects on the official criminal justice system if it continues to operate primarily as local, unorganized grassroots activities. It is doubtful whether any program can be truly restorative in a system based on retributive values. Even if restorative justice principles cannot completely transform the justice system, they may turn criminal justice policy and values in another, arguably better, direction.

Increased Control and Punishment

Advocates argue that if crime is seen in both traditional and restorative ways—as an offense against the state and as harm to the victim and the community—a double system of punishment may be created. Offenders will first be processed through the traditional system and receive punishment and then move to the informal restorative programs to agree to a reparative contract. As a consequence, they often will be subjected to greater social control and more sanctions.

Deschutes County, Oregon: Reinventing Community Corrections

Deschutes County, Oregon, is attempting to apply community justice principles throughout its correctional system. In 1996 the County Board of Commissioners passed a Community Justice Resolution, which recognizes community justice as "the central mission and purpose of the county's community corrections effort." It calls for incorporating community justice principles into corrections by striking a balance among prevention, early intervention, and correctional efforts; ensuring participation by and restoration of victims; including community decision-making in crime prevention and reduction; and fostering offender accountability. In recognition of this major change, the Community Corrections Department, headed by Dennis Maloney, was renamed the Department of Community Justice.

Basic Principles

A lay citizen body, the Commission on Children and Families, was assigned authority over the department's budget. In 1998, it set budget principles that for the first time included:

- Enhancing public safety.
- Paying particular attention to offender accountability, responsibility, and skill development.
- Incorporating the findings of research on cost-effective interventions.
- Focusing on restoration and defining offenders' accountability as meeting their obligations to victims and the community.
- Encouraging volunteer involvement and reducing dependence on service delivery by professionals.
- Managing crime problems as cost effectively as possible.
- Directing reallocated resources to crime prevention.
- Viewing investment in prevention as the first order of business.

State law permits the county to apply any savings in juvenile detention to crime prevention.

Community Action and Other Initiatives

A number of former juvenile probation officers constitute a Community Action Team, which devotes most of its time and resources to neighborhood crime prevention. The new Community Justice Center contains space for juvenile custody facilities, houses a number of criminal justice agencies as well as victim service and other nonprofit organizations, and has a meeting room available for community groups.

Deschutes County also offers victim-offender mediation in criminal cases and dispute resolution in other conflicts. Merchant Accountability Boards, consisting of local business owners, adjudicate minor shoplifting cases. Reparative community service projects are operated through the collaboration of business owners, neighborhood residents, and community leaders. As part of these projects, offenders have built houses for Habitat for Humanity, cut and distributed firewood for elderly citizens, and built and maintained parks.

Trivialization of Restorative Programs

If the criminal justice system endorses restorative justice principles but does not participate in designing, implementing, and monitoring programs based on them, it is not likely to refer other than trivial cases. Criminal justice agencies and officials understandably do not want to rely heavily on practices whose outcomes they cannot comprehend, influence, predict, or trust. For the same reason, judges often are reluctant to divert offenders to these programs.

No Resource Savings

Although restorative justice advocates emphasize that the goal is not decreased criminal justice caseloads or costs, it is unrealistic not to consider resource savings in the current climate of exploding correctional costs. Few resources will be saved if restorative solutions only supplement traditional punishments or are used only for minor crimes.

Inconsistent Practices and Outcomes

The most common argument against restorative justice is that practices and outcomes vary with the particular program, and that fairness requires comparable crimes and criminals to be punished equally. Restorative justice involves individualized responses to crimes.

Proportionality and equality in punishment are often understood narrowly as calling for the same sentence for people who have committed similar crimes. However, they could just as well be interpreted as requiring comparable sentences for comparable offenses. This would mean punishment or responses may vary as long as they are meaningfully related to the nature and effects of the crime. Thus, in principle, there is no reason restorative justice cannot respect the tenets of proportionality and equality.

In practice, responses to crime will be different and inconsistent as long as restorative justice is not implemented systemwide. Many people are concerned that assigning substantial punishment power to lay volunteers will mean random, inequitable, and capriciously severe sanctions. Restorative justice, with its positive, constructive goals, attempts to move in the opposite direction. If participants, including the offender, understand and accept restorative justice principles, the requirements of fairness will not be circumvented and there will be no extreme consequences.

If there is no systemwide shift, programs based on restorative justice will probably continue to handle only minor offenses, and problems of inequity will likely not become serious. It will not much matter whether one offender is sentenced to 10 h of community service and $50 in restitution and another, who commits a similar crime, to 20 h of service and $100 in restitution. However, the more serious the crimes, the more unjust the differences could become and the greater the need for consistent practices.

Other matters of equity relate to socioeconomic considerations. Without official encouragement and support, restorative justice initiatives are likely to be concentrated in middle-class white neighborhoods or rural areas, and volunteers will disproportionately be white, middle-class, and middle-aged and older individuals, as these are the demographic groups from which activists tend to emerge. Moreover, if citizen activists work on their own, new practices may be concentrated in areas with relatively minor crime problems. By contrast, disadvantaged urban neighborhoods with large proportions of minority group members and immigrants—who are disproportionately affected by serious crime—would be unlikely to benefit.

The Future of Restorative and Community Justice

How deeply restorative and community justice ideas will penetrate the traditional justice system remains to be seen. So far, restorative justice approaches are used much more for juveniles than for adults, and for minor offenses rather than for serious crime. Experience with community justice has consistently shown that generating citizen involvement and building relationships with the community is a challenge. Both movements have spread rapidly, however, and both are increasingly reaching out to encompass adult offenders, more serious crime, and disadvantaged urban communities where, arguably, the need is greatest.

Leena Kurki, who holds law degrees from the University of Turku, Finland, and the University of Minnesota, is a Research Associate at the University of Minnesota Law School and the Project Association of the Executive Sessions on Sentencing and Corrections.

This study was supported by cooperative agreement 97-MUMU-K006 between the National Institute of Justice and the University of Minnesota.

Findings and conclusions of the research reported here are those of the author and do not necessarily reflect the official position or policies of the U.S. Department of Justice.

The National Institute of Justice is a component of the Office of Justice Programs, which also includes the Bureau of Justice Assistance, the Bureau of Justice Statistics, the Office of Juvenile Justice and Delinquency Prevention, and the Office for Victims of Crime.

This and other NIJ publications can be found at and downloaded from the NIJ web site (http://www.ojp.usdoj.gov/nij).

NCJ 175723

Questions

1. Describe how the case study illustrates the five basic steps of criminal justice systems assessment. Give one example of each of the following steps:
- Mapping the system.
- Documenting and assessing current policy and practice.
- Gathering information on the offender population.
- Identifying sanctions, services, and programs.
- Identifying community resources.

2. Assume now that the following hypothetical circumstances occur:
The governor makes an announcement that restorative and community justice is about to become the preferred practice in your state. The governor states that a new law will require all counties within the state to reduce the number of their court commitments to state prison by 50% within 2 years. There will be substantial financial incentives for compliance and substantial financial penalties for noncompliance. Assume you have been assigned to a county planning committee that has been asked to respond to this change in law.
Now, using force field analysis, do the following:
- (a) Identify "driving forces" and "restraining forces." Try to identify at least two of each.
  - (b) Analyze one of the restraining forces in part (a) in terms of its: amenability, potency, and consistency.
  - (c) Describe two possible strategies to reduce this source of resistance.

References

Akers, R. L., & Sellers, C. S. (2008). *Criminological theories: Introduction, evaluation, and application* (5th ed.). New York: Oxford University Press.

Barajas, E. (1996). Moving toward community justice. In *Community justice: Striving for safe, secure, and just communities.* Washington, DC: U.S. Department of Justice, National Institute of Corrections.

Bazemore, G. (1997). The "community" in community justice: Issues, themes, and questions for the new neighborhood sanctioning models. *Justice System Journal, 19,* 193–228.

Bernard, T. J., Snipes, J. B., & Gerould, A. L. (2009). *Theoretical criminology* (6th ed.). New York: Oxford University Press.

Biderman, A. D., & Lynch, J. P. (1991). *Understanding crime incidence statistics.* New York: Springer-Verlag.

Blomberg, T. G. (2010). Advancing criminology in policy and practice. In N. A. Frost, J. D. Freilich & T. R. Clear (Eds.), *Contemporary issues in criminal justice policy: Papers from the American society of criminology conference* (pp. 25–30). Belmont, CA: Wadsworth.

Blumstein, A., Wallman, J., & Farrington, D. (Eds.), (2000). *The crime drop in America.* New York: Cambridge University Press.

Bonta, J., Rooney, J., & Wallace-Capretta, S. (1998). *Restorative justice: An evaluation of the restorative resolutions project.* Ottawa: Solicitor General of Canada.

Braithwaite, J. (1999). Restorative justice: Assessing optimistic and pessimistic accounts. In M. Tonry (Ed.), *Crime and justice: A review of research.* Vol. 25. Chicago: University of Chicago Press.

Bureau of Justice Statistics, (2004). *The justice system: What is the sequence of events in the criminal justice system?* Retrieved February 5, 2008, from the BJS web site at: http://www.ojp.usdoj.gov/bjs/justsys.htm.

Burke, P., Cushman, R., & Ney, B. (1996). *Guide to a criminal justice system assessment: A work in progress* (p. 7). Washington, DC: National Institute of Corrections.

Buzawa, E. S., & Buzawa, C. G. (2002). *Domestic violence: The criminal justice response* (3rd ed.). Newbury Park, CA: Sage.

Community Research Associates, (1996). *Disproportionate confinement of minority juveniles in secure facilities: 1996 national report.* Washington, DC: Office of Juvenile Justice and Delinquency Prevention. Retrieved January 24, 2008, from the NCJRS web site at: http://www.ncjrs.gov/App/Publications/abstract.aspx?ID=169882.

Devine, P., Coolbaugh, K., & Jenkins, S. (1998). *Disproportionate minority confinement: Lessons learned from five states.* Washington, DC: Office of Juvenile Justice and Delinquency Prevention. Retrieved January 24, 2008, from the NCJRS web site at: http://www.ncjrs.org/94612.pdf.

Eisenstein, J., Flemming, R. B., & Nardulli, P. F. (1999). *The contours of justice.* New York: Rowan and Littlefield.

Feinblatt, J., & Berman, G. (1997). *Responding to the community: Principles for planning and creating a community court.* Washington, DC: U.S. Department of Justice, Bureau of Justice Assistance.

Galaway, B., & Hudson, J. (Eds.), (1996). *Restorative justice: International perspectives.* Amsterdam: Kugler.

Gustafson, D. (1997). Facilitating communication between victims and offenders in cases of serious and violent crime. *The International Community Corrections Association Journal on Community Corrections, 8,* 4–49.

Hsia, H. M., Bridges, G. S., & McHale, R. (2004). *Disproportionate minority confinement: 2002 update.* Retrieved January 24, 2008, from the NCJRS web site at: http://www.ncjrs.gov/pdffiles1/ojjdp/201240.pdf.

Hsia, H. M., & Hamparian, D. (1998). *Disproportionate minority confinement: 1997 update.* Washington, DC: Office of Juvenile Justice and Delinquency Prevention. Retrieved January 24, 2008, from the NCJRS web site at: http://www.ncjrs.gov/pdffiles/170606.pdf.

Joint United Nations Programme on HIV/AIDS (UNAIDS) and World Health Organization (WHO). (2010). *UNAIDS global report 2010: Press kit.* Retrieved August 5, 2011, from the UNAIDS web site at: http://www.unaids.org/documents/20101123_FS_Global_em_en.pdf.

Kettner, P., Daley, J. M., & Nichols, A. W. (1985). *Initiating change in organizations and communities: A macro practice model.* Monterey, CA: Brooks/Cole.

Kettner, P. M., Moroney, R. K., & Martin, L. L. (2007). *Designing and managing programs: An effectiveness-based approach* (3rd ed.). Thousand Oaks, CA: Sage.

Kurki, L. (1999). *Incorporating restorative and community justice into American sentencing and corrections. Sentencing & Corrections: Issues for the 21st Century.* Papers from the Executive Sessions on Sentencing and Corrections, No. 3 (NCJ 175723). Washington, DC: U.S. Department of Justice, Office of Justice Programs, National Institute of Justice. Retrieved January 30, 2008, at http://www.ncjrs.org/pdffiles1/nij/175723.pdf.

Kurz, G., & Schumacher, M. (2000). *The 8% solution: Preventing serious, repeat juvenile crime.* Thousand Oaks, CA: Sage.

LaFree, G. (1998). *Losing legitimacy: Street crime and the decline of social institutions in America.* Boulder, CO: Westview.

Lewin, K. (1947). Group decision and social change. In T. M. Newcomb & E. L. Hartley, et al., *Readings in social psychology* (pp. 202–203). New York: Holt and Company.

Lewin, K. (1951). *Field theory in social science.* New York: Harper and Row.

Lilly, J. R., Cullen, F. T., & Ball, R. A. (2006). *Criminological theory: Context and consequences* (4th ed.). Thousand Oaks, CA: Sage.

Lösching-Gspandl, M., & Kilchling, M. (1997). Victim/offender mediation and victim compensation in Austria and Germany—Stock-taking and perspectives for future research. *European Journal of Crime, Criminal Law and Criminal Justice, 5,* 58–78.

Maxwell, G., & Morris, A. (1993). *Family, victims, and culture: Youth justice in New Zealand.* Wellington, New Zealand: Social Policy Agency and Institute of Criminology, Victoria University of Wellington.

McCold, P., & Wachtel, B. (1998). *Restorative policing experiment: The Bethlehem Pennsylvania police family group conferencing project.* Pipersville, PA: Community Service Foundation. This evaluation was sponsored by the National Institute of Justice.

McGarry, P., & Ney, B. (2006). *Getting it right: Collaborative problem solving for criminal justice.* Silver Spring, MD: Center for Effective Public Policy (CEPP). Retrieved January 30, 2008, from the CEPP web site at: http://www.nicic.org/Library/019834.

Messmer, H., & Otto, H. U. (1992). *Restorative justice on trial: Pitfalls and potentials of victim-offender mediation.* Dordrecht, Netherlands: Kluwer.

Messner, S., & Rosenfeld, R. (2006). *Crime and the American dream* (4th ed.). Belmont, CA: Wadsworth.

Midtown Community Court. (1997). *The Midtown Community Court experiment: A progress report.* New York: Midtown Community Court.

National Institute on Drug Abuse. (2011). *NIDA InfoFacts: High school and youth trends.* Retrieved August 5, 2011 from the NIDA web site at: http://drugabuse.gov/infofacts/hsyouthtrends.html.

Nellis, A. M. (2005). *Seven steps to develop and evaluate strategies to reduce disproportionate minority contact (DMC).* Juvenile Justice Evaluation Center, Justice Research and Statistics Association (JRSA). Retrieved January 24, 2008, from the JRSA web site at: http://www.jrsa.org/pubs/juv-justice/dmc-guidebook.pdf.

Office of Juvenile Justice and Delinquency Prevention. (2006). *DMC technical assistance manual* (3rd ed.). Washington, DC: Office of Juvenile Justice and Delinquency Prevention. Retrieved January 24, 2008, from the NCJRS web site at: http://www.ncjrs.org/html/ojjdp/dmc_ta_manual/index.html.

Office of Juvenile Justice and Delinquency Prevention. (2008a). *A disproportionate minority contact (DMC) chronology: 1988 to date.* (Updated by Andrea R. Coleman, OJJDP DMC Coordinator.) Retrieved August 11, 2011, from the OJJDP web site at: http://www.ojjdp.gov/dmc/chronology.html.

Office of Juvenile Justice and Delinquency Prevention. (2008b). *A catalog of state research reports on disproportionate minority contact.* Retrieved January 24, 2008, from the NCJRS web site at: http://ojjdp.ncjrs.org/dmc/tools/index.html.

Petersilia, J. (1991). Policy relevance and the future of criminology: The American society of criminology 1990 presidential address. *Criminology, 29,* 1–15.

Pope, C., & Feyerherm, W. (1995). *Minorities and the juvenile justice system: Research summary.* Washington, DC: Office of Juvenile Justice and Delinquency Prevention. Retrieved January 24, 2008, from the OJJDP web site at: http://www.ncjrs.org/pdffiles/minor.pdf.

Pope, C. E., Lovell, R., & Hsia, H. M. (2002). *Disproportionate minority confinement: A review of the research literature from 1989 through 2001.* Washington, DC: Office of Juvenile Justice and Delinquency Prevention. Retrieved January 24, 2008, from the NCJRS web site at: http://ojjdp.ncjrs.org/dmc/pdf/dmc89_01.pdf.

President's Commission on Law Enforcement and Administration of Justice. (1968). *The challenge of crime in a free society.* New York: Avon Books.

Reiss, A. J., & Roth, J. A. (Eds.) (1993). *"Appendix B: Measuring and counting violent crimes and their consequences." Understanding and preventing violence, v. 4* (p. 404). Washington, DC: National Academy Press.

Riedel, M., & Welsh, W. (2011). *Criminal violence: Patterns, causes, and prevention* (3rd ed.). New York: Oxford University Press.

Riveland, C. (1999). Prison management trends, 1975–2025. In M. Tonry & J. Petersilia (Eds.), *Prisons. Crime and justice, a review of research.* Vol. 26 (pp. 163–203). Chicago: University of Chicago Press.

Robers, S., Zhang, J., & Truman, J. (2010). *Indicators of school crime and safety: 2010 (NCES 2011-002/NCJ 230812).* Washington, DC: National Center for Education Statistics, U.S. Department of Education, and Bureau of Justice Statistics, Office of Justice Programs, U.S. Department of Justice. This publication can be downloaded from the World Wide Web at: http://nces.ed.gov or http://bjs.ojp.usdoj.gov.

Roscoe, M., & Morton, R. (1994). *Disproportionate minority confinement: FACT SHEET # 11 (FS-9411).* Retrieved January 24, 2008, from the NCJRS web site at:http://www.ncjrs.org/txtfiles/fs-9411.txt.

Rosenfeld, R. (2010). Raising the level of public debate: Another view of criminology's policy relevance. In N. A. Frost, J. D. Freilich & T. R. Clear (Eds.), *Contemporary issues in criminal justice policy: Papers from the American society of criminology conference* (pp. 31–36). Belmont, CA: Wadsworth.

Rossum, R. A. (1978). *The politics of the criminal justice system. An organizational analysis.* New York: Marcel Dekker.

Sherman, L., Strang, H., Barnes, G., Braithwaite, J., Ipken, N., & Teh, M.-M. (1998). *Experiments in restorative policing: A progress report to the national police research unit in the Canberra reintegrative shaming experiments (RISE).* Canberra: Australian Federal Police and Australian National University.

Skogan, W. G., & Hartnett, S. M. (1997). *Community policing, Chicago style.* New York: Oxford University Press.

Snyder, H. N., & Sickmund, M. (1999). *Minorities in the juvenile justice system.* Washington, DC: Office of Juvenile Justice and Delinquency Prevention. Retrieved January 24, 2008, from the NCJRS web site at: http://www.ncjrs.gov/pdffiles1/ojjdp/179007.pdf.

Spector, M., & Kitsuse, J. (2001). *Constructing social problems.* New Brunswick, NJ: Transaction.

Truman, J. L., & Rand, M. R. (2010). *Criminal victimization, 2009.* Washington, DC: U.S. Department of Justice, Office of Justice Programs, Bureau of Justice Statistics. Retrieved August 5, 2011, from the Bureau of Justice Statistics web site at: http://bjs.ojp.usdoj.gov/content/pub/pdf/cv09.pdf.

Umbreit, M. (1994). *Victim meets offender: The impact of restorative justice and mediation.* Monsey, NY: Criminal Justice Press.

Van Ness, D., & Strong, K. H. (2006). *Restoring Justice* (3rd ed.). Newark, NJ: LexisNexis Matthew Bender.

Walker, S. (2005). *Sense and nonsense about crime and drugs* (6th ed.). Belmont, CA: Wadsworth.

Wellford, C. (1998). Changing nature of criminal justice system responses and its professions. U.S. Department of Justice. In: *The challenge of crime in a free society: Looking back, looking forward* (pp. 58–71). *Symposium on the 30th Anniversary of the President's Commission on Law Enforcement and Administration of Justice (NCJ-170029).* Washington, DC: U.S. Department of Justice, Office of Justice Programs.

Wellford, C. F. (2010). Criminologists should stop whining about their impact on policy and practice. In: N. A. Frost, J. D. Freilich & T. R. Clear (Eds.), *Contemporary issues in criminal justice policy: Papers from the American Society of Criminology Conference.*

Welsh, W. N. (1995). *Counties in court: Jail overcrowding and court-ordered reform.* Philadelphia: Temple University Press.

Welsh, W. N., Leone, M. C., Kinkade, P. T., & Pontell, H. N. (1991). The politics of jail overcrowding: Public attitudes and official policies. In J. A. Thompson & G. L. Mays (Eds.), *American jails: Public policy issues.* Chicago: Nelson-Hall.

Welsh, W. N., & Pontell, H. N. (1991). Counties in court: Inter-organizational adaptations to jail litigation in California. *Law and Society Review, 25,* 73–101.

Welsh, W. N., & Zajac, G. (2004). Building an effective research partnership between a university and a state correctional agency: Assessment of drug treatment in Pennsylvania prisons. *The Prison Journal, 84,* 143–170.

Wing, J. (2008). Idaho's statistical analysis center helps state police solve personnel allocation problem. *Geography and Public Safety: A Quarterly Bulletin of Applied Geography for the Study of Crime & Public Safety, 1*(2), 11–13. Washington, DC: U.S. Department of Justice, Office of Community Oriented Policing Services (COPS). Retrieved August 5, 2011 from: http://www.nij.gov/pubs-sum/gps-bulletin-v1i2.htm.

Wundersitz, J., & Hetzel, S. (1996). Family conferencing for young offenders: The South Australian experience. In J. Hudson, A. Morris, G. Maxwell & B. Galaway (Eds.), *Family group conferences: Perspectives on policy and practice.* Monsey, NY: Willow Tree Press.

2

Setting Goals and Objectives

CHAPTER OUTLINE

- *Write goal statements* specifying the general outcome to be obtained. Goals are abstract statements of purpose.
- *Write specific outcome objectives for each goal.* Unlike goals, objectives are specific and measurable statements of intended outcomes. Each objective should include a time frame for measuring impact, a target population, a key result intended, and a specific criterion or measure of impact.
- *Seek participation* from different individuals and agencies in goal setting. Goal setting that includes a broad range of stakeholders helps to ensure that interventions receive necessary resources and support.
- Consider "top-down" versus "bottom-up" approaches.
- *Specify an impact model.* This is a description of how the intervention will act upon a specific cause so as to bring about a change in the problem. Successful interventions target causes of problems, not problems themselves. An impact model is an explanation of how the intervention will affect the causes and, consequentially, how changes in causes of the problem will affect the problem.
- *Identify compatible and incompatible goals in the larger system.* Where do values of different stakeholders overlap or conflict?
- *Identify needs and opportunities for interagency collaboration.* Whose cooperation and participation is needed to achieve the goals of this program or policy?

Many interventions fail not because they lack good ideas, but because of vague goals or disagreement about goals. Defining goals and objectives is crucial to the rest of the planning process. It is amazing how many expensive and otherwise well-designed interventions fail to define the desired outcomes of the intervention adequately. Without specific, agreed-upon criteria for success, it is impossible to measure whether any intervention works. It is also likely that without agreed-upon goals, program staff, directors, and various stakeholders will frequently disagree on the mission of the program and the type of intervention approach to use.

■ ■ Goals ■

Broad, abstract purposes of an intervention.

Every intervention attempts to achieve some kind of outcome—some desired change in the problem. Both goals and objectives refer to desired outcomes, but objectives are much more specific. *Goals* are broad aims of the intervention (e.g., to reduce drug abuse); *objectives* specify explicit and measurable outcomes (e.g., in a 1-year follow-up of ex-offenders who participated in a drug treatment program while in prison, researchers predict that participants will have a lower rearrest rate than nonparticipants).

■ ■ Objectives ■

Explicit and measurable aims of an intervention.

Identifying Goals and Values

Goals describe desired future states, some intended change in the problem. Generally, goals are broad statements intended to provide direction for change. While goals lack the specificity needed to measure actual outcomes of the intervention, they provide some sense of mission that may be crucial to gaining political support for the intervention. For example, the goals of a shelter for abused women might be "to provide temporary shelter for victims of domestic violence and reduce spouse abuse"; the goals of a drug treatment program might be "to reduce drug dependency and help clients lead productive, drug-free lives." Goal statements should be relatively brief (one or two sentences), but at the same time they should accurately capture the intent of a particular program or policy and explain the rationale (reasons) for its creation and its particular structure.

Writing goal statements can be difficult, particularly where relevant stakeholders (individuals, groups, and organizations) have widely differing viewpoints about the desired results of a proposed change. Formulating goal statements requires disclosure and discussion of personal beliefs and values. It requires officials to be clear about what they are doing and why they are doing it. Sometimes their political positions and aspirations interfere with the need for transparency.

We present below a few brief examples of the most common goals of criminal sanctions, and then some of the most common normative values guiding the formulation of criminal justice programs and policies. Case studies at the end of this chapter ask you to consider these issues further and apply the concepts to specific examples. The change agent and relevant stakeholders involved should seek to explicitly identify and acknowledge the goals and values that underlie any specific program or policy being considered.

The Goals of Criminal Sanctions

Often referred to as purposes of sanctioning, five different goals (retribution, rehabilitation, deterrence, incapacitation, and restoration) are commonly asserted as reasons for punishing particular offenders and offenses in particular ways. Some authors (Rothman, 1980) have suggested that our society alternates or cycles through punitive and rehabilitative extremes over time, while others (Richard, 2005; Von Hirsch, 1985) have argued that a more discrete progression from one set of goals (e.g., rehabilitation in the 1950s and 1960s) to another (e.g., incapacitation in the later 1980s and early 1990s) has occurred. More recent policy developments emphasize offender accountability to victims and their communities. Regardless of the historical perspective that one adopts, the dominance of any one goal at any one time in history is never complete. The five goals below are currently relevant and are likely to be hotly debated for some time.

Retribution

According to advocates of this position, the rightful purpose of punishment is to assign blame and punishment to the wrongdoer. No future good for society is intended, only that the balance of justice be restored by making the offender pay for his or her transgression against society. Advocates of the death penalty often justify its use on such grounds.

Rehabilitation

The purpose of punishment, according to this view, is to reduce the likelihood of future offending by diagnosing and treating its causes within the individual. Implicit are theoretical notions that criminal behavior is learned and can be unlearned, and that individual deficits can be corrected. Programs may attempt to alter educational deficits or psychological factors such as anger control, social, and problem-solving skills.

Deterrence

According to *general deterrence,* the purpose of punishment is to send a message to other potential lawbreakers that the specific offense being punished will not be tolerated. Potential lawbreakers, as a result of fearing the punishment they see inflicted on others, should be "deterred" from committing similar acts. This approach assumes that people make a rational calculation of costs and benefits associated with specific actions, and its advocates intend that the "pain" (of apprehension, prosecution, and punishment) outweigh the "gain" (the benefits of criminal behavior). For *specific deterrence,* the message is not to others who might be deterred, but to the specific individual being punished. The individual is expected to learn his or her lesson and refrain from future criminal acts. Many "shock incarceration" programs such as Scared Straight and boot camps have been based on such premises.

Incapacitation

The simple purpose of incapacitation is to physically restrain the offender from committing further crimes. The logic is simple: a person cannot commit further crimes against society during the time they are locked up or incapacitated. Long prison sentences for certain offenses are often based, at least in part, upon such notions. Less severe forms of incapacitation might include curfews, house arrest, intensive supervision probation, and day reporting centers. Advocates often believe that crime rates can be reduced by incarcerating (incapacitating) the worst offenders ("career criminals") for long periods of time (Auerhahn, 2001).

Restoration

More recent than the other four types of goals, restoration or reparation attempts to restore the victim and or the community to his or her (its) prior state before the crime occurred. It is similar to retribution in the sense that crime is viewed as a disruption of the peace. However, restoration seeks to repair the harm that resulted from the offense, where retribution seeks only to apply blame and punishment. Many current programs are exploring options such as financial restitution to victims, as well as requiring offenders to perform community service work. Still others involve the offender, the victim, and family members and friends of both parties in face-to-face encounters during which reparation steps are negotiated and empathy is encouraged (Braithwaite, 2002).

Normative Values

Normative values are guiding assumptions held by individuals about how the justice system *should* work. For example, Packer (1968) discusses two very broad, competing value orientations of the criminal justice system. To some officials, criminal case processing is like an "assembly line," through which cases should be processed and disposed of as quickly as possible. Proponents of this view, the *crime control model*, believe that for the most part, police, prosecutors, judges, and juries make correct decisions, and the system effectively ferrets out the guilty from the innocent. In contrast, those who lean more toward the *due process model* view believe that the system is imperfect, and that individual officials frequently make hasty and incorrect decisions. As a result, many safeguards are needed to protect the interests of the accused against the much greater power of the state. Criminal case processing, according to this view, is more like an "obstacle course" than an assembly line. We warn the reader that neither model truly represents reality. No individual should completely adopt one or the other orientations. In Packer's own words, "A person who subscribed to all of the values underlying one model to the exclusion of all of the values underlying the other would be rightly viewed as a fanatic" (Packer, 1968).

Criminal justice officials hold normative values about what type of change should be pursued and why, how important specific goals are, and what results should be expected from a specific program or policy. For example, the discussion of restorative justice at the end of Chapter 1 illustrated that a value orientation toward handling criminal cases was dramatically at odds with the orientation of using traditional law enforcement strategies to protect public safety. Any potential solution had to account for at least the values and interests of police and court personnel. Four very broad value orientations common to criminal justice are described below.

Proportionality

Proportionality is a principle that punishment for criminal behavior should not be any more onerous, intrusive, or painful than warranted by the severity of the crime. At least in theory, this principle holds that there is some logical hierarchy of crimes, and a corresponding ("proportional") hierarchy of appropriate punishments. One does not give the death penalty to jaywalkers, for example. A fine might be more appropriate.

Equity

Equity is the principle that similarly situated offenders should be treated similarly. For example, those accused of committing the same criminal offense should receive similar punishments, unrelated to their personal or demographic characteristics (e.g., age, race, gender, or income).

Parsimony

Parsimony is the principle of using the least drastic and expensive measure needed to produce a specific objective. For example, if a 1-year driver's license suspension and probation term is sufficient to motivate a first-time offender to abstain from drunk driving, a 3-year suspension and probation term would be overly harsh and wasteful.

Humane Treatment

Humane treatment is a principle meaning that the decision about appropriate punishment is guided by a preference to seek the least painful and intrusive method to achieve specific objectives. One attempts to avoid unnecessary humiliation, pain, and discomfort. For example, incarceration and its associated deprivations of liberty can be considered appropriate punishment in and of itself. Only considerations of appropriate sentence length, security classification, and perhaps rehabilitation opportunities should guide the decision about where and how the offender serves his or her sentence, and for how long. Under this principle, one would not impose additional punishment by making prison conditions as unbearable as possible (e.g., by denying inmates a heated facility in cold weather).

What are the "Right" Goals and Values?

Mine, of course! Actually, we do not advocate any particular set of punishment goals or values in this book; we want to give you the tools you need to make such decisions explicit. We also caution that different goals and values are not necessarily mutually exclusive: it is possible that a specific program or policy could address more than one goal or value simultaneously. Excellent discussions of competing views and related research evidence are provided elsewhere (Walker, 2001). Do rehabilitation programs work sufficiently well to serve as a basis for correctional policy? Does retributive justice result in satisfaction of the victim that justice was done? Does the threat of punishment deter others from committing crimes? Consulting the body of research that addresses these questions will help to avoid unrealistic expectations and increase our capacity to clearly identify and evaluate the intended outcomes of our programs and policies.

It is important to understand that the pursuit of specific goals may be driven by values, in spite of past failures to achieve these goals. The goal of rehabilitation, for example, has been challenged consistently over the past three decades, and yet we continue to believe that people can change and that positive change can be facilitated by well-designed interventions (Lipsey & Cullen, 2007). Similarly, in spite of consistent evidence that capital punishment does not deter others from committing murder, death penalty statutes continue to be supported because of the perceived deterrent effect of executions (Lipsey & Cullen, 2007).

Stating Specific Objectives for Each Goal

Objectives are much more specific than goals. Objectives should define clearly and concisely exactly what outcome is to be achieved by the intervention. Objectives precisely describe the intended results of the intervention in measurable terms.

An intervention should have at least one specific goal, and each goal should be accompanied by at least one specific objective. It is possible, therefore, to have more than one objective for each goal. Because goals are broadly defined, any program may have several specific objectives. For example, the goal of a new drug treatment program is "to help clients lead drug-free lives." Two objectives are possible:

- Objective #1: Six months after leaving the program, fewer clients will have been rearrested on drug charges, compared to those who didn't go through the program.
- Objective #2: After 6 months, treated clients, relative to untreated clients, will score higher (on average) on a "personal and family responsibility" scale.

Objectives, therefore, must always be *measurable* and *specific*. Objectives should include four major components:

1. *A time frame:* date by which the objective will be completed.
2. *A target population:* who will exhibit the intended change?
3. *A result:* the key outcome intended; a specific change in the problem (or one of its causes).
4. *A criterion:* a standard for measuring successful achievement of the result.

> **Example 2–1   Four Components of an Objective: The Minneapolis Domestic Violence Experiment**
>
> In the Minneapolis Domestic Violence Experiment (Sherman & Berk, 1984), researchers reviewed major studies of police response to domestic violence. In various jurisdictions, they found a rather low rate of arrest out of all calls reported to the police. Other more frequently used police responses included: separation (ordering the offender to leave the house for a cooling-off period, often overnight) and mediation (officers encourage a couple to resolve the conflict).
>
> The researchers hypothesized that, due to greater deterrent effects, mandatory arrest for misdemeanor domestic assault would result in fewer repeat offenses (recidivism) than either separation (order the suspect to leave for at least 8 h) or mediation (try to restore peace, informally solve the conflict). Researchers convinced police to randomly assign all misdemeanor domestic violence cases in two precincts to one of these three interventions. Six months later, researchers predicted, there would be a lower rate of repeat incidents of domestic assault for cases where mandatory arrest was used. We can summarize the four components of the objective as follows:
>
> 1. *Time frame:* six months.
> 2. *Target population:* the experiment included only misdemeanor assaults, where police were empowered (but not required) to make arrests under a new state law. Police had to have probable cause, and felonies (e.g., obvious or serious injury) were excluded (i.e., felony suspects were always arrested). Two precincts with the highest density of domestic violence were selected for the study.
> 3. *Result:* fewer repeat incidents of domestic abuse.
> 4. *Criteria:* two measures were used: (1) police arrest records (incident reports over a 6-month period); and victim self-reports (follow-up interviews were conducted with victims every 2 weeks for 24 weeks, asking about frequency and seriousness of any victimization).
>
> Note that these four components could have been quite different depending upon the results of the problem analysis. First, a different time frame could have been specified (e.g., one year? Two years? Three years?). Second, a different target population could have been specified (e.g., different demographic and income groups could have been studied in different neighborhoods). Third, a different result could have been specified (e.g., victim satisfaction with the police response they received). Finally, different criteria (measures) could have been used (e.g., hospital records of injuries, incidents reported to social service agencies or crisis lines). Any change agent should define the four components of an objective, and explain the reasoning behind these specifications.

Another distinction is sometimes made between process and outcome objectives. *Process objectives* refer to short-term tasks that must be completed in order to implement a program (e.g., within 30 days, all police agencies will hold orientation sessions to acquaint officers with a new domestic violence policy). Strictly speaking, these are not objectives of the intervention at all, because they do *not* define any specific change in the problem. We note this distinction only because it is likely to arise as one reads published reports of interventions, and one should be aware of the difference. We are concerned here with *outcome objectives* (specific, measurable changes in the problem or their causes).

Seeking Participation in Goal Setting

Is it necessary that everyone agree on the same goals of a specific program or policy? What are the implications if they don't? At the most basic level, the implications are that different individuals (stakeholders) perceive that they are each working toward some specific end point. They may believe, correctly or incorrectly, that they are working toward the same desired end. The problem is: if they have not articulated or discussed their own goals and values with each other, they may find out after considerable expenditure of energy and resources that they are working toward very different ends. Certainly no effective program or policy can be constructed if those responsible for designing the program or policy hold widely disparate or conflicting goals. Participants need some basic agreement about what it is they are trying to achieve, and why. Not every single stakeholder needs to agree on the final goals, but those responsible for implementing the program or policy must be held accountable for articulating what it is they are doing and why.

Once again, we stress the virtues of participation in program planning. Having the relevant stakeholders involved in setting program goals is crucial to gaining the support and cooperation necessary to make the intervention work. An important step, if it has not already been accomplished (see Chapter 1), is to identify relevant participants for inclusion in the goal-setting and objective-setting phase.

The change agent (e.g., the person responsible for coordinating the program planning effort) should involve various participants in the planning process, not just agency administrators. Participants might include program staff, potential clients, citizens in the surrounding community, representatives from justice and social service agencies, schools, and so on. This requires patience and negotiating skills, as there are likely to be different assumptions and opinions regarding the problem, its causes, and the type of intervention needed.

Targets and clients are often overlooked at this stage, as are front-line workers: what should *they* expect to see result from this planned change? A major question to ask at this point is whether goal-setting should proceed from a "top-down" or "bottom-up" approach.

Typically, change follows a top-down format. This is often the case because the change agent is likely to be working for, or contracted by, the agency that is funding the intervention, and the change agent owes some obligation to weight their definitions of goals more heavily. There may be advantages to this situation, as well as costs. It may be the case that those in the higher levels of the organization have the most experience with interventions of this type, and they might indeed be in the best position to state realistic, feasible outcomes to be expected. They might also be best equipped to formulate goals that can garner widespread political support for the program (e.g., support from other stakeholders). However, there is a very real danger in ignoring the views of program staff and clients. The danger is that the goals handed down from above may be unrealistic to program staff, or irrelevant to the clients. In either case, the impact of the intervention could be severely compromised. The goals might prove unrealistic, in which case the program would be held accountable for unreachable goals; or clients and program staff might refuse to cooperate with a new policy or provide information to program evaluators.

■ ■ Goal Setting: Top-Down versus Bottom-Up Approaches ■

Top-Down

The change agent begins by getting goal definitions from top officials at the administrative level of his or her organization (e.g., the Chief of County Probation, the Chief of Police, the Director of Social Services, etc.), and then gets responses from lower levels of the organization: perhaps from agency supervisors, then program staff, and eventually from potential clients. Thus, those at the top of the organizational hierarchy have more "say" in defining the program's goals, because their definition is the first one, and it carries more weight and more power as subordinates and clients are asked to respond to it.

Bottom-Up

The change agent begins by seeking goal definitions at the client or staff level. In contrast to the top-down approach, here the change agent first gets definitions from clients and staff about what the program goals are or should be, and then gets responses to these goal definitions from successively higher levels of the agency responsible for implementing the intervention, as well as the agency that is funding the intervention. Other stakeholders to approach may include agency supervisors, administrators, and government representatives. The views of clients and program staff are given more priority using this format; their definitions guide subsequent responses. Obviously, this approach is favored when it is widely viewed that so-called "experts" are out of touch, and that front-line program staff and/or clients are in a better position to state the needs and goals of the target population. Many "grassroots" organizations follow this format.

Regardless of which approach is used to formulate initial goals, therefore, it is crucial that all stakeholders eventually have some input into defining program goals. These issues are examined in more detail in Case Study 2–1 at the end of this chapter.

Specifying an Impact Model

We discussed causes and theories in Chapter 1. Examination of theories helps us to formulate what is called an *impact model:* a prediction that a particular intervention will bring about a specific change in the problem. Formulating such a model forces us to answer several important questions: What is the intervention? Why would a proposed intervention work? Which causes of the problem will it address? In other words, through what process will change occur, and why? What outcome (a change in the problem) is expected? Thus, the impact model is made up of three key elements we've discussed: the intervention (policies and programs); the cause(s) to be addressed by the intervention (theories about what causes the problem); and some specific outcome, a desired change in the problem (goals and objectives). We can analyze an existing intervention by working backward, first specifying the intervention, then the causes of that problem, and finally the problem the intervention addresses. Program or policy creation, on the other hand, proceeds from problem analysis to causal analysis to formulation of goals and objectives and then to intervention design (Figure 2–1).

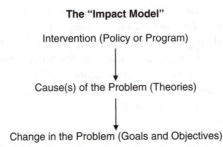

The "Impact Model"

Intervention (Policy or Program)

Cause(s) of the Problem (Theories)

Change in the Problem (Goals and Objectives)

FIGURE 2–1 The "Impact Model."

Example 2–2   An Impact Model for a Reentry Program

THE PROBLEM

Texas has a prison population well in excess of 162,000. As far back as 1984, researchers in Texas reported that 38% of parolees were reincarcerated within a period of 3 years. Both the huge corrections costs and the failure of parolees to succeed in the community produced a demand for solving the parole failure problem.

THE PROGRAM

Project RIO (Re-Integration of Offenders) was started as a joint effort of the Texas Department of Corrections and the Texas Workforce Commission. Originally started in two cities as a federally funded pilot project, it is now a statewide and state-funded program. Project RIO has assembled 12,000 employers who hire parolees, and every parolee in the state has access to its services. Preparatory work with parolees begins while they are still in prison. Six months prior to release, Project RIO staff conduct assessments of skills and work history, and initiate job-readiness training. Vocational training is made available, and many employers come to the prison to meet with inmates and to encourage them during this difficult time of transition back to the community. Once released from prison, parolees receive more preparation and help with job placement.

THE CAUSE(S)

Several research studies have found that parolees with jobs are less likely to reoffend and be returned to prison. Those with higher incomes were found to reoffend less than those with low incomes. The lack of a job and means of support is one factor that drives parolees back into crime.

Example 2–2   An Impact Model for a Reentry Program—Cont'd

THE INTENDED CHANGE IN THE PROBLEM

A study of recidivism conducted by a research team from Texas A&M University found that participants in Project RIO were less likely to recidivate than nonparticipants. For example, among high-risk parolees, 48% of Project RIO parolees were arrested during the first year of parole, compared with 57% of nonparticipants. Among this same group, 23% of the Project RIO participants were returned to prison, compared to 38% of nonparticipants.
(summarized from Finn, 1998)

Identifying Compatible and Incompatible Goals in the Larger System

As we discussed in Chapter 1, criminal justice programs and policies are shaped by the interactive actions of various decisionmakers and agencies in any jurisdiction. We argued that a "systems assessment" provides a common language for describing the structure, policies, practices, and norms of the system in which the problem has been identified, in order to shape a common vision for the future, and to make that vision a reality.

It is the notion of shaping a common vision that is relevant to this chapter. Based upon information collected in Stage 1, Problem Analysis, we should be able to identify and describe the competing interests of different individuals and agencies. We try to determine where agreement and disagreement about goals exist, and we try to get stakeholders to articulate and discuss their desired goals for any specific program or policy.

In Case Study 1–3 (Incorporating Restorative and Community Justice into American Sentencing and Corrections), for example, we saw that government control over criminal justice has not resulted in safer and more closely knit communities. Proponents of restorative and community justice strategies argue that communities should exercise control over certain justice processes. On the one hand, communities feel safer when there is a significant police presence and when the courts imprison wrongdoers. But the problems that generate crime don't go away because of these criminal justice system responses, and victims generally feel left out of the process. Community justice strategies engage members of the community in the business of solving community crime problems. Restorative justice strategies involve victims in the process of deciding on an appropriate sanction. Even members of the offender's family can have a role in efforts to restore victims to preoffense conditions (further information on restorative justice is available at: http://www.realjustice.org).

In another example, contracting out prison operations to private companies (i.e., privatization of prison operations) is often seen by elected officials as superior to public correctional organizations due to assumed cost savings. Other stakeholders disagree about whether cost savings are likely, and whether cost savings should be the goal at all. Several major objections to privatization have emerged (Shichor, 1995).

- Correctional officers have initiated lawsuits alleging violation of their collective bargaining agreements. Privatization, they argue, is designed to drive down wages and benefits that were won through hard-fought, legitimate union negotiations.
- Inmate advocates and attorneys, concerned with civil rights, argue that turning over the power to punish from government to the private sector is absolutely unethical. Private corporations are motivated to make profits, not to rehabilitate prisoners, protect public safety, or provide constitutionally mandated, humane conditions of confinement.
- Private interests, many argue, will attempt to use inmates as a source of cheap labor, or worse, indentured slavery. Such conditions would mark a return to the barbaric days of inmate exploitation and abuse prior to court intervention.
- Cost-cutting motivations, it is feared, will lead to lapses in prison security that threaten public safety (e.g., higher inmate-to-guard staffing ratios).

The change agent, consultant, or analyst guiding the change effort should constantly carry a systems perspective throughout the seven-stage planned change process. A systems perspective is no less important at the goal-setting stage than any other stage, and perhaps more so because the fundamental assumptions developed at this stage will critically shape the design and structure of the entire program or policy. Case Study 2–2 at the end of this chapter further examines these issues, using mandatory sentencing as a context for analysis.

We offer six guidelines for identifying compatible and incompatible goals or values in the larger system:

1. Have the appropriate stakeholders been identified via a thorough problem analysis (see Chapter 1)?
2. Review the five goals and four values described earlier in this chapter: Do different stakeholders disagree over specific goals and values? Have their assumptions about the problem, its possible causes, and possible solutions been described?
3. Do individuals within the same agency agree or disagree about the goals or values of the proposed change? How?
4. Do individuals within different agencies agree or disagree about the goals or values of the proposed change? How?
5. Has a systems analysis been conducted to provide stakeholders with relevant information about criminal case processing in this jurisdiction? Is all the information needed to make decisions about goals available, or does some information need to be developed?
6. Do any group mechanisms (e.g., a Criminal Justice Cabinet) exist for bringing stakeholders together to discuss the goals of a proposed change? Is it necessary to create or further develop such a group before proceeding?

Identifying Needs and Opportunities for Interagency Collaboration

It is highly likely that any criminal justice intervention will at some point require the cooperation of other agencies to achieve its goals. Many criminal justice interventions, to be successful, require the participation of police, courts, and corrections to carry out their program plans. Other public agencies such as public health or social service agencies may also be called upon, depending upon the problem to be addressed (e.g., gun violence) and the type of intervention to be attempted. The change agent, as part of the planning process, needs to consider his or her agency's "external environment" when attempting any kind of change. Different types of collaboration or support may be required: political support, shared information, exchange of services, joint client intake or assessment, and perhaps even cross-referrals of clients among different agencies (Rossi, Gilmartin, & Dayton, 1982). Such forms of cooperation, obviously, must be negotiated and agreed upon. Each agency must perceive tangible benefits from undertaking such cooperation.

Interagency cooperation is not always possible or even desirable, however. Political conflicts and administrative hierarchies occasionally preclude opportunities for collaboration.

Example 2–3   Agency Politics: Roadblocks to Collaboration?

In a recent project, we found that the juvenile court, part of a state agency, was resistant to participating in the development of an information system that would benefit a group of city agencies. The purpose of the information system project was to create an integrated system that would link the databases of the juvenile court, the department of human services, the police, the district attorney, the public defender, and the school district. Sharing information electronically was viewed as a primary means of supporting effective decisions and avoiding fragmented planning for individual youths and families. The juvenile court resisted involvement because preexisting political conflicts with other agencies had not been resolved and because of its stated desire to protect confidential court data from misuse by other agencies.

The Benefits of Goal Conflict

Under some circumstances, planning partnerships may not be desirable. Kevin Wright, for example, argues that a complex justice system in a complex society cannot and should not have any common set of goals and values (Wright, 1999). There is (and should be) a certain tension between some criminal justice agencies, because they do not (and should not) all have the same goals. For example, prosecutors tend to emphasize goals of crime control while defense attorneys emphasize due process. Such goal "tension" helps protect the competing interests of victims and suspects. Moreover, distinctions need to be made between goal conflicts and agency conflicts. Opposition on specific goals does not imply that agencies cannot work together under all circumstances. There will be many situations in which collaboration will serve the purposes of agencies that represent different interests. Plea bargaining between prosecutors and defense attorneys is perhaps the classic example of such exchange relations.

Example 2–4   Goal Conflict in Criminal Justice: Roadblocks or Speedbumps for Interagezncy Collaboration?

According to Wright, there are at least three reasons why goal conflict within the criminal justice system is desirable: (1) reflective diversity, (2) mediation of interests and system adaptation, and (3) efficient offender processing.

1. *Reflective Diversity:* Fragmentation and lack of integration allow different interests to be incorporated into the system. Conflict may be necessary to mediate among conflicting interests in the community, including competing demands for crime prevention, public order, justice, due process, efficiency, and accountability.
2. *Mediation of Interests and System Adaptation:* Conflicting goals promote a system of checks and balances. No single component of the system can dominate others, nor can any unitary interest be overemphasized. Conflict establishes and maintains a balance of power within the structure of the system [e.g., a prosecutor gives an overly stiff sentence in reaction to public sentiment, but corrections (parole) may modify that sentence and balance out the fairness (and vice versa)].
3. *Offender Processing:* Conflict and fragmentation may actually promote and support rather than hinder the processing of offenders. Prosecution, for example, may be smoother and more efficient precisely because police officers do consider decisions about prosecution, and that tension reduces the likelihood that prosecutors will need to void illegal, improper, or weak arrests.

Loose Coupling and Criminal Justice Agencies

The concept of *loose coupling* further illustrates the need for interagency cooperation in criminal justice. Loose coupling refers to agencies that are responsive to one another and yet maintain independent identities (Cohen, March, & Olsen, 1972; Hagan, 1989; Weick, 1976; Welsh, 1992). In such systems, "structural elements are only loosely linked to one another and to activities, rules are often violated, decisions often go unimplemented, or if implemented have uncertain consequences, and techniques are often subverted or rendered so vague as to provide little coordination" (Hagan, 1989). In other words, the criminal justice "system" has been called a "nonsystem" due to its decentralized and fragmented nature (Wagenaar et al., 2007; Berman & Aubrey, 2010; Eisenstein & Herbert, 1977; Forst, 1977; President's Commission on Law Enforcement and Administration of Justice, 1968). For example, prosecutors and defense attorneys may appear together in criminal trials, but each group answers to a different administrative head, and their goals reflect very different missions. Different agencies interact with one another, but only rarely do different agencies cooperate effectively or efficiently to process criminal cases.

For example, narcotics enforcement and white-collar crime prosecution require a departure from the loose coupling that dominates criminal justice organizations (Hagan, 1989). While reactive police work based on loosely coupled processes is the norm, proactive policing requires more tightly coupled interagency relations. Narcotics work requires police to use more controversial tactics to obtain evidence, including undercover work, entrapment, and informants (Skolnick, 1966). Police officers are more dependent upon prosecutors for feedback on the legal permissibility of evidence, and prosecutors are more dependent upon police officers for extensive information and cooperation in the preparation of cases. Such information exchange influences charging decisions and plea bargains engineered to develop cooperation from informants and codefendants. Hagan argues that the proactive prosecution of white-collar criminals requires similar leverage to "turn witnesses." Judges must participate in these decisions as well, because their approval is necessary to implement charge reductions or negotiated sentences.

Using loose coupling as an explanatory concept, Hagan describes how sudden changes in the external environment of an organization (e.g., a riot; a murder committed by an escaped prisoner; court orders to reduce jail overcrowding) create demands for tighter coupling (Hagan, 1989). The distinction between proactive and reactive problem solving is crucial. For example, proactive policing or prosecution implies that officials actively target certain problems for attention. Proactive problem solving, however, requires a departure from the norm of "loose coupling": it necessitates cooperation and planning from multiple agencies and actors. In an analysis of urban riots in Los Angeles and Detroit, Balbus (1973) suggested that black suspects were rounded up en masse, at least initially, to serve an ostensible order maintenance function ("clearing the streets"). This initial increase in restrictiveness was followed by "uncharacteristic leniency" as bail release became much more frequent than usual ("clearing the jails"). This shift from "normal" court operations required a tightening of the relations between the police, prosecutorial, and judicial subsystems, so that bail decisions became more consistent.

Similarly, most criminal justice agencies today have computerized information systems that are used to gather, analyze, and provide reports. In many jurisdictions, the same information on offenders is collected and stored by several agencies, producing considerable waste of resources. More critically, important information about an offender may be available inside of an agency such as a police department but may never reach the court where important decisions need to be made. The implications of this agency fragmentation perspective are illustrated in Example 2–5 below.

Example 2–5   Reorganizing the Federal Government to Meet the Threat of Terrorist Attacks (Office of Homeland Security, 2002)

In the aftermath of the attacks on the World Trade Center and the Pentagon on September 11, 2001, the Bush administration proposed the reorganization of those federal agencies responsible for protecting U.S. citizens and the creation of a Department of Homeland Security. Those attacks demonstrated the vulnerability of our country to terrorist attacks and caused our leaders to perform a quick analysis of our sources of weakness. The problems identified included an inability to share and use existing intelligence information, lack of strategic coordination of resources among those agencies responsible for our national security, and a lack of technical preparedness for the kinds of weapons likely to be used by terrorists. In fact, several federal agencies, including the FBI and CIA, had information relevant to this tragedy, but this information was not shared. Competition and administrative barriers among these agencies had created a security system that was so loosely coupled that it was incapable of adequately meeting national security needs.

The proposal to create a Department of Homeland Security was passed quickly by Congress, and former Pennsylvania Governor Tom Ridge was appointed to head the new agency. The "impact model" looks like this:

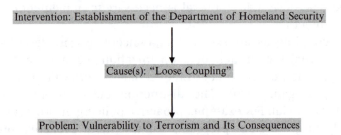

Intervention: Establishment of the Department of Homeland Security

Cause(s): "Loose Coupling"

Problem: Vulnerability to Terrorism and Its Consequences

The overall Homeland Security strategy was designed to enhance resources that are designed to prevent terrorist attacks, such as increased airline security; to reduce our vulnerability to attacks by doing such things as increasing border controls; and to increase our capacity to respond to attacks if and when they occur. Under the Department of Homeland Security, 22 smaller agencies were brought together under one administrative entity, thus eliminating some of the "loose coupling" that existed. The Department of Homeland Security also was made an intelligence analysis and reporting hub for all intelligence-gathering agencies, including state and local law enforcement agencies. In addition to creation of this new agency, other agencies such as the CIA and FBI were restructured in light of the mission laid out by the White House in its National Strategy for Homeland Security.

Conclusion

Failure to clearly identify the goals, values, and expectations guiding the development of an intervention can spell certain failure. At best, continued disagreement over intended goals and outcomes can be expected long after the program or policy is implemented. While discussion between stakeholders of competing goals and values can initially heighten conflict, it may also direct us toward eventual compromise or collaboration, more effective planning, and a reduction in the problem of concern. Similarly, failure to specify measurable objectives makes accountability elusive and measuring effectiveness impossible.

Discussion Questions

1. At the end of the Introduction, we asked you to write a short essay describing one possible intervention to address a specific problem in criminal justice. You are also likely to be doing one of the following in this course: (a) writing about a specific problem and/or intervention as a class assignment, or (b) participating in the development of a specific program or policy within the agency you work for. Briefly describe a specific criminal justice program or policy, and then describe one goal and one objective for this intervention.
2. Define: (a) *goal,* and (b) *objective.* (c) Describe the difference between the two.
3. Describe the four components of an objective.
4. Some argue that goal-setting should proceed from the bottom up; others argue it should proceed from the top down. (a) Describe each of these positions. (b) Which position do you agree with? Why?
5. Describe five common goals of punishment. Which of these goals appeals to you most?
6. Describe four common value orientations in criminal justice.
7. Describe an example of incompatible goals within the criminal justice system, and explain why it is important.
8. Discuss advantages and disadvantages of interagency collaboration. Give specific examples.
9. Describe the concept of "loose coupling," and explain why it is important, using a specific example.

■ ■ ■ ━━

Case Study 2–1 Top-Down versus Bottom-Up Goal Setting: Responding to Negative Information about Conditions of Juvenile Confinement

Instructions

Read the case study below, and then answer the following questions.

1. *Was the original goal-setting in this example top-down or bottom-up? Explain, and give evidence to support your answer.*
2. *How are performance standards similar to and different from objectives? How were goals and objectives developed?*
3. *What kinds of resistance to the creation of performance standards did the designers of Performance-based Standards (PbS) face? How did they address this resistance? Be specific, using concepts discussed in this chapter.*

By the early 1990s, the juvenile justice system was declared "broken," and delinquent youths were labeled "super predators" needing the severity of criminal prosecution and adult prison. What happened within the walls and razor wire of the "kiddie prisons" was little known or cared about. The public perception of juvenile justice was formed by the media coverage of a single horrendous crime committed by a youth. Juvenile justice leaders (nationally and locally) and youth workers were highly frustrated with the inability to demonstrate the positive things they do for delinquents. The public was similarly frustrated with the inability to hold the facilities and government agencies accountable for operations and expenditures of tax dollars.

In 1994 the Office of Juvenile Justice and Delinquency Prevention (OJJDP) of the Office of Justice Programs, U.S. Department of Justice, released a report that showed deplorable conditions in the facilities housing juvenile delinquents across the country (Parent et al., 1994). The congressionally mandated study found that in the nearly 1,000 facilities operating at that time, there were "substantial and widespread deficiencies" in living space, security, control of suicidal behavior, and health care. The facilities were overcrowded, youths and staff were suffering high rates of injuries, suicidal behavior was frequent, and health and mental health care was inadequate and sometimes unavailable. The report also found that the conditions were no better in facilities that met correctional accreditation standards. Joining businesses and government in the movement toward standards that indicate performance rather than process, OJJDP called for the development and implementation of national PbS and a new way of doing business for juvenile corrections.

The PbS for Juvenile Correction and Detention Facilities project developed and directed by the Council of Juvenile Correctional Administrators (CJCA) directly addresses the problems cited in the COC report (for information on the Performance Based Standards Project, see the CJCA web site page at http://cjca.net/initiatives/performance-based-standards-pbs). PbS is a system for juvenile agencies to demonstrate improvement and success in treating confined youths through national standards and performance outcome measures. The PbS data collection-analysis-improvement planning and implementation cycle provides a quality improvement structure and monitoring tools. The supporting PbS tools—the table of practices and processes that are expected to lead to better outcomes and performance, visits and support by experienced consultants, and links to other resources—provide facilities and agencies with a blueprint to move from deplorable conditions to safe, productive, and cost-effective management of youths in government care. PbS capitalized on Internet advances to build a secure national data-collection and reporting system that provides easy access across the country and quick feedback to facilities.

PbS asks facilities to report data twice a year on 106 outcomes that indicate performance toward meeting 30 standards derived from seven goals—one goal for each of the following components of facility operations: safety, security, order, programming (including education), health/mental health, justice, and reintegration. In this case, standards are objectives that are defined in terms of the values of the system and best practices among facilities nationally. Facilities collect the data from administrative records, youth records, youth exit interviews, incident reports, and climate surveys of youths and staff. The information is entered into the web portal and is reported back in easy-to-read bar graph reports. Each outcome is reported for the current data-collection period as well as any past data collections, allowing for comparison over time. The reports also include the average outcome of the field, indicated by a vertical intersecting the bar graph, which provides a quick analysis of whether the facility is doing better or worse than other PbS facilities. The outcomes include critical rates such as injuries, suicidal behavior, assaults, time in isolation, percentages of youths receiving suicide and mental health screenings, changes in academic achievement from admission to release, and percentages of youths completing educational, life skills, behavior management, and other programming curriculum.

Leaders at the Office of Juvenile Justice and Delinquency Prevention (OJJDP) conceived PbS following the release of the Conditions of Confinement Study. OJJDP at that time envisioned the development of national PbS setting the highest goals for facilities and providing outcome measures (numbers such as rates, percentages) to monitor progress meeting the standards. CJCA was awarded the competitive bid on September 30, 1995.

As part of the proposal, OJJDP required the creation of a project Advisory Board with members representing national organizations and relevant government entities. OJJDP believed that the major government entities and national organizations should define and guide PbS' development in order to create widely accepted and supported national standards and encourage voluntary participation. The strategy was effective in creating a comprehensive set of standards and establishing a respected group of leaders to initiate and promote PbS. The breadth of the Advisory Board continues as a solid basis for PbS' unique position as the only PbS for juvenile facilities. The Advisory Board membership included a seat for:

- CJCA, representing the juvenile correctional agencies;
- American Correctional Association (ACA), representing the adult agencies and staff of both adult and juvenile facilities;
- National Juvenile Detention Association (NJDA), representing county detention centers;
- National Association of Juvenile and Family Court Judges (NAJFCJ), representing the judicial branch;
- National Commission on Correctional Health Care (NCCHC), representing the correctional medical field;
- The National GAINS Center for People with Co-Occurring Disorders in the Justice System, representing the mental health and substance abuse field;
- American Bar Association, Juvenile Justice Center, working to improve access to counsel and the quality of representation for children in the juvenile justice system;
- Youth Law Center, representing juvenile advocates; and
- Correctional Education Association, representing correction teachers.

OJJDP has served throughout the development and implementation of PbS as an active contributor. The federal project monitor has participated in all major meetings and project discussions since 1995. OJJDP has worked with CJCA each funding cycle to assess progress, identify expansion opportunities and discuss priorities for resources. Additionally, OJJDP separately funded the ongoing evaluation by the National Academy of Public Administration to help PbS succeed.

Government agencies have found tremendous benefit to PbS data. Historically agencies feared data because it counted mistakes and poor practices without a vehicle to show how they responded. For example, if a facility screened youths for risk of suicide and the screen indicated the youth was at risk, the facility would be liable for addressing the needs of any youth and keeping him or her safe. Lacking data to demonstrate activities to keep the youths safe, too many facilities in the past opted not to collect data and relied in part on good luck to protect youths. PbS gives facilities the opportunity to show how they deal with and improve negative data. In South Dakota, a federal court judge approved the settlement agreement (*Christina A. v. Bloomberg*), giving the agency 1 year to abolish the use of restraints as punishment, limit the use of isolation, and increase mental health and education services for the youths—and demonstrate that the practices had changed. Under the watchful eye of the Youth Law Center, the agency implemented less punitive behavior management systems and presented to the court its PbS data demonstrating no incidences of restraints, reduced use of isolation, and increased services delivered to the youths. In December 2001 the federal court judge found the state in substantial compliance and ended its involvement.

The state agency directors (CJCA's members) have played a very significant role, beginning with letters of support for CJCA's application to OJJDP from 25 state and county governments. The juvenile correctional CEOs have served as advisors to development strategies and volunteered employees in expertise areas when needed. The juvenile CEOs also were instrumental in opening their facilities to the first PbS pilot test visits and data collection. The positive experience of those agencies opened doors and peaked interest in other states and counties so PbS could grow and learn. Continually CJCA members volunteer to participate in PbS and educate their peers, staff, legislator, and the public about its value. Because PbS is not mandated and is not attached to funding, the reason to participate was because an administrator wanted to improve. But the risks were high—data could discover problems. It was the encouragement and belief in PbS by other juvenile CEOs that moved many agencies to join PbS. The support and leadership of CJCA members was critical to PbS' development and continues to aide PbS' goals of expansion and self-sustainability within the field.

■ ■ ■

■ ■ ■

Case Study 2–2 The Goals of Mandatory Sentencing

Instructions

Read the case study below, and then answer the following questions.

1. *What goals and normative values guided the creation of mandatory sentencing policies? Explain and give evidence.*
2. *Identify and describe any incompatible goals or values of different stakeholders.*
3. *Describe one objective that could be used to evaluate the effectiveness of mandatory sentencing policies. Pay careful attention to the four components of an objective discussed in Chapter 3.*

By 1994 all 50 states had enacted one or more mandatory sentencing laws (Tonry, 1995), and Congress had enacted numerous mandatory sentencing laws for federal offenders. Furthermore, many state officials have recently considered proposals to enhance sentencing for adults and juveniles convicted of violent crimes, usually by mandating longer prison terms for violent offenders who have a record of serious crimes.[1]

A second frequently mentioned mandatory sentencing enhancement is "truth-in-sentencing," provisions for which are in the Violent Crime Control and Law Enforcement Act of 1994.

---

[1]In mid-1996 the California Supreme Court ruled the state's three-strikes law an undue intrusion on judges' sentencing discretion. State legislative leaders immediately announced plans to introduce legislation that would reinstate the law.

States that wish to qualify for federal aid under the Act are required to amend their laws so that imprisoned offenders serve at least 85% of their sentences.

Rationale for Mandatory Sentencing

Mandatory sentences are based on two goals—deterrence and incapacitation. The primary purposes of modest mandatory prison terms (e.g., 3 years for armed robbery) are specific deterrence, which applies to already sanctioned offenders, and general deterrence, which aims to deter prospective offenders. If the law successfully increases the imprisonment rate, the effects of incapacitation also will grow because fewer offenders will be free to victimize the population at large. The intent of three-strikes (and even two-strikes) is to incapacitate selected violent offenders for very long terms—25 years or even life. They have no specific deterrent effect if those confined will never be released, but their general deterrent effect could, in theory, be substantial.

By passing mandatory sentencing laws, legislators convey the message that certain crimes are deemed especially grave and that people who commit them deserve, and may expect, harsh sanctions. These laws are a rapid and visible response to public outcries following heinous or well-publicized crimes. The high long-term costs of mandatory sentencing are deferred because the difficult funding choices implicit in this policy can be delayed or even avoided.

Impact of Mandatory Sentencing Laws

Mandatory sentencing has had significant consequences that deserve close attention, among them its impact on crime and the operations of the criminal justice system. The possible differential consequences for certain groups of people also bear examination.

Crime

Evaluations of mandatory sentencing have focused on two types of crimes—those committed with handguns and those related to drugs (the offenses most commonly subjected to mandatory minimum penalties in state and federal courts). An evaluation of the Massachusetts law that imposed mandatory jail terms for possession of an unlicensed handgun concluded that the law was an effective deterrent of gun crime (Pierce & Bowers, 1981), at least in the short term.

However, studies of similar laws in Michigan (Loftin, Heumann, & McDowall, 1983) and Florida (Loftin & McDowall, 1984) found no evidence that crimes committed with firearms had been prevented. An evaluation of mandatory gun-use sentencing enhancements in six large cities (Detroit, Jacksonville, Tampa, Miami, Philadelphia, and Pittsburgh) indicated that the laws deterred homicide but not other violent crimes (McDowall, Loftin, & Wiersema, 1992). An assessment of New York's Rockefeller drug laws was unable to support the claim for their efficacy as a deterrent to drug crime in New York City (Joint Committee on New York Drug Law Evaluation, 1978). None of the studies examined the incapacitation effects of these laws.

The Criminal Justice System

The criminal courts rely on a high rate of guilty pleas to speed case processing and thus avoid logjams. Officials can offer inducements to defendants to obtain these pleas. If only in the short term, mandatory sentencing laws may disrupt established plea-bargaining patterns by preventing a prosecutor from offering a short prison term (less than the new minimum) in exchange for a guilty plea. However, unless policymakers enact long-term mandatory sentences that apply to many related categories of crimes, prosecutors usually can shift strategies and bargain on charges rather than on sentences.

The findings of research on the impact of mandatory sentencing laws on the criminal justice system have been summarized by a prominent scholar (Tonry, 1987). He found that officials make earlier and more selective arrest, charging, and diversion decisions; they also tend to bargain less and to bring more cases to trial. Specifically, he found that:

- Criminal justice officials and practitioners (police, lawyers, and judges) exercise discretion to avoid application of laws they consider unduly harsh.
- Arrest rates for target crimes decline soon after mandatory sentencing laws take effect.
- Dismissal and diversion rates increase at early stages of case processing after mandatory sentencing laws take effect.
- For defendants whose cases are not dismissed, plea-bargain rates decline and trial rates increase.
- For convicted defendants, sentencing delays increase.
- Enactment of mandatory sentencing laws has little impact on the probability that offenders will be imprisoned (when the effects of declining arrests, indictments, and convictions are taken into account).
- Sentences become longer and more severe.

The research review concluded that mandatory sentencing laws:

- Do not achieve certainty and predictability because officials circumvent them if they believe the results are unduly harsh.
- Are redundant with respect to proscribing probation for serious cases because such cases generally are sentenced to imprisonment anyway.
- Are arbitrary for minor cases.
- May occasionally result in an unduly harsh punishment for a marginal offender (Tonry, 1987).

Racial and Ethnic Minorities

One issue that has received considerable attention in recent years is whether racial or ethnic minorities are treated unfairly in the courts' application of mandatory minimum sentences. The question cannot be answered simply by comparing the proportion of minority offenders sentenced before and after introduction of, or changes in, mandatory sentencing laws. If, for example, it is objectively determined that minorities are more likely than the general population to commit offenses that carry mandatory sentences, an equitable application of the law would result in an increase in the proportion of imprisoned minorities—and probably in the lengths of their average sentences.

Consequently, the central question is whether criminal justice officials' discretionary choices in the application of mandatory sentencing laws are made in a racially neutral manner.

Results of particular studies are relevant. In one study involving cases of federal offenders sentenced for crimes subject to mandatory minimums, the researcher examined whether sentencing severity varied by amount and type of drugs involved in the current crime, weapons, offense record, role in offense, history of drug use, age, gender, and race (Meierhoefer, 1992a,b). She found sentencing differences associated with the offender's race, even after accounting for differences associated with these other characteristics. However, the magnitude of this difference was small.

The U.S. Sentencing Commission expanded this study and found significant differences in the proportion of whites (54%), Hispanics (57%), and African Americans (68%) who received mandatory minimum sentences for the most serious offense charged against them (U.S. Sentencing Commission, 1991). A reanalysis of the U.S. Sentencing Commission data drew different conclusions, however (Langan, 1992). The reanalysis showed that when legally relevant case-processing factors were considered, a defendant's race/ethnicity was unrelated to the sentence. Also examined in the reanalysis was why more than 40% of the cases apparently eligible for mandatory sentences did not receive them. Reasonable explanations include evidentiary problems and instances in which defendants provided substantial assistance to prosecutors in preparing cases against others.

In an analysis of the federal sentencing guidelines, other researchers found that African Americans received longer sentences than whites, not because of differential treatment by judges but because they constituted the large majority of those convicted of trafficking in crack cocaine—a crime Congress had singled out for especially harsh mandatory penalties (McDonald & Carlson, 1993). This pattern can be seen as constituting a "disparity in results" and, partly for this reason, the U.S. Sentencing Commission recommended to Congress that it eliminate the legal distinction between crack and regular cocaine for purposes of sentencing (a recommendation Congress rejected; Greenwood et al., 1994).

Future Issues

In the interviews conducted for this review of mandatory sentencing, state policymakers expressed the need to respond to the public's fear of crime and call for tougher sanctions, but also recognized the need to rein in spiraling costs of corrections. If the costs of government are cut, spending more on prisons means spending less on other public purposes. The fiscal analysis of California's three-strikes law, for example, has implications for that state's future.

In a major study of sentencing policy, Michael Tonry of the University of Minnesota suggested that states consider the following options (Tonry, 1995):

- Pursue presumptive rather than mandatory sentences.

Presumptive sentences, which are developed by sentencing commissions and set forth as guidelines, can shift overall sentencing patterns in ways acceptable to policymakers. For example, they can seek to imprison more violent offenders and fewer property offenders. A sentencing commission can help maintain sentencing policy while still preserving ultimate legislative control. Presumptive sentences have generally achieved their intended goals, and research shows high rates of conformity to the sentences by judges.

In the rare instance in which a presumptive sentence is inappropriate (i.e., either too harsh or too lenient, given the facts of the case), judges can depart from the guidelines by providing in writing reasons that can be reviewed by higher courts. If legislatures so instruct sentencing commissions, they can craft the guidelines to control future costs and, at the same time, toughen sentences for repeat violent offenders.

- Include "sunset provisions" to require periodic reconsideration of the propriety of the laws, if mandatory sentencing laws are enacted.
- Limit the duration and scope of mandatory sentencing laws.

Crime is, quite literally, an activity of young men. As the study of the California law emphasized, extremely long mandatory sentences (e.g., 25 years to life) are inefficient because they confine offenders for long periods (at great cost) after they would have "aged out" of crime. Sentencing could be mandated for only a few especially serious crimes. If such laws are aimed at repeat serious offenders, they could include a requirement that only particularly serious prior and current convictions trigger them.

- Conduct some form of periodic administrative review to determine if continued confinement of the offender is required, in the event mandatory sentences are imposed.
- Closely link sentencing and fiscal policy decisions to enhance the legislative process. Legislatures could ensure that they know the financial impact of proposed sentencing legislation and, where substantial long-term costs will be incurred, a funding plan might be a required provision of the enabling law. This would prevent today's legislature from avoiding the fiscal implications of its sentencing policies.

Cultivating Alternative Sanctions

Legislatures also may want to develop policy that makes more effective and systematic use of intermediate sanctions, if the twin objectives of punishment and lower correctional costs are to be achieved. Such policy might specify goals for each particular sanction, locate each category of intermediate sanctions along the continuum between standard probation and total confinement, and define target populations for each category. For example, it could specify which confined offenders will be considered for early release, which sanctions should enhance standard probation, and which offenders need treatment or services.

In addition, states may want to develop a financial structure to steer development of intermediate sanctions in intended directions. This could be a variant of current community corrections acts, for which a central state agency sets standards for local programs and administers performance-based financial aid to local governments. For intermediate sanctions, the state could provide greater support to jurisdictions whose program met or exceeded the performance objectives specified by the agency.

Finally, states that make greater use of intermediate sanctions may want to develop policies that govern their use in individual cases. Examples are the development of presumptive guidelines for nonconfinement as well as confinement sanctions. Such policies could be designed to ensure that overall use of nonconfinement sanctions is consistent with goals established by the legislature and broad principles that govern sentencing generally (e.g., proportionality, uniformity, and neutrality). In particular, guidelines could limit additive use of sanctions (imposing two or three nonconfinement sanctions on a particular offender) and control revocation decisions in order to minimize needless confinement for minor rule violations.

(excerpted from: Parent, Dunworth, McDonald, & Rhodes, 1997)

References

Auerhahn, K. (2001). *Incapacitation, dangerous offenders, and sentencing reform.* Albany: State University of New York Press.

Balbus, I. (1973). *The dialectics of legal repression.* New York: Russell Sage.

Berman, Greg, & Aubrey, Fox (2010). *Trial and error in criminal justice reform: Learning from failure.* Washington, DC: Urban Institute Press.

Braithwaite, J. (2002). *Restorative justice and responsive regulation.* Oxford: Oxford University Press.

Cohen, M. D., March, J. G., & Olsen, J. P. (1972). A garbage can model of organizational choice. *Administrative Science Quarterly, 17*, 1–25.

Eisenstein, J., & Herbert, J. (1977). *Felony justice: An organizational analysis of criminal courts.* Boston: Little, Brown.

Finn, P. (1998). *Texas' project RIO (re-integration of offenders).* Washington, DC: U.S. Department of Justice, Office of Justice Programs, National Institute of Justice.

Forst, M. L. (1977). To what extent should the criminal justice system be a "system"? *Crime & Delinquency, 23*, 403–416.

Greenwood, P. W., Rydell, C. P., Abramse, A., Caulkins, J. P., Chiesa, J., Model, K., & Klein, S. P. (1994). *Three strikes and you're out: Estimated benefits and costs of California's new mandatory-sentencing law.* Santa Monica, CA: RAND.

Hagan, J. (1989). Why is there so little criminal justice theory? Neglected macro- and microlevel links between organization and power. *Journal of Research in Crime and Delinquency, 26*, 116–135.

Joint Committee on New York Drug Law Evaluation, (1978). *The nation's toughest drug law: Evaluating the New York experience.* Washington, DC: U.S. Government Printing Office (A project of the Association of the Bar of the City of New York, the City of New York and the Drug Abuse Council, Inc).

Langan, P. (1992). *Federal prosecutor application of mandatory sentencing laws: Racially disparate? Widely evaded?* Washington, DC: U.S. Department of Justice, Bureau of Justice Statistics.

Lipsey, M. W., & Cullen, F. T. (2007). The effectiveness of correctional rehabilitation: A review of systematic reviews. *The Annual Review of Law and Social Science, 3*, 297–320.

Loftin, C., Heumann, M., & McDowall, D. (1983). Mandatory sentencing and firearms violence: Evaluating an alternative to gun control. *Law and Society Review, 17*, 287–318.

Loftin, C., & McDowall, D. (1984). The deterrent effects of the Florida Felony Firearm Law. *Journal of Criminal Law and Criminology, 75*, 250–259.

McDonald, D. C., & Carlson, K. E. (1993). *Sentencing in the courts: Does race matter? The transition to sentencing guidelines, 1986-90.* Washington, DC: U.S. Department of Justice, Bureau of Justice Statistics.

McDowall, D., Loftin, C., & Wiersema, B. (1992). A comparative study of the preventive effects of mandatory sentencing laws for gun crimes. *Journal of Criminal Law and Criminology, 83*, 378–394.

Meierhoefer, B. S. (1992a). Role of offense and offender characteristics in federal sentencing. *Southern California Law Review, 66*, 367–404.

Meierhoefer, B. S. (1992b). *General effect of mandatory minimum prison terms: A longitudinal study of federal sentences imposed.* Washington, DC: Federal Judicial Center.

Office of Homeland Security. (2002). *National strategy for homeland security.* Washington, DC: The White House.

Packer, H. L. (1968). *The limits of the criminal sanction.* Stanford, CA: Stanford University Press.

Parent, D., Dunworth, T., McDonald, D., & Rhodes, W. (1997). *Key legislative issues in criminal justice: Mandatory sentencing (NCJ-161839).* Washington, DC: U.S. Department of Justice, Office of Justice Programs, National Institute of Justice.

Parent, D., Leiter, V., Kennedy, S., Livens, L., Wentworth, D., & Wilcox, S. (1994). *Conditions of confinement: Juvenile detention and correctional facilities (research report).* Washington, DC: Office of Juvenile Justice and Delinquency Prevention, U.S. Department of Justice.

Pierce, G. L., & Bowers, W. J. (1981). The Bartley-Fox gun law's short-term impact on crime in Boston. *Annals of the American Academy of Political and Social Science, 455*, 120–132.

President's Commission on Law Enforcement and Administration of Justice. (1968). *The challenge of crime in a free society.* New York: Avon Books.

Richard, F. S. (2005). Punishment purposes. *Stanford Law Review, 58*–84.

Rossi, R. J., Gilmartin, K. J., & Dayton, C. W. (1982). *Agencies working together. A guide to coordination and planning.* Beverly Hills, CA: Sage.

Rothman, D. J. (1980). *Conscience and convenience: The asylum and its alternatives in progressive America.* Boston: Little, Brown.

Sherman, L. W., & Berk, R. A. (1984). The specific deterrent effects of arrest for domestic assault. *American Sociological Review, 49*, 261–272.

Shichor, D. (1995). *Punishment for profit: Private prisons/public concerns.* Thousand Oaks, CA: Sage.

Skolnick, J. (1966). *Justice without trial.* New York: John Wiley.

Tonry, M. (1987). *Sentencing reform impacts.* Washington, DC: U.S. Department of Justice, National Institute of Justice.

Tonry, M. (1995). *Sentencing matters.* Oxford, England: Oxford University Press.

U.S. Sentencing Commission. (1991). *Federal sentencing guidelines: A report on the operation of the guidelines system and short-term impacts on disparity in sentencing, use of incarceration, and prosecutorial discretion and plea bargaining.* Washington, DC: U.S. Sentencing Commission.

Von Hirsch, A. (1985). *Past or future crimes: Deservedness and dangerousness in the sentencing of criminals.* New Brunswick, NJ: Rutgers University Press.

Wagenaar, A. C., Maldonado-Molina, M. M., Erickson, D. J., Ma, L., Tobler, A. L., & Komro, K. A. (2007). General deterrence effects of U.S. statutory DUI fine and jail penalties: Long-term follow-up in 32 states. *Accident Analysis & Prevention, 39*(5), 982–994.

For example, see: Walker, S. (2001). *Sense and nonsense about crime and drugs* (5th ed.). Belmont, CA: Wadsworth.

Weick, K. (1976). Educational organizations as loosely coupled systems. *Administrative Science Quarterly, 21*, 1–19.

Welsh, W. N. (1992). The dynamics of jail reform litigation: A comparative analysis of litigation in California counties. *Law and Society Review, 26*, 591–625.

Wright, K. N. (1999). The desirability of goal conflict within the criminal justice system. In S. Stojkovic, J. Klofas & D. Kalinich, et al., *The administration and management of criminal justice organizations* (pp. 37–49). (4th ed.). Prospect Heights, IL: Waveland.

3

Designing the Program or Policy

CHAPTER OUTLINE

- ***Choosing an intervention approach*** involves integrating the information assembled in previous stages to decide how a policy or program can best achieve the goals that have been specified. How can the information collected at previous stages be used to decide what the substance of an intervention will be? How will specific goals be achieved?

- ***Major activities for program design*** include the following: (1) Identifying the target population: Who is the intervention aimed at? (2) Defining participant selection and intake procedures: How are program participants recruited and selected for the intervention? (3) Defining program components: the precise nature, amount, and sequence of activities provided must be specified. Who does what to whom, in what order, and in what amounts? (4) Writing job descriptions of staff, and define the skills and training required in order to deliver services well.

- ***Major activities for policy design*** include the following: (1) Identifying the target population of the policy. Which persons or groups are to be affected by the policy? (2) Identifying the responsible authority. Who is required to carry out the policy, and what will their responsibilities be? (3) Defining the provisions and procedures of the policy. Provisions specify the sanctions or services that will be delivered, and the conditions that must be met in order for the policy to be carried out. Individuals responsible for implementing a specific set of rules must also clearly understand the specific sequence of actions to be taken (procedures) to ensure that the policy is carried out consistently.

Keep in mind that the kinds of collaboration we discussed in Chapter 3 with regard to setting goals and objectives is just as important at this stage of the planning process. Eventually, support and, perhaps, participation of these key stakeholders will be essential to the long-term success of the intervention.

You will recall that policies differ from programs in that policies are rules, principles, or guidelines that govern actions, while programs are structures created to address specific needs or problems of a target population (see "Introduction"). Stage 4 involves specifying all of the program's activities or the policy's rules and procedures. Although planning for programs and for policies share many common features (e.g., analyzing the problem, setting goals and objectives), the two types of intervention are quite different in substance (design). This chapter will treat *program design* and *policy design* separately in order to keep these two intervention approaches clear.

Choosing an Intervention Approach

Choosing between a policy and program involves integrating the information assembled in previous stages. For example, your goal might be to reduce gun violence, but how will that goal be accomplished? What will be the substance of the intervention—creating a boot camp, creating more restrictive gun laws, developing a community antiviolence campaign, suppressing gang activity, or something else? How do you decide? Up to this point, you have collected and analyzed data, you have an idea of the intervention options that fit the problem or need, and your goals and objectives have been established. Your *force field analysis* (see Chapter 1) has revealed critical sources of resistance and support, and your *systems analysis* (Chapter 1) has identified important characteristics of the organizational environment in which the change effort will take place. These data help inform choices about which intervention approach to choose.

Another critical ingredient is the cost of the option selected. We can learn about the potential costs of an option by examining its use in other settings. In cases in which the policy results in the creation of a new agency, the costs can be very high. The Juvenile Justice and Delinquency Prevention Act of 1974 was developed to improve state-level planning for combating juvenile crime and to halt the practice of confining status offenders with delinquents. One of the Act's provisions was the creation of the Office of Juvenile Justice and Delinquency Prevention within the Department of Justice. Between 1974 and 1980, Congress increased funding for this act from $25 million to $100 million. By 2005, the OJJDP budget had risen to $362.9 million.

Program and policy options are often weighed in terms of cost. One option is to compare to another in terms of its expected benefits in relation to its costs, and its costs in relation to available resources. In 2001, the average cost of incarcerating a person in prison was $22,650 (Stephan, 2004). Figure 3–1 shows, however, that these costs vary greatly from state to state. Obviously, a number of categories of expenditure are contained within the overall cost of corrections. These include salaries and benefits, construction and equipment, medical care, food service, and utilities. Some people are surprised to learn that a residential treatment program can be more costly than imprisonment or that an in-home drug treatment program can cost more than a boot camp. Similarly, many states have chosen to invest in developing community-based correctional programs to reduce

State	Cost
States with highest reported average costs:	
Maine	44,379
Rhode Island	38,503
Massachusetts	37,718
Minnesota	36,836
New York	36,835
States with lowest reported average costs:	
Alabama	8,128
Mississippi	12,795
Missouri	12,867
Louisiana	12,951
Texas	13,808

FIGURE 3–1 States with highest and lowest reported average costs.

dependency on costly prisons. But these community programs, if run well, can be costly too. Are offenders in these programs expected to work or go to school? If so, will it be necessary to purchase training, assist with job searches, monitor their behavior on the job, or intervene when conflicts occur at the place of employment? Programs that include treatment are considerably more expensive than those that do not, and yet treatment improves the effectiveness of intensive probation programs (Bonta, Wallace-Capretta, & Rooney, 2000; Petersilia & Turner, 1993). These are facts that must be known in order to avoid wasteful planning or eventual program failure because of inadequate resources.

Designing a Program

In general, in designing a program we must answer the following questions as specifically as possible: Who does what to whom, where, in what order, how much, and how often? How will the program be set up? How are participants selected? What activities are delivered, and how? What training and qualifications are required for staff? By the time you reach this stage of analysis, you should have information about:

- The problem or need to be addressed
- It's etiology (causes) and theory that explains how these causes work to produce the problem
- Possible interventions, including interventions that have already been tried
- Potential barriers or sources of resistance to change
- Goals and objectives (remember that objectives are specific and measurable)

If you were acting as a program "analyst," you would look at an existing program and specify in detail exactly what it does. When designing a *new* program, however, the change agent's task is to design the "nuts and bolts" of the new program. The goals and objectives that have previously been specified must now be translated into specific tasks and activities, and the appropriate sequencing and timing of each activity must be defined. Case Study 3–1 at the end of this chapter illustrates these points.

Identifying the Target Population of the Program

Who is to be targeted, or changed? This process often involves specifying some level of need on the part of potential targets (e.g., level of drug involvement) and the characteristics of the intended target population (e.g., age, gender, geographic residence, type of offense, prior criminal record, etc.). In Chapter 1, recall that we discussed five levels of causality. We now need to clarify exactly who or what is the target of change. Are we trying to change:

- Individuals? (e.g., via intensive monitoring, counseling, teaching problem-solving skills)
- A group or groups? (e.g., via support groups, peer groups, family counseling)

- An organization? (e.g., via police training)
- A community? (e.g., via community policing, neighborhood watch, community service)
- Social structural conditions? (e.g., via welfare reform, job training, employment assistance)

In order to specify the target population, two major steps are required: defining eligibility and specifying numbers to be served.

1. *Define Eligibility:* Who is eligible for the program? What kind of individuals is the program intended for, and which targets are best suited to the intervention approach? Eligibility is often based on age, residence, income, gender, ethnicity, or other demographic variables. It is also based on level of need: What is the appropriate population to be targeted, in terms of how significant or urgent their needs are?
2. *Specify Numbers to be Served:* Given scarce resources, how are program funds most wisely spent? How many people can be served with available resources? How many individuals can the program accommodate over a time period of 6 months? One year?

Assessing Risk and Needs

One of the most common tools for defining a target population and matching individual needs with appropriate programming is a *risk/needs assessment.* Risk typically refers to the likelihood of a negative outcome, like rearrest, while *needs* pertain to modifiable problems that may be causing them to engage in antisocial behavior. The risk/needs assessment tools most commonly used are empirically based; that is, they were developed from research on actual individuals from the targeted population. Among the most widely used of these tools with delinquent youths are the Youth Level of Service/Case Management Inventory, developed by Robert Hoge and Don Andrews (Hoge & Andrews, 1996; Onifade, Davidson, Campbell, Turke, & Turner, 2008), The Massachusetts Youth Screening Instrument, Second Version (MAYSI-2), developed by Grisso and Barnum (2000), and The Psychopathy Checklist—Youth Version (PCL-YV), developed by Hare, McPherson, and Forth (1988). The YLS/CMI is a general screening tool designed to assess a youth's criminogenic needs and the risk that the youth will commit an offense in the future. The MAYSI-2 is a tool for identifying youths who may have mental health problems and require further diagnostic testing. The Psychopathy Checklist is used to identify the extent to which a youth's delinquent behavior is due to ways of thinking about antisocial acts.

Defining Participant Selection and Intake Procedures

Now that we know who the targets of change are, the next question is: How are program participants recruited and selected for the intervention? Given that targeted individuals and potential referral sources (e.g., police, courts, schools, probation, social services, etc.) are initially unaware of the program (or perhaps hostile toward it), how will we make them aware of this program, and how will we encourage them to use it? For example, boot camp programs are often intended for first-time, nonviolent offenders. The court might identify eligible offenders; an application from the individual may be required; an interview and screening process may be required to determine the applicant's suitability for the program.

Keep in mind that eligibility does not guarantee selection. A number of issues aside from being eligible affect selection for a program. The following five issues should be considered when defining how participants will be selected.

1. *Access:* How are potential participants "recruited" (i.e., how do they become aware of the program)? How are they informed of program operations and activities? Are referrals made to the program by any outside agencies? If so, by whom and for what reasons? How do referral sources learn about the program?
2. *Screening:* How are referrals or applicants screened for eligibility? Is some kind of needs assessment or other assessment tool used? Are application procedures required? How do they work? How is it decided which eligible referrals or applicants will be admitted to the program and who will be excluded?
3. *Intake:* Is an intake form used to record basic information when an individual is referred to the program, such as name, age, source of referral, reason for referral, etc.?
4. *Individual Records:* Is information to be recorded or stored throughout an individual's participation in the program? What kinds of information are needed for agency reporting purposes? For feedback to the individual? For treatment planning?
5. *Retention:* How long are participants to be retained in the program? What procedures will encourage them to complete the program?

Defining Program Components

Program components fall into the following categories: services, service delivery, dosage levels, and outputs. First, the precise nature, amount, and sequence of activities provided by a program must be specified. *Service delivery* refers to all those parts of the program that involve the dispensing of some "services" to targets. Who does what to whom, where, in what order, how often, and how much? What is the sequence of activities?

A boot camp program, for example, might contain several components: rigid military-style drills and physical training; academic or vocational education; life skills or problem-solving training; drug awareness education; social skills training, and so on. We need to describe how frequently each activity is provided (e.g., how many times a week?) and how much (e.g., 1 h/session?). Program evaluators often refer to these measures of exposure to a service as *dosage.* We need to specify which staff will be responsible for providing each activity, and exactly how it will be done (e.g., how are "life skills" taught? What approach is used: text, lectures, speakers, films, role plays, individual, or group counseling?). We need to describe the sequence of activities: What happens when an individual is first admitted? What order of activities is followed: upon admission? In a daily routine? On a weekly basis? How long does the program last (e.g., six weeks? six months?). How are targets "graduated" from the program?

Output refers to criteria for defining when the program has been completed (some unit of intervention provided to a specific individual). For example: 10 counseling sessions, 8 weeks of boot camp, 12 problem-solving skills training sessions, and so on.

When we review applications for funding, general program descriptions, or even academic articles, we are often surprised by the vagueness of the actual activities specified by the program. For example, we are told only that a program offers "counseling for battered women." We ask: How are women referred to this program? By whom? How is eligibility determined? Who delivers counseling? How? What kind of counseling (e.g., psychotherapy? Behavior modification? Cognitive restructuring?) How often is counseling given? For how long? In what setting (inpatient, outpatient)? Obviously, the simple information that "counseling" is provided is, by itself, insufficient to understand anything about the program's services or how they are delivered.

Writing Job Descriptions of Staff, and Defining the Skills and Training Required

How many and what kinds of staff are required to operate the program? What specific duties will they carry out? What kind of qualifications do they need to possess, and what further training will be necessary? How much money is needed for staff salaries and training? *Service tasks* include writing job descriptions of all program staff, their qualifications and training, and the major activities that are to be completed by them. Of course, an additional question is whether applicants for a job must possess all of the needed qualifications or if some required knowledge will be addressed through internal training.

Designing a Policy

Policies are rules, principles, or guidelines that govern actions taken by ordinary citizens as well as people in positions of authority, while programs are organizational units created to address specific needs or problems of a target population. Often programs are created to carry out large-scale policies. For example, the policy of requiring drug-abusing defendants in criminal court to participate in drug treatment has produced both new drug treatment programs and, more recently, drug courts (Goldkamp, 2003; Gottfredson, Najaka, & Kearley, 2003; Harrell, 2003). Drug courts possess more specialized knowledge of drug addiction and are better equipped to address the unique problems of the addicted defendant.

Policies are never designed by individuals working alone. Instead, because the decisions of a great many people will be affected, policy design occurs within a legislative process. Elected legislators of government bodies typically vote on policies designed by subcommittees. In private organizations, a similar process occurs through the board of directors. In other words, the creation of rules is usually the business of a legitimate body of rule-makers.

In the Introduction, we noted that policies vary in terms of their complexity. For example, a policy states that visitors to the offices of a program must sign a visitors' log. This is not a rule that typically requires discussion by a legislative body. Instead, these lower-level policies are handled at an administrative level. We will concern ourselves here, however, with broader policies created to address significant criminal justice problems.

The design of a policy involves specifying in detail the elements of the policy that make it possible for others to use it appropriately. In other words, if the provisions and procedures of the policy are not laid out clearly, actions may be taken that are inconsistent with the intent of the policymakers. In addition, if elements of the policy are missing, then incomplete implementation may result.

As an example, in the early 1980s, Philadelphia's Municipal Court initiated a new policy for handling drunk drivers. The idea was that small amounts of punishment combined with education and treatment would be more effective than punishment alone. Consequently, new penalties that included jail sentences of only a few days were created, requirements were added that immediately after sentencing the offender would be tested for alcohol abuse problems, and contracts were established with private programs to provide alcohol abuse treatment and education. But a critical piece was missing. No one was made responsible to see that the sentence was carried out, and no record of participation was maintained. Sentenced offenders were expected to show up for education and counseling sessions and to serve jail time. The problem was that authorities receiving these offenders had no list of who to expect, so there was no way for them to know who was missing. Over time, offenders learned that if they ignored the sentence, nothing would happen. Consequently, the more times an offender was sentenced, the less likely it was that the sentence was completed (Rourke & Harris, 1988).

In designing a policy, the change agent typically identifies:

* The *target population,* or who will be affected by the policy,
* The *decision authority,* or who has the authority to carry out the policy,
* The *provisions* of the policy (what members of the target population will receive), and the steps that must be followed (procedures).

Identifying the Target Population of the Policy

Policies affect people. Much like programs, they are intended to benefit or punish specific groups of people through the actions of decisionmakers. A policy that certain juveniles will be automatically tried as adults ("direct file" or "automatic exclusion") must clearly specify the characteristics of individuals and their offenses that will make them ineligible for trial in juvenile court. How old must they be? What offenses are excluded? Do they need to have a record of prior offenses? Must the prior offenses be serious? Is there any way that these juveniles can be tried in juvenile court?

For other types of policies, the question is often one of selection: whether the rule applies to everyone or whether only certain persons or groups are being targeted. For example, police pedestrian stops are often suspected of targeting members of minority groups. The amount of racial bias in these stops seems to be small or nonexistent, however, suggesting that the policy targets all persons found walking in areas where street crime rates or rates of violent crime are high (Ridgeway, 2007).

Identifying the Responsible Authority

Who is to carry out the policy, and what will the responsibilities of those persons be? Many states, for example, have implemented sentencing guidelines that limit the ranges of sentences that judges can give to offenders, depending on current and prior offense information. Judges are required to stay within the specified reasons or to provide written justification for giving a sentence that is outside the range. In this case, the judge is the responsible authority, and the judge must consult the guidelines before assigning the sentence. This assignment of responsibility to an organizational unit or to persons occupying a specific role in an organization is important to the policy's success. It assures that relevant knowledge, credibility, and lines of authority are consistent with other policies.

In some cases, a new policy results in the creation of new agencies. In the case of sentencing guidelines, many states have created commissions that monitor implementation of the guidelines, including training judges, prosecutors, defenders, and others who need to know the new rules. Importantly, these sentencing commissions monitor use of the guidelines and learn from the application of the guidelines how to improve them. For example, if judges routinely make exceptions to the guidelines in cases involving use of a weapon or drug addiction, then the commission needs to review the guidelines to see if changes are needed. It may be that the justifications provided by judges are consistent and convincing, and that the guidelines should reflect the values and beliefs being expressed by these judges. This example shows how important it is to assign responsibility for carrying out a policy to the right persons. Not only will implementation be more effective; the policy itself has a better chance of being improved.

Specifying Policy Provisions and Procedures

In order for a set of principles or rules to be implemented well, individuals responsible for carrying them out must understand what is to be done (provisions) and the steps that must be taken (procedures) so that the policy is carried out consistently. In the case of a curfew for juveniles, the rule about "who gets what and in what order" is clear. In other cases, however, the policy statement must be more detailed. It is critical that provisions and procedures be developed and stated clearly in order to ensure consistency, fairness, and control of costs associated with the policy's implementation. Typically the policy identifies:

- *Provisions:* What is to be done: the goods, services, opportunities, or interventions that will be delivered to members of the target population.
- *Procedures:* The steps that need to be followed and the conditions that must be met to apply the policy.

For example, state Community Corrections Acts (CCAs) are policies that specify how community correctional programs should be developed to control the growth of prison populations. The provisions of state CCAs vary on at least four dimensions (Harris, 1996):

1. The degree of decentralization of authority from state to local levels (e.g., administrative control granted to city/county networks vs. state-run programs).
2. The nature of citizen participation in the design, governance, and operation of community corrections programs (e.g., citizen advisory board, role in case screening).
3. Relative emphasis on deinstitutionalization of offenders (e.g., the degree to which reductions in local or state prison populations are explicitly mandated; funding incentives or disincentives are tied to prison populations).
4. The nature and scope of individualized sanctions and services to be offered (e.g., relative emphasis on rehabilitation, reintegration, restitution, restoration, or control).

We see that provisions may overlap to some degree with decision authority and target identification. The decision authority that chooses to keep some prison-bound offenders in the community may be compelled by strict selection criteria that include type of crime the offender committed, the offender's prior court history, and their employment situation. In another setting the policy may specify a requirement (provision) that a certain proportion of prison-bound offenders must stay in the community. How these offenders are selected may not be left to the sole discretion of decisionmakers.

When specifying the provisions of a policy, it is also important to delineate the specific steps or procedures to be followed. For example, Emergency Release Acts are controversial policy options that require a local or state correctional agency to release certain prisoners in order to bring the population down to an acceptable level (Welsh, 1993). Obviously, such a policy is not popular with everyone. In fact, in 2011, the U.S. Supreme Court had to order California to reduce its prison population because of extreme overcrowding.[1] Letting prisoners out before their sentence is completed may be regarded as cheating. After all, the judge handed down a sentence that seemed fair. The fact that the prison is crowded doesn't change the appropriateness of the sentence. The fact is, however, that criminal justice agencies are not given infinite resources. They must do the best that they can with limited resources. In designing an Emergency Release policy, then, it is important to state clearly the sequence of actions (procedures) that must be taken when the prison population reaches a specified level. These procedures can include:

- Prison populations are to be monitored daily.
- Projections are made about immediate crowding problems.
- Responsible persons are designated to make release decisions.
- The governor's office must be consulted in specific cases.
- Persons with specific authority must sign orders.

[1]*Brown v. Plata* (No. 09-1233), (563 U S ____ 2011 1).

- Arrangements must be made for those inmates about to be released.
- Notification to other agencies (e.g., law enforcement) that these releases are about to occur.

These steps are especially important when the rights of individuals are affected, eligibility might be challenged, resources are limited, and public objections are likely. Clear procedures help to ensure consistency and fairness in the application of a policy (Figure 3–2).

	Program Design	Policy Design
Who (does)	Staff	Decision authority
What	"Services" (program components and activities)	Provisions
To whom	Target population	Target population
In what order	"Service delivery" (sequence of program activities)	Procedures
How much and	"Service delivery" (dosage of each service)	Provisions
How often	"Service delivery" (frequency of program activities)	Procedures

FIGURE 3–2 Critical elements of program and policy design.

Conclusion

Once the intervention approach is chosen, it is necessary to specify clearly and in detail the design of the program or policy. Vague descriptions are not sufficient. Not all "boot camps" provide the same programming, for example, nor do all mandatory sentencing policies contain the same provisions. We want to know, in detail, who does what to whom in what order, how much, and how often (see the summary figure above). Only when the program or policy design has been clearly defined are we ready to move to the next stage of planning or analysis.

Discussion Questions

1. (a) Briefly describe the design of a program discussed in class, or use one that you have found while doing library research for a class paper. (b) Do you have enough published material to do this analysis? If not, what information do you need, and how might you get it?
2. What factors should you consider in choosing an intervention approach? Give a brief example to illustrate your answer.
3. What is meant by the term "service tasks"? Describe the different aspects that need to be specified.
4. What is meant by the term "service delivery"? Describe the different aspects that need to be specified.

5. What is meant by the term "policy provisions"? Give an example.
6. What kinds of factors are considered in defining the target population?
7. Identify a criminal justice policy and outline its major components, including its target population, provisions, responsible authority, and procedures.
8. Describe each of the following concepts:
   • Access
   • Screening
   • Needs/Risk Assessment
   • Intake
   • Retention
   • Emergency Release Acts

■ ■ ■ ────────────────────────────────

Case Study 3–1 Program Design: The Philadelphia Drug Treatment Court

Instructions

Read the case study below, and then answer the question at the end of the material.

Drug Courts

Many individuals enter the criminal justice system on drug-related charges. Recently, instead of just punishing these offenders, specialized drug courts have been implemented in order to respond to the offense and interrupt the cycle of drugs and crime. By merging court processing with substance abuse treatment, such courts serve as an alternative to sending individuals to prison. The specialized courts usually provide diversionary or deferred sentencing programs, meaning that successful completion of the program results in dismissal of charges.

The Philadelphia Treatment Court

The Philadelphia Treatment Court was developed through a collaboration of several criminal justice agencies, treatment agencies, and key stakeholders (Goldkamp, Weiland, Collins, & Moore, 1999). A Drug Court Planning Committee was formed in December 1995 under supervision of Judge Louis Presenza, Supervising Judge for the Criminal Division of the Philadelphia Municipal Court. The committee consisted of representatives of the Philadelphia Municipal Court, the Court of Common Pleas, the Philadelphia District Attorney's Office, the Defender Association of Philadelphia, Pretrial Services, the Public Health Department, and Temple University. A comprehensive plan for a drug court in Philadelphia was completed in December 1996 and set into execution in April of 1997.

Goals

The development of a drug court in Philadelphia was initiated to address high levels of drug involvement among the adult offenders. This court was designed as an alternative to incarceration to provide treatment to substance-abusing defendants. Its goal is to reduce a defendant's involvement in crime and recidivism, to reduce the overcrowding of Philadelphia's prison population, and to increase offenders' chances of functioning more productively as citizens by providing treatment as a part of the criminal justice process. The Treatment Court is structured as a partnership between the criminal justice system and a network of treatment providers that respond to the clinically determined needs of participants. It delivers treatment and other supportive services to more fully address treatment, health, housing, literacy, educational, and other social service needs presented by drug-involved defendants.

Target Population

The Planning Committee defined a target population and specific criteria for selecting participants. Eligible participants were limited to nonviolent, seriously drug-involved felony offenders who had been recently arrested. Medium to high-risk individuals were targeted. Defendants with more than two prior nonviolent convictions (including juvenile adjudications) or diversion dispositions did not qualify, and neither did those offenders with any prior violent conviction. Strong objections by a victim could also preclude participation.

Participation Selection Procedures

Potential candidates are identified immediately following arrest, triggered by eligible charges. Pretrial Services then continues the screening through an interview with the defendant. The Municipal Court Bail Commissioner is then alerted by Pretrial Services and determines eligibility by assigning a medium-high-risk release. Referrals are assessed for drug abuse treatment needs and appear before the Treatment Court. Defendants determined not to be in need of drug treatment are returned to the normal processing. Final eligibility of defendants in need of treatment is decided by the district attorney's office by reviewing the current charges, criminal history, and social history. Participation is also voluntary on the part of the defendant.

Program Components

As soon as a plea is entered, the participant begins an intensive drug treatment program designed to last for 12 months. Frequent drug testing and visits to an Intensive Supervision Center (ISC) are regular components of the court's requirements. This component is staffed by members of the Pretrial Services Unit of the court. The treatment itself is divided into five phases: (1) nonmedical detoxification, (2) intense treatment, (3) life skills training, (4) pregraduation, and (5) aftercare. Treatment services are provided by private providers, through contracts with the court.

Throughout these phases, participant behavior is acknowledged by means of rewards and sanctions. Sanctions include writing essays, court hearings, increased drug testing, restarting a phase, electronic monitoring, brief incarceration, and treatment termination with plea entered. Rewards include recognition in court, less frequent court appearances, unobserved drug testing, graduation, dismissing of case, and expungement of the offender's record. Although expected time periods are defined for each phase, moving from one phase to the next requires completion of the previous stage. Let's look at each phase in a bit more detail.

Phase I: Orientation, nonmedical detoxification, and assessment takes 1 month. During this phase participants must comply with pretrial release conditions, attend all hearings, and complete substance abuse assessment. They must attend treatment intake, where an initial treatment plan determined by the assessment is implemented. They must attend all treatment sessions, making up ones they have missed, and supply five consecutive negative drug tests.

Phase II: Intense Treatment is planned to last 3 months. Services include substance abuse treatment, mental health treatment, life skills training, and counseling. Participants are required to attend and participate in required treatment sessions and be actively involved in meeting treatment goals. They must maintain 90 consecutive days with negative drug tests and attend self-help sessions at least twice a week. They must not accumulate more than two sanctions. Drug testing is administered twice a week, court appearances are monthly, and ISC visits are once or twice a month.

Phase III: Focus on Life Skills, and *Phase IV:* Pregraduation. Phase III and Phase IV are similar. Each phase lasts about 4 months. Life skills training, vocational and housing assessment, relapse prevention, and an aftercare plan are all addressed during these two phases. Clients must continue substance treatment and attend all court hearings. They are required to attend AA/NA meetings at least once a week and participate in relapse prevention at least 2 h/week. They also must be drug-free for 120 days. Weekly random drug testing is given, monthly court hearings are set, and monthly ISC contacts are required. Graduation follows the successful completion of Phase IV.

Finally, an aftercare phase lasts about 12 months. Participants follow an aftercare plan agreed on with the court. Participants must attend Treatment Court alumni/support groups and NA/AA meetings. If participants are not arrested with convictions and there is no evidence that the defendant is engaging in drug use, their arrest is expunged from their record. If they are arrested or it becomes apparent that they are abusing drugs, their arrest remains on record.

Questions

1. Review the program description in Case Study 3–1, and critically evaluate it. How well is the design of this program described? Is there any other information about the program design that should be included? What questions might you ask to gain more information about the program design?
2. Is the program design logically linked to its goals? Why or why not?

Case Study 3–2

Instructions

Read the material below, and then answer the questions at the end of the case study.

Model Domestic Violence Law Enforcement Policy

Division of Child Abuse and Domestic Violence Services
Department for Human Support Services Cabinet for Health and Family Services State of Kentucky
Created by the Kentucky Justice and Public Safety Cabinet in conjunction with the Governor's Council on Domestic Violence

I. Introduction

Domestic violence is a serious crime against the individual and the community. The failure of any law enforcement officer to properly respond and handle a domestic call, no matter how frequent, will expose individuals and the community to danger up to and including death. Because domestic violence can and does result in the death of individuals, every response to a domestic call, no matter how often, shall be treated the same as any other crime against a person.

Every response to a domestic call shall include a substantive investigation of the incident which shall involve the gathering of background information, the gathering of physical evidence including pictures, clothing, and statements from direct and indirect witnesses including children and neighbors.

Every response to a domestic call, no matter how frequent, requires that every step possible be taken to insure the safety of the victim including providing a safety plan to the victim and, if necessary, transporting the victim and children, if appropriate, to another site for safekeeping.

II. Purpose

This domestic violence policy is designed to provide officers and support personnel with clear definitions, direction, and guidelines for providing and promoting a consistent, effective response to domestic violence crime in order to accomplish the following goals:

- make an arrest for any violation of an Emergency Protective Order ("EPO"), any violation of a Domestic Violence Order ("DVO"), any violation of a Foreign Protective Order ("FPO") or any violation of a condition of release or bond when authorized by state law;
- reduce the incidence and severity of domestic violence crime;
- afford maximum protection and support to adult and child victims of domestic violence through coordinated services of law enforcement and victim assistance; and
- reduce the risk of civil liability for officers, supervisors and administrators, and the employing unit of government.

III. Policy

A. To Accomplish These Goals, Every Officer Shall:
- make an arrest when authorized by state law as the preferred response, instead of using dispute mediation, separation or other police intervention techniques;
- treat all acts of domestic violence as criminal conduct;
- respond with the same protection and sanctions for every domestic violence incident, regardless of race, religion, creed, national origin, gender, sexual orientation, disability, and socio-economic status, including cases where any of the alleged parties may be a law enforcement officer, public official or prominent citizen;
- immediately report all known or suspected cases of domestic violence and abuse, adult abuse, or child abuse as required by state law; and
- receive training on domestic violence as required by state law.

Note: Every officer shall document action taken (arrest or nonarrest) on the JC-3 form.

B. The following facts shall not be considered as an independent compelling reason not to arrest the perpetrator. These facts may be used as background information to complete a domestic violence investigation for prosecution:
- the marital status of the suspect and the victim;
- whether or not the suspect lives on the premises with the victim (except as may be necessary to qualify the parties as "members of an unmarried couple");

- whether the victim has not obtained a protective order against the perpetrator;
- the potential financial consequences of arrest;
- whether there have been previous law enforcement responses to domestic calls at this address;
- verbal assurances that the violence will cease;
- the victim's emotional status;
- whether or not physical injuries suffered by the victim can be personally observed at the time of the law enforcement response;
- the location of the incident (i.e., public or private);
- speculation that the victim may not follow through with the prosecution, or that the arrest may not lead to a conviction;
- the victim's initial reluctance regarding an officer-initiated arrest;
- the fact that the victim and suspect are of the same gender; or,
- the use of alcohol or drugs by either or both parties.

IV. Procedures

A. Communications: General Responsibilities

1. In progress domestic violence calls shall receive a high priority response. Communications will:
   - use professional communications skills, obtain all pertinent critical information;
   - promptly relay all important information to the law enforcement officer including any information available through the LINK-Domestic Violence File;
   - update the responding officer with additional information obtained from the caller by keeping them on the line unless they perceive themselves to be in danger.

2. Communications personnel should request the following information:
   - location of incident, victim, and perpetrator;
   - type of incident (verbal/physical);
   - need for emergency medical assistance including injuries and severity;
   - weapons involved and descriptions;
   - name and telephone number;
   - dispatch two officers when available;
   - other people involved including children/witnesses;
   - perpetrator's dob/soc, previous history of domestic violence including previous law enforcement responses outstanding warrants;
   - alcohol and or drug use;
   - has perpetrator left scene, vehicle description, direction of travel;
   - apparent hazards to responders including animals.

3. Safety of Complainant
   - communications personnel should attempt to maintain telephone contact with the complaining party in order to monitor the situation and provide the most recent information until the officer arrives;
   - if the complainant must leave the telephone to seek safety, advise the caller to lay the phone down and not disconnect so the communications personnel can monitor the situation;
   - if the complainant is calling away from the scene advise them to remain there until the law enforcement officer arrives. Advise the responding officer of their location;

- for officer safety update the responding officer with all new information so he may approach the scene with as much information as possible;
- *advise the responding officer of additional calls from the residence including those requesting to cancel the call but do not advise the officer to cancel the call;*
- any interrupted or disconnected calls should be responded to if the location is known.

B. On-Scene Investigation, Arrest, and Postarrest Procedures

    1. General Responsibilities at the Scene: When responding to domestic violence calls, officers should:

- respond promptly to the call—utilize two officers when available;
- establish control;
- assess the situation for risks to all parties including children;
- attend to the emergency medical needs of those involved;
- interview parties/witnesses separately and away from the line of sight and hearing of the perpetrator (use direct quotes of witnesses about their fears and concern);
- effect an arrest of the perpetrator as the preferred response, if legally possible;
- seize any weapons used in the incident;
- inform the victim of rights;
- provide victim information on legal remedies and community services available for protection and safety planning;
- assist the victim in securing medical attention which shall include arranging for the transporting of the victim to obtain medical attention;
- assist the victim in securing legal protection (warrant, protective order) which may include transporting the victim to obtain the legal protection, if appropriate;
- report all actual and suspected incidents of abuse to the Cabinet for Families and Children, Department for Social Services, using the "Child Abuse, Adult Abuse, and Domestic Abuse Standard Report" form (JC-3);
- if the exigent circumstances have ceased, obtain a consent to search or obtain a search warrant when appropriate;
- collect and photograph all relevant evidence required for successful prosecution [use body map with checklist to document injuries];
- arrange for follow up photographs of the victim in order to demonstrate the extent of the injuries that may later become more obvious;
- attend to any children or dependent adults;
- check LINK and NCIC for outstanding warrants, history file on protective orders and whether there are any active "EPO's," "DVO's," or Foreign Protective Orders ["FPO's"].

    2. Arrests a. Arrest is the preferred response to domestic violence. All arrests shall be made in conformity with Kentucky state law, agency policy and procedures. b. Warrantless arrest for domestic violence related felonies is the preferred response.

Questions

1. Examine this policy in terms of the elements of a policy described in this chapter. Is anything missing?

2. Are the provisions of this policy consistent with its goals?

3. What do you see as the main concerns of the stakeholder that influenced the content of this policy?

■ ■ ■

■ ■ ■

Case Study 3–3 Getting Tough with Juvenile Offenders

Instructions

Read the material below, and then answer the questions at the end of the case study.

The juvenile court underwent a number of changes, largely through legislation, during the 1980s and 1990s. Both the media and some academic scholars portrayed delinquents as increasingly violent, predicting a wave of violence as the adolescent population increased in size. During the 1990s, almost every state passed new legislation making it easier to transfer juveniles to the criminal courts for trial and removing many protections, such as the confidentiality of juvenile court records. The waiver of juvenile cases to the criminal court was facilitated by removing the decision from the juvenile court and making transfer automatic under certain circumstances, thus placing the decision in the hands of prosecutors. Moreover, the language of these new laws indicated that the purpose of the juvenile justice system had shifted from one of rehabilitation to the protection of public safety and holding youths accountable for their offenses. Thus, legal and social scholars and researchers raised questions about the "rehabilitative ideal" on which the system was founded (Harris, Welsh, & Butler, 2000).

The experience of Pennsylvania illustrates well these changes (information on juvenile laws in other states can be found at the web site of the National Center for Juvenile Justice: http://www.ncjj.org/stateprofiles). In 1994, the state's District Attorney's Association asked the legislature to change the Juvenile Act. The recommended change was to give prosecutors the option of filing criminal charges directly in adult court when the offense was serious, violent, or if the offender was at least 16 and a chronic offender. Armed with factual evidence of increasing youth violence and arguments that the juvenile justice system was inadequate to deal with the problem, they pressed their case even harder when a new governor was elected in November of 1994.

The juvenile court judges of the state strongly opposed this proposed change. Instead, the judges proposed enhancements of the juvenile justice system that would support a comprehensive, community-focused effort to control violent juvenile delinquency. With greater resources and continued control over the decision to transfer juveniles to the adult system, the judges believed that youth violence could be reduced.

The new governor, Tom Ridge, addressed these initiatives aggressively when he came into office in January of 1995. Within a year, new legislation had been passed that changed the purpose of the juvenile court from one of rehabilitation to one of "balanced and restorative justice," or "balanced attention to the protection of the community, the imposition of accountability to victims for offenses committed and the development of competencies to enable children to become responsible and productive members of the community." Importantly, this legislation shifted the status of beneficiary of programs from the child to the community. Other major changes also were brought into law:

- The police were now authorized to fingerprint and photograph any child alleged to have committed a misdemeanor or felony,
- Parents could now be required to participate in summary offense hearings,

- Schools and the police must now be notified of the disposition of a case,
- Juvenile records of former juvenile offenders could now be used at bail hearings, and
- Juvenile hearings were now open to the public in cases in which the juvenile was charged with a felony.

The District Attorney's Association also got what it wanted: a number of offenses were excluded from juvenile court jurisdiction, thus enabling prosecutors to try these cases in adult court. The excluded offenses, which apply only to youths 15 and older, are: rape, involuntary sexual intercourse, aggravated assault, robbery, robbery of a motor vehicle, aggravated indecent assault, kidnapping, voluntary manslaughter, and an attempt to commit murder. If the juvenile can demonstrate that a trial in juvenile court would be better for the public, then the criminal court can choose to transfer the case back to juvenile court. In addition, juvenile court judges are now to consider primarily the "public interest" when deciding to transfer other cases. Again, it is the public, not the juvenile, which now is seen as the beneficiary of the law.

Obviously, each of the provisions listed above requires detailed procedures for judges, administrators, prosecutors, and probation staff to follow. Let's take the direct file provision, known as Act 33. This act not only specifies what offenses are excluded from juvenile court jurisdiction, but it defines in detail each offense so that fairness can be achieved. For example, aggravated assault includes an intentional attempt to cause bodily harm to a public official, an attempt to cause bodily harm with a deadly weapon, or an attempt to cause bodily harm to a teacher or student while he or she is engaged in school activities.

One of the most difficult implementation issues regarding this law has been translating the goals of public safety, victim restoration, and competency development into operational terms. In particular, if the development of youth competencies is a goal, what does it mean in practice? Is competency development the same thing as rehabilitation? Is it just education, vocational training, and the acquisition of life skills? Questions as to how courts and programs should translate the concept of competency development into concrete objectives and program services took some effort to resolve. The results can be found in a white paper produced by the National Center for Juvenile Justice at: http://ncjj.servehttp .com/ncjjwebsite/publications/topical/topicalbalance.htm.

Questions

1. Review the policy description given in Case Study 3–3 and critically evaluate it. Is the policy design (as described here) adequate? Why or why not? Is anything missing?
2. Consider what decision issues are raised by shifting the emphasis of the juvenile justice system from "the best interests of the child" to "the protection of the community," and what cost considerations should be addressed.
3. For Pennsylvania's Juvenile Act, what is the law's target population? What are its provisions? Who is the authority responsible for carrying it out? What procedures have been provided, and what procedures still need to be addressed?

References

Bonta, J., Wallace-Capretta, S., & Rooney, J. (2000). A quasi-experimental evaluation of an intensive reha-bilitation treatment program. *Criminal Justice and Behavior, 27*, 312–329.

Goldkamp, J. (2003). The impact of drug courts. *Criminology and Public Policy, 2*, 197–206.

Goldkamp, J. S., Weiland, D., Collins, M., & Moore, J. (1999). *The implementation of the Philadelphia treat-ment court: A descriptive analysis of early stages of implementation.* Philadelphia: Temple University, Crime and Justice Research Institute (Technical Report).

Gottfredson, D., Najaka, S. S., & Kearley, B. (2003). Effectiveness of drug treatment courts: Evidence from a randomized trial. *Criminology and Public Policy, 2*, 171–196.

Grisso, T., & Barnum, R. (2000). *Massachusetts youth screening instrument-2: User's manual and technical report.* Worcester, MA: University of Massachusetts Medical School.

Hare, R., McPherson, L., & Forth, A. (1988). Male psychopaths and their criminal careers. *Journal of Con-sulting and Clinical Psychology, 56*, 710–714.

Harrell, A. (2003). Judging drug courts: Balancing the evidence. *Criminology and Public Policy, 2*, 207–212.

Harris, M. K. (1996). Key differences among community corrections acts in the United States: An overview. *The Prison Journal, 76*, 192–238.

Harris, P. W., Welsh, W. N., & Butler, F. (2000). A century of juvenile justice. In G. LaFree (Ed.), *Criminal justice 2000.* Vol. 1 (pp. 359–426). Washington, DC: U.S. Department of Justice, Office of Justice Pro-grams, National Institute of Justice (NCJ-182408).

Hoge, R., & Andrews, D. A. (1996). *The youth level of service/case management inventory (YLS/CMI).* Ottawa, Ontario: Carleton University.

Onifade, E., Davidson, W., Campbell, C., Turke, G., Malinowski, J., & Turner, K. (2008). Predicting reci-divism in probationers with the youth level of service/case management inventory (YLS/CMI). *Criminal Justice and Behavior, 35*(4), 474–483.

Petersilia, J., & Turner, S. (1993). Intensive probation and parole. In M. Tonry (Ed.), *Crime and justice: A review of research.* Vol. 17. Chicago: University of Chicago Press.

Ridgeway, G. (2007). *Analysis of racial disparities in the New York police department's stop, question, and frisk practices.* Santa Monica, CA: RAND Corporation. http://www.rand.org/pubs/technical_reports/TR534.

Rourke, N. E., & Harris, P. W. (1988). Evaluating your DUI system: It can be sobering. *Judicature, 27*(14-18), 45–49.

Stephan, J. J. (2004). *Bureau of justice statistics special report: State prison expenditures, 2001.* http://www.bjs.gov/index.cfm?ty=pbdetail&iid=1174.

Welsh, W. N. (1993). Changes in arrest policies as a result of court orders against county jails. *Justice Quarterly, 10*, 89–120.

4 Action Planning

CHAPTER OUTLINE

- ***Identify resources needed and make cost projections.*** How much funding is needed to implement a specific intervention? Identify the kinds of resources needed, estimate costs and make projections, and develop a resource plan.

- ***Plan to acquire or reallocate resources.*** How will funding be acquired? Identify resource providers, and be prepared for making adjustments to the resource plan.

- ***Specify dates by which implementation tasks will be accomplished,*** and assign responsibilities to staff members for carrying out tasks. A "time line" or *Gantt chart* is particularly useful for this purpose.

- ***Develop mechanisms of self-regulation.*** Create mechanisms to monitor staff performance and enhance communication, including procedures for orienting participants, coordinating activities, and managing resistance and conflict.

- ***Specify a plan to build and maintain support.*** Anticipate sources of resistance and develop responses.

Action planning is Stage 4 of the seven-stage model used in this book. We assume that the first three stages of analysis have been completed at this point in time: Stage 1 (problem analysis), Stage 2 (goals and objectives), and Stage 3 (program or policy design). Recall that the steps involved for developing a new program or policy or analyzing an existing one are similar (see "Introduction"). If developing a new program or policy (Table 1–1), you now have the program or policy design specified, and it is time to develop a plan to put it into motion. If analyzing an existing program or policy (Table 1–2), you want to collect information to determine how critical decisions were made to implement the program (e.g., how resources were estimated and acquired, how support was built).

■ ■ Action Planning ■

Charting the entire sequence of activities and completion dates required to implement the program or policy design. It involves specifying, in clear and concise detail, the steps required to implement the program or policy design. It is, in essence, a "blueprint" explaining how to translate a vision of the program or policy into reality.

Developing an *action plan* is like writing the instructions explaining how to assemble a new computer system. Let's say you're about to assemble a complex system of electronic equipment by carefully following all the manufacturer's instructions. You have all the necessary components laid out in front of you; you hook up all the wires and cords according to the instructions, and you hook up the power supply. Now it is time to turn on the switch. Then: *Will it run at all? If so, will it run effectively and efficiently? What do you do if it doesn't?* Needless to say, simply having all the components doesn't do much good unless the instructions effectively explain what is needed to get the thing going. One needs a plan for putting the system into operation and making sure that it is working properly.

Here's another analogy: developing an action plan is like the blueprint for building a house. In addition to the *description* of the house (e.g., a four-bedroom, two-story brick house with a deck, modern kitchen, and landscaped yard), you need a *blueprint* that specifies all the necessary materials, supplies, and tools required, what goes where, and how things are supposed to fit together. Without the blueprint, you can't even begin. We find out how good the blueprint is when we actually put it into action step-by-step. Alas, the blueprint didn't just fall out of the sky into our waiting hands. Someone (the architect) put considerable thought and effort into explaining how to translate her vision of a house into reality. In essence, developing an action plan is like writing a blueprint.

■ ■ Implementation ■

The initiation, management, and administration of the action plan (see Chapter 5). Once the program or policy actually begins, we want to minimize discrepancies between what was planned (i.e., the program or policy design) and what was actually done (i.e., the "program or policy in action").

Programs and policies are similar—we need a blueprint. We may have the program or policy design on paper (i.e., descriptions of target selection procedures, job descriptions and qualifications of staff, and all the program/policy components or services to be delivered), but that is not sufficient. You need to develop an action plan, a blueprint that methodically specifies the sequence of tasks that need to be completed in order to launch or implement the program or policy successfully. These include technical and interpersonal tasks (e.g., identifying and acquiring the necessary resources for the program or policy; locating office space and/or meeting space; hiring and training staff; designing client intake and reporting forms; purchasing equipment and supplies; setting dates and assigning responsibility for the completion of specific tasks).

Naturally, as with the hypothetical computer system above, you want the program or policy to run properly after you've spent time, money, and energy on it. If you have planned carefully, you can minimize unanticipated problems that can surface when the program or policy actually begins operations.

Identify Resources Needed and Make Cost Projections

We need to identify all the specific resources necessary to implement an intervention. In real life, this is extremely important. One cannot launch any program or policy without the fiscal and personal resources needed to translate a vision into reality. One needs to start by developing a *resource plan,* which enumerates all the specific costs associated with each program or policy component, including staff salaries, benefits, training, supplies, physical space, and so on.

■ ■ Resource Plan ■

A comprehensive statement of the specific fiscal, material, and social resources required to implement an intervention. All program or policy costs are estimated, including personnel, training, equipment, supplies, facilities, travel, and so on.

A resource plan attempts to achieve the following goals:

- It matches resources to objectives. One must carefully ensure that all the resources necessary to achieve the objectives of the program or policy are in place. It forces us to impose a test of feasibility: either resources must rise to the level needed to achieve the stated objectives of the program or policy, or the objectives must be downscaled to match the level of resources available.
- It identifies the availability of current resources and resources still needed to implement the program or policy design properly.
- It attempts to control expenditures, usually by specifying how much money is to be spent over specific periods of time, such as each quarter (a 3-month period) and year.
- It provides data for monitoring fiscal aspects of the program or policy and providing feedback to funding sources and other stakeholders (e.g., annual reports, or quarterly grant reports).

We offer a few simple guidelines for developing the resource plan. We emphasize that one need not be a financial wizard, an economist, or an accountant to understand and use basic principles of resource planning. We will not be discussing professional budgeting models such as incremental models, performance-based budgeting, program budgeting, or zero-based budgeting. The interested reader can find detailed discussions on these specialized techniques elsewhere (Kettner, Moroney, & Martin, 2008; Miller, Rabin, & Hildreth, 2001). Instead, we present two basic principles of resource planning. First, we identify the kinds of resources needed. Second, we estimate costs for each type of resource needed.

First, list the different categories of resources that are needed to achieve each program or policy objective. Work closely from the program or policy design (see Chapter 3). The resource list should include everything that costs anything. For example:

- Staff: how many, with what qualifications?
- Staff training: what kind, and how much will be needed?
- Supplies: for example, paper, printing and copying, office supplies?
- Advertising: for example, brochures, flyers, public service announcements?

- Equipment: for example, computers, telephones, copiers?
- Rental costs: office space, meeting space, and other specialized space, if required (e.g., private interviewing rooms)?
- Utilities: telephone, electrical, heat, and water bills?

Some types of costs can be anticipated and calculated fairly precisely (e.g., salaries, rent); others may vary a great deal (e.g., telephone, photocopying, supplies). How do you find out? Ask around; do some research on similar programs or policies. Consult directors of other programs and agencies; see if it is possible to look at proposals that other agencies have prepared. Contact potential funding sources (e.g., state or federal government) to see if they will allow you to look at selected proposals they have funded in the past (probably with confidential financial information such as individual salaries removed, but with basic categories of costs such as personnel costs intact). For an example, see Case Study 4–1, which presents a sample grant application to the National Institute of Justice (NIJ) DNA Backlog Reduction Program. Many evidence-based program databases also include basic resource estimates.[1]

Those involved with the day-to-day operations of the program or the implementation of the policy (e.g., program or agency staff, coordinators, and directors) should have some input into what fiscal and social resources are needed to run the program or administer the policy. Too often, especially in applications to government agencies for funding, we see resource plans that were developed entirely by professional grant writers outside of the agency. The problem is that those grant writers have had little or no contact with the daily operations of the program or its clients, and their estimates of resources may not correspond very closely with the experience of the staff or the clients. Again, we emphasize the value of participation: do not exclude the input of staff or clients to aid resource planning.

Next, we ask how much of each kind of resource is needed. It is very important to be realistic about cost estimates. If you estimate too little, the program or policy is likely to fail. If you estimate too much, the proposal may not get funded, or the agency may face accusations of waste. A good budget will not only describe all estimated costs, but will provide a clear justification for each expenditure item.

In general, we attempt to estimate all the costs involved with processing all clients or targets through all phases of the program or policy over a specific period of time (e.g., 1 year). As we are trying to estimate these costs associated with each program or policy design component, we try to be as thorough as possible. In addition to paying staff salaries, how much will it cost to train staff? How much will it cost to print and duplicate the client intake forms and other record-keeping forms needed? How much will it cost to acquire the supplies needed to deliver

[1]See, for examples: (1) the *OJJDP Model Programs Guide,* available at: http://www.dsonline.com/mpg2.5/mpg_index.htm; (2) *Blueprints for Violence Prevention,* available at: http://www.colorado.edu/cspv/blueprints/; (3) the Center for Program Evaluation and Performance Measurement, available at: http://www.ojp.usdoj.gov/BJA/evaluation/index.html; (4) Crime Solutions.gov, available at: http://www.crimesolutions.gov/; and (5) *SAMHSA: National Registry of Evidence-based Programs and Practices (NREPP),* available at: http://www.nrepp.samhsa.gov/.

specific services (e.g., textbooks, learning aids, computer software, etc.)? How much will it cost to pay electrical, telephone, and water bills for the rooms or offices that are to be used?

Start-up costs are generally higher than costs for subsequent years. This is because we need to purchase new equipment and supplies, and set up management systems, staff recruitment systems, and referral systems. Often the flow of clients into a program is below capacity for the first year, or is unstable for the first couple of years. This creates fiscal instability that needs to be planned for.

Some funding sources are limited to a short period of time: 1-3 years. These funders often want to know how their funds will be replaced once their grant ends. They won't want to invest in a program that can't sustain a flow of needed resources.

Again, we recommend working closely from the program or policy design. Estimate the costs involved for each program or policy design component. For example, conducting DNA analysis on DNA samples collected from all convicted felony and misdemeanor offenders requires highly specialized equipment as well as highly trained staff (see Case Study 4–1). How much staff time will be needed over a specific time period, and how much will the necessary equipment cost? Some will complain that in this era of scarce resources and shrinking budgets, funding agencies expect programs to do more for less, that is, provide comprehensive, intensive services on a shoestring budget. Program directors may complain that they are already committed to providing services far beyond what their meager budgets actually pay for. But how can they possibly provide more services than what their budgets allow for? By overworking and burning out their most motivated staff persons, by pushing untrained staff to provide specialized services (e.g., life skills training, conflict-resolution training), by constantly training and recruiting new staff to replace the ones who left, by working hard to provide the impression (a "front") that the program is really "working," and by actively covering up any negative information that might threaten the program's survival. Such a situation is untenable. A good resource plan would never allow such a fiasco.

Plan to Acquire or Reallocate Resources

The task of obtaining funds to implement the program or policy requires a combination of experience, dedication, persistence, and patience. In most cases, the change agent or another specifically appointed individual (e.g., the program director or the agency's executive director) will scour the grant announcements of government, private, and nonprofit agencies, attempting to find some match between the interests of potential funding providers and the type of services the program is designed to provide. The interests of funding providers are usually clearly spelled out in Annual Program Announcements, Grant Announcements, or Solicitations for Proposals. In other cases, the change agent will lobby to get individuals or agencies interested in putting up funding for the program, arguing that it addresses a compelling problem or need within the mission of the funding provider. Consider the following types of funding sources (Figure 4–1).

- *Local, state, or federal government agencies:* Does the program or policy address a compelling need or problem that fits within the mission statement and jurisdiction of a government agency? Federal agencies are most likely to have specific grant announcements; local (city or county) agencies are most likely to fund specific programs that address their mission.
- *Governmental funds designated for special purposes:* Find out if city, state, or federal agencies have designated specific funds for certain programming areas (e.g., crime prevention, drug awareness education, violence prevention, etc.). Funding priorities or targeted programming areas change from year to year, so one must stay up-to-date with each agency's funding priorities.
- *User fees:* In some cases, nominal fees may be charged to the clients, although these fees are usually far less than actual program costs. In many criminal justice programs, such "user fees" are unpopular, but we have seen more creative user fees in recent years (e.g., a probation agency charges a daily fee to all participants to help offset costs of electronic surveillance; the incentive to pay such fees resides in offenders' motivations to be supervised in the community, rather than prison, to maintain full-time employment, and be closer to their families).
- *Private and nonprofit agencies* (e.g., the MacArthur Foundation, the United Way, the Pugh Foundation): These agencies often provide funding for programs that address their specific mission statements.
- *Donations from businesses:* Many large corporations and even many small community businesses have become increasingly involved in providing support for programs or policies that address community needs. In addition to "giving something back to the community" by being good citizens, many business people may qualify for valuable tax breaks by making donations of equipment, goods, services, or money.
- *Volunteers:* Many programs and agencies make extensive use of volunteers to provide some services (e.g., tutoring and mentoring in after-school delinquency prevention programs). Of course, volunteers need to be qualified and trained to provide specific services, and the program or agency must be prepared to support its volunteers.
- *Fund-raising projects:* Special projects may occasionally be undertaken to raise money for the program's services.

FIGURE 4–1 Potential funding sources.

Acquiring the necessary resources to implement the program may involve any or all of a combination of activities: writing a formal funding application to a government or nonprofit agency; lobbying local, state, or federal politicians for funding; making informal inquiries, presentations, and solicitations to various agencies; and familiarizing oneself with the entire funding terrain of potential funding sources.

Specify Dates by Which Implementation Tasks Will Be Accomplished

The next task, probably the most important one at this stage, is to develop a program or policy time line, sometimes called a *Gantt chart* (see Example 4–1), which specifies three elements: (1) all the specific implementation activities that need to be accomplished, (2) assignment of responsibility for each specific task to one or more individuals, and (3) a specific date by which each task is to be completed. This process may seem tedious, but it is a far more effective alternative than merely "winging it" or improvising program/policy implementation. Without a specific plan that incorporates all three elements listed above, the program or policy is likely to experience difficulty (or even mortality) before it even gets off the ground. A Gantt chart is a blueprint for putting all the program or policy elements into operation: step-by-step instructions explaining how to implement the program.

Example 4–1   A Gantt Chart for a Delinquency Prevention Program

Recall Example 4 ("Introduction"). We examined an excerpt from a funding proposal submitted by a delinquency prevention program applying for state funds. Major program components included: a 7-day challenge course in which juveniles were encouraged to examine their lives and set goals; one-to-one mentoring of youths by adult "committed partners"; and weekly "follow-through" meetings of all mentors and clients. The proposal spelled out exactly who was responsible for completing numerous activities required to launch the program. Activities included training, travel, site costs, 7-day course costs, and follow-through costs.

Here is the time line (Gantt chart) submitted with that proposal. While specific completion dates are not shown here, the time line clearly indicates a time period for beginning and ending each task; it also indicates clearly the sequence of activities to be accomplished (and by whom) in implementing the program. Note that the "consultants" referred to are subcontractors, trainers from a well-established national youth program. Note that additional technical tasks (e.g., acquiring office space, meeting space, etc.), while not shown, could easily be specified in such a chart.

Activity	Person Responsible	Time Schedule (in months)											
		1	2	3	4	5	6	7	8	9	10	11	12
1. Hire Program Coordinator.	Consultant.	X											
2. Project Coordinator training and coaching.	Consultant.	X											
3. Recruit and train volunteers (Youth Enrollment Coaches, Outreach, Facilitators).	Three trainers provided by consultant.	X											
4. Market the program.	Project Coordinator; Outreach volunteers.		X	X									
5. Youth enrollment training.	Youth Enrollment Coaches.		X										
6. Recruit and orient youth participants.	Project Coordinator; Youth Enrollment Coaches.		X										
7. Conduct precourse volunteer orientation.	Three trainers provided by consultant.	X	X	X									

Continued

Example 4–1   A Gantt Chart for a Delinquency Prevention Program—Cont'd

Activity	Person Responsible	Time Schedule (in months)											
		1	2	3	4	5	6	7	8	9	10	11	12
8. Conduct youth violence clearance, medical exams.	Specialists, professionals provided by consultant.		X										
9. Conduct 10-day intensive curriculum.	Facilitators, Coaches, Course Production Team, Situation Intervention Team, Security.			X									
10. Conduct parents' orientation.	Project Coordinator.			X									
11. Assign adult mentors and introduce to their youth partners.	Project Coordinator.			X									
12. Conduct monthly mentor coaching sessions.	Project Coordinator.				X	X	X	X	X	X	X	X	X
13. Conduct monthly youth and partner follow-through sessions.	Project Coordinator; two Workshop Leaders provided by consultant.				X	X	X	X	X	X	X	X	X
14. Manage weekly youth/partner communications.	Project Coordinator.				X	X	X	X	X	X	X	X	X
15. Provide life skills counseling, educational and job training, referral and placement.	Project Coordinator; adult mentors.				X	X	X	X	X	X	X	X	X

Develop Mechanisms of Self-Regulation

Orienting Participants

All participants, both staff and clients, must understand their respective roles. Leaders must: (1) clearly communicate the program's rationale, values, and intent; (2) clarify the staff's job descriptions; (3) spell out behavioral expectations, and specify rewards and punishments; and (4) allow staff to ask questions.

Coordinating Activities

Like the conductor of an orchestra, the change agent (with assistance from the individuals and agencies comprising the action system described in Chapter 1) must coordinate the activities of several different individuals and groups. A program's departments and individual staff need to be monitored and managed on a regular basis. Program managers must hire and train their staff; they must build good relations with potential referral sources (e.g., police, schools, probation); they must train staff to use required intake forms and keep client records; they must build good relations with citizens and businesses in the neighborhood; and they must provide regular reports of program progress to their funding providers. Three guidelines help ensure smooth coordination (see Figure 4–2).

---

1. *Maintain consistency:* Make sure that the actual job duties of staff are consistent with their job descriptions. Develop reward systems and incentives for good performance, and communicate to staff what these rewards are. Poor managers tend to wait until something goes wrong, and then blame (or punish) their staff. Proactive managers find that better performance results from communicating clear expectations and rewards. Such rewards include not just money, but privileges, responsibilities, and access to resources. For example, most staff are interested in professional development, and a paid trip to a local or national conference could be a substantial, appreciated reward. Staff development activities are usually permissible budget items, if someone had the forethought to include them in a grant proposal.
2. *Maintain clear and frequent communication among staff members, and between staff and supervisors:* Various means can be used: staff meetings, memos, conferences, informal conversations, and performance evaluations. Such mechanisms need to be explicit, though, and must be done on a regular basis. Staff must also feel that their opinions count. The program or agency director should encourage honest opinions and reporting about difficulties as well as successes. Some of the worst programs we have seen are those in which the director communicates a "don't rock the boat" philosophy, with the result that staff are afraid to report any problems until they reach crisis proportions.
3. *Keep an eye on the time line:* Make sure that activities required for successful progression from one step to the next are carried out on time (e.g., make sure that staff are hired and trained by the dates specified in the action plan, make sure that all record-keeping forms are printed, and procedures are clearly understood by staff). Imagine if 100 clients had to be turned away because a program was not ready to open when it was supposed to. Perhaps a required staff position was not filled, the office space or meeting space was not ready, or the referring agency had specific reporting requirements that were not met by the program. Such events, although relatively rare, are tragic: the program suffers irreparable damage to its credibility and reputation.

FIGURE 4–2 Three guidelines for coordinating activities.

Managing Resistance and Conflict

Some resistance is inevitable with the start-up of any new program or policy (recall *force field analysis* from Chapter 1). Resistance may come from any of the participants involved: clients, targets, even the program or agency's own staff (i.e., the action system). Any kind of change threatens people because it creates discomfort and uncertainty. Change challenges long-standing values and views of the world; it introduces risk. If participants have had input into the planning process, resistance can be anticipated and perhaps minimized. However, if resistance surfaces it should be dealt with fairly and seriously.

Conflict is not something to be avoided at all costs. It may provide the opportunity to identify and resolve misunderstandings, and it may also point out difficulties in implementation that deserve attention. Four general guidelines for conflict resolution are often helpful (see Figure 4–3).

Specify a Plan to Build and Maintain Support

With all the different interests represented by stakeholders and participants, one can expect that some public relations work goes with managing any program or policy, especially criminal justice interventions. The program or agency director is always trying to strengthen sources of support for the program or policy: within the staff, the community, across other agencies with which the program links, with his or her superiors, with the funding agency, with the news media, and with clients. Time for maintaining and increasing support needs to be built into one's schedule, and the person responsible for doing it needs to make sure that different stakeholders are contacted on a regular basis throughout the year.

---

1. *Avoid the use of force or coercion:* Using force is not often very effective, even when one has legitimate power and authority. Attempts to stifle opposition often create or increase resistance, produce unintended side effects, and lead to intentional subversion of the program's long-term goals.
2. *Try to work for a "win-win" solution, not a "win-lose" outcome:* Look for common ground, if possible. There may be options based upon a principle of exchange (i.e., each party gives up something in order to get something) that would reduce resistance at little cost.
3. *Generate alternatives and options to deal with problems* (i.e., brainstorming): Identify all possible options before evaluating them. Only after a list of options is developed should parties begin discussing costs and benefits of specific strategies or negotiating outcomes (e.g., brainstorming).
4. *Use "principled negotiations":* There are four basic rules for negotiating fairly (Fisher, Ury, & Patton, 2003). First, separate the people from the problem (don't take it personally). Second, focus on interests, not positions: each party should identify and communicate their needs, preferences, values, or concerns. Each party should understand what elements need to be included in a reasonable solution. Third, invent options for mutual gain: generate new options that are based on shared interests or an exchange of divergent interests. Finally, insist on objective criteria: both parties should agree on what criteria will be used to evaluate possible solutions.

FIGURE 4–3 Four guidelines for conflict resolution.

Conclusion

The program or policy in action will never perfectly match the program or policy on paper (i.e., the program or policy design). Developing a good "blueprint," or action plan, however, should markedly reduce subsequent problems with program or policy implementation and will help launch and maintain an effective intervention. So does looking for implementation difficulties, as we will see in the next chapter 5.

Discussion Questions

1. Define and describe the following terms: (a) "action planning," and (b) "resource plan."
2. Describe the purposes (goals) of a resource plan.
3. What does it mean to "estimate the costs involved for each program component"? How does one do this?
4. What is a "time line" or "Gantt chart"? What does it attempt to do?
5. Describe three guidelines for coordinating activities. Give an example.
6. Describe four guidelines for conflict resolution. Give an example.

■ ■ ■ ▬▬▬▬▬▬▬▬▬▬▬▬▬▬▬▬▬▬▬▬▬▬▬▬▬▬▬▬▬▬▬▬▬▬

Case Study 4–1 A Sample Grant Application to the National Institute of Justice[2]

Instructions

Many criminal justice agencies and nonprofit groups apply to the National Institute of Justice for funding to develop or improve specific projects and programs. These funding applications usually require a detailed breakdown of the anticipated costs for personnel, project materials, and other costs, and require a justification for all items in the budget. Please read the case study below; then answer the questions at the end. The application is broken into two parts. First, the *Program Narrative* describes the problem, the need for change, goals and objectives, and a plan for implementing the project. Second, the *Budget Narrative* describes specific costs for personnel and materials, and explains why each resource is needed.

FY11 DNA Backlog Reduction Program

Redrum State Bureau of Investigation: Division of Forensic Services (RSBI-DFS)

I. Program Narrative

Project Abstract

The Redrum State Bureau of Investigation, Division of Forensic Services (RSBI-DFS) is the agency that is responsible for analyzing evidential material associated with criminal

---

[2]"Redrum" is a hypothetical state somewhere in the U.S. The information in this case study was excerpted from a sample application available on the NIJ web site at: http://www.nij.gov/funding/welcome.htm #sampleapps.

investigations for all state and local law enforcement agencies and medical examiners within the state of Redrum. The RSBI-DFS maintains two regional laboratories—the East laboratory and the West laboratory. The Code of Redrum designates the RSBI-DFS as the agency responsible for conducting DNA analysis on DNA samples collected from all convicted felony and misdemeanor offenders as well as all felony arrestees in the state of Redrum; the RSBI-DFS is responsible for storing and maintaining the resultant profiles in the Redrum DNA Data Bank. The West regional laboratory maintains the DNA Database Unit.

The RSBI-DFS is facing budgetary constraints and is facing new DNA database expansion legislation that will be going into effect on May 1, 2011, that will increase the number of DNA database samples it will have to analyze. The Federal funding from this award will be used for the following goals:

1. Reducing the forensic DNA case backlog through analyst overtime, purchasing supplies, and outsourcing.
2. Reducing the DNA database sample backlog through analyst overtime and purchasing supplies.
3. Increasing the capacity of the laboratory by purchasing equipment (genetic analyzers, thermal cyclers, and a DNA extraction robot) and by hiring one evidence technician for each regional laboratory.
4. Providing the required continuing education for each analyst, purchasing text books for each analyst, and purchasing a subscription to the *Journal of Forensic Sciences*.

The RSBI-DFS can expect to reduce the DNA case backlog by at least 236 cases (206 in-house, 30 outsourced) by the end of the award period. The agency also expects to work at least 6800 DNA database samples (which includes 340 QC samples) using Federal funding. The turnaround time is expected to be reduced to 60 days or less, and the analyst throughput in the casework sections is expected to increase 10%.

Expected Results

1. The RSBI-DFS expects to decrease the backlog by at least 206 cases through in-house testing using federal overtime and supplies, and by at least 30 cases through outsourcing for a total of at least 236 cases over the award period.
2. The RSBI-DFS expects to analyze at least 6800 DNA database samples and QC samples through overtime and supplies.
3. The RSBI-DFS expects to decrease the turnaround time to 60 days or less through the introduction of new equipment and the addition of an evidence technician in each laboratory.
4. The expected increase in analyst throughput by the end of the award period is 10% with the addition of new equipment.
5. By the end of the award period, it is expected that all 10 analysts will have fulfilled their required continuing education through this grant.

Goals and Objectives

Goal 1: Reduce the casework backlog through overtime and outsourcing.

- Objective A: Fund overtime and purchase supplies for analysts to work backlogged cases
- Objective B: Outsource 30 cases to Orchid Cellmark

Goal 2: Reduce the backlog of DNA database samples

- Objective A: Fund overtime for the CODIS analyst to analyze, review, and upload samples
- Objective B: Purchase supplies to be used in the analysis of DNA database samples
- Objective C: Purchase collection kits for convicted offender and arrestee DNA samples

Goal 3: Increase capacity in the forensic casework laboratories

- Objective A: Purchase 2 ABI 3500 xl genetic analyzers, and service contacts
- Objective B: Purchase an AutoMate Express DNA extraction robot for the East laboratory
- Objective C: Purchase thermal cyclers to replace aging equipment
- Objective D: Purchase laptops for each analyst to replace aging desktop computeres
- Objective E: Hire evidence technicians to help with reagent preparation, QA/QC, and evidence intake

Goals 4: Provide required continuing education

- Objective A: Fund analysts' travel to conferences and training opportunities
- Objective B: Purchase texts
- Objective C: Purchase a subscription to the *Journal of Forensic Sciences* (JFS)
- Objective D: Provide an in-house training program on DNA Mixture interpretation

What Current Challenges Will This Project Address?

The RSBI-DFS is facing budgetary challenges as well as the challenge of implementing new legislative changes of the DNA database expansion. The state has lowered its personnel budget and has not allowed state-funded overtime for over a year nor have they allowed out of state travel for state employees, making the required continuing education for our analysts difficult to obtain. The state has also cut the budget for equipment for the crime laboratories and the labs have not been able to purchase equipment for 2 years. The Code of Redrum, Chapter 10, section 32 and 33 went into effect on May 1, 2010. Section 32D requires a DNA sample be collected from all offenders convicted of a Class A or Class B misdemeanor. Sections 32D and 33A went into effect immediately. Section 33B is an extension of the felony arrestee legislation and will go into effect May 1, 2011. The first section, 33A, required a DNA sample be collected at arrest for all persons arrested for violent felonies such as homicide, felonious assault, felonious sexual assault, and arson. Section 33B will require all persons arrested of any felony to have a DNA sample collected at the time of arrest. The legislative constraints also allow for automatic expungement of the records within 60 days if charges are not brought against the person; therefore, the arrestee sample must be analyzed, uploaded, and searched within 20-30 days.

How Will This Project Be Implemented?

This award will be used to fund overtime for forensic casework analysts to work forensic DNA cases. The funds will also be used to purchase supplies needed to work forensic DNA cases. The overtime for these analysts will be started immediately and the supplies will be purchased as necessary.

Monies from this award will also fund overtime for the CODIS analyst responsible for all database samples, and the funds will be used to purchase supplies to work database samples. The award will also fund the purchase of buccal swab DNA collection kits from Bode in order to ease the anticipated large influx of samples from the new legislation. The overtime for the CODIS analyst will start immediately and the supplies will be purchased as needed.

The funds will also be used for outsourcing 30 cases to Orchid Cellmark. The outsourcing contract is already in place and we will start to outsource cases immediately.

In order to increase the efficiency of the laboratories as a whole, two evidence technicians will be hired within 3 months of receiving the award. One evidence technician will be placed in the West laboratory, the other one in the East laboratory. The evidence technician in the East laboratory will assist in the quality assurance measures of the lab such as bleaching common work areas, monitoring temperatures of water baths, refrigerators, and freezers, and random laboratory inventory checks. The technician will also be responsible for the intake of evidence to the laboratory and entering the evidence into the LIMS. The technician assigned to the West laboratory is assigned to the Database Unit, and will perform similar duties for that unit as described for the technician assigned to the East laboratory as well as be responsible for the intake of database samples.

The funds will be used to purchase two genetic analyzers and service contracts, two thermal cyclers, and an extraction robot. The purchase of the 3500 xl genetic analyzers, 9700 thermal cyclers, and AutoMate Express will take place within 6 months of receiving the award. The 3500 xl analyzers will replace a 3130 xl in the West laboratory and will be an additional instrument in the East laboratory. Both thermal cyclers will go to the East laboratory because the instruments in the West laboratory were recently replaced. The RSBI-DFS has already evaluated extraction robots and decided that the AutoMate Express from ABI is the robot most suited for our laboratory system; previous award monies were used to validate the technology and develop Standard Operating Procedures for our laboratories. The extraction robot purchased with this award will be placed in the East laboratory.

The funds will also be used to purchase 10 laptops, one for each forensic analyst in the laboratory system. The laptops will allow easy access to the LIMS from anywhere and will allow each analyst to interpret data at his or her desk. The laboratory has a set of very old desktop computers that it would cost too much to update. A previous grant will be used to purchase GMIDX and LIMS licenses for each laptop. Laptops will be evaluated by our IT department and we expect the purchase of the laptops within 8 months of receiving the award.

The funds from this award will also be used to fulfill our analysts' continuing education requirements. Five analysts will travel to the American Academy of Forensic Sciences (AAFS) meeting in Atlanta in 2012 and will attend the DNA workshop. Four analysts will travel to the Promega conference—International Symposium on Human Identification—in October 2011 in the Washington D.C. area. One analyst who wishes to take over the West lab CODIS responsibilities in the future will attend the CODIS conference in November 2011. Each analyst will also be supplied with a copy of John Butler's "Fundamentals of Forensic DNA Typing." These books will be purchased within 3 months of receiving the award. We also plan to have an in-house training in DNA mixture interpretation for all analysts. This training will be set up as soon as possible and will take place as soon as an expert in Mixture Interpretation Training can be available to travel to our state.

In order to allow analysts to have access to scientific articles, an institutional subscription to the *Journal of Forensic Sciences* (JFS) will be purchased within 4 months of receiving the award.

List of Key Personnel

Grant Point of Contact:
Jack Torrance, RSBI-DFS Forensic Commander, jtorrance@redrumstate.gov

Redrum State Bureau of Investigation Headquarters
555 North Arson Street
Homicide, Redrum 00001
jtorrance@redrumstate.gov
555-555-5000

Key Personnel at West Regional Laboratory
500 South Robbery Boulevard
Battery, Redrum 00002
511-555-0005

Wendy Jones
West Regional Laboratory DNA Technical Leader
wtorrence@redrumstate.gov

Stephen Kingsly
Redrum State CODIS administrator
skingsly@redrumstate.gov

Key Personnel at East Regional Laboratory
5 East Hijack Avenue
Assault, Redrum 00003
501-555-5050
Dick Hallorann
East Regional Laboratory DNA Technical Leader
dhallorann@redrumstate.gov

II. Budget Narrative

Note: *Casework* totals are used to calculate how many cases have to be worked. *Database* totals are used to calculate the actual cost/database sample worked.

A. *Personnel: $149,000*

Salaries for technicians will be funded through this award. One technician will assist the casework laboratory with evidence transfers and returns. One technician will be assigned to the database laboratory to assist in the accessioning of new samples and transfer of samples to the laboratory to test. The salaries for these positions are based on current salaries for state-funded employees of the RSBI-DFS with equivalent levels of experience and training.

This award will also fund overtime for 10 forensic analysts. The forensic analyst I level is funded at $32/hr. for 250 hr. per individual for five (5) individuals. The forensic analyst II level is funded at $36/hr. for 250 hr. per individual for four (4) individuals. The CODIS analyst is funded at $35/hr. for 250 hr. of overtime. All nine forensic analysts will be directly involved in the handling and analysis of backlogged forensic cases. They will also be reviewing results from outsourced cases on overtime. The CODIS analyst will be analyzing all DNA database samples that are collected in the state of Redrum, and will be doing analysis, review, and upload on overtime.

B. Fringe Benefits: $32,343.60

The fringe benefits in this category are based on current State of Redrum values for FICA (6%), retirement (12%), Medicare (1.46%) and health (22%). For the technicians' salary total of $66,000, their benefits come to $27,496. In the state of Redrum, only FICA is assessed on overtime at the regular rate of 6%. For this project, the FICA for overtime for the casework analysts comes to $4560 and the FICA for overtime for the CODIS analyst comes to $420.

Casework: The total overtime salaries and fringe benefits costs that will be used by the casework laboratory come to $80,560. *Database*: The total overtime salary and fringe costs for the database laboratory come to $7420.

C. Travel: $14,021

Travel expenses in this category are for nine analysts to attend one national conference each, and for one analyst to attend the annual national CODIS administrator's conference where continuing education opportunities include workshops at the American Academy of Forensic Sciences and the Promega Symposium. The rates are based on the GSA allowable per diem for lodging and dining/other expenses for each location. All expenditures follow Federal and state regulations.

D. Equipment: $401,460

The equipment budget includes the following items:

- Two ABI 3500 xl genetic analyzers at $165,000 per instrument—This is the next generation of capillary electrophoresis instruments and the purchase of two of these instruments will replace an aging model 3130 xl genetic analyzer in the West laboratory and increase the capacity of the East laboratory by being an additional instrument. Both instruments will be purchased with installation, training, and all analytical software necessary for RSBI-DFS analysts to complete analysis. This instrument will be purchased as a sole source based upon existing training and validation using the Applied Biosystems instrument platforms and the fact that Applied Biosystems is the only manufacturer of these instruments.
- Two ABI thermal cyclers model 9700 at $8730 per instrument. Both of these instruments will be purchased to replace aging thermal cyclers at the East laboratory. These instruments are necessary in the amplification step of DNA analysis.
- One AutoMate Express DNA extraction robot from Applied Biosystems at a cost of $43,000. Using previously awarded Federal funds, DNA extraction robots were evaluated and the AutoMate Express was chosen as the instrument the RSBI-DFS would be using. Validation services provided by Federal funding have helped to develop Standard Operating Procedures (SOP) for this instrument. This instrument will be purchased with the full installation and set-up for the East laboratory. Along with the genetic analyzers, this instrument will be purchased as a sole source based upon existing SOPs and platforms in the laboratory system.
- Ten laptops. The RSBI-DFS IT department will evaluate laptops and will determine which brand and model will be the most useful for our analysts to use to access the LIMS from any place in the laboratory and to use data interpretation software as well as use as their personal work computer.

E. Supplies: $330,310

The RSBI-DFS budget for supplies includes a total of 34 kits of Promega PowerPlex 16 HS. The costs will be split up as follows:

- The database unit will use 17 of the kits for a total of 6800 samples to be analyzed. The actual cost to this award to analyze these 6800 database samples (which includes 340 QC samples) based on supply and overtime requests is $120,955 or $18.88 per sample.
- The casework unit will use 17 of the kits to analyze backlogged forensic DNA cases. This budget also includes 8 kits each of the PrepFiler reagents and PrepFiler plastics to be used with the AutoMate Express. These supplies will be used in casework on the AutoMate Express extraction robot that is already online in the West laboratory. Between the overtime and supplies requested under this award to assist in the processing of forensic cases, at least 206 backlogged DNA cases will be analyzed.

The budget in this category also includes 400 cases of Bode's buccal swab collection kit to be used at law enforcement agencies throughout the state for the collection of arrestee samples. Due to the DNA database expansion legislation that will go into effect on May 1, 2011, there is a need for more collection kits. The RSBI-DFS already has a contract with Bode for these collection kits, and that contract was previously competitively bid.

F. Construction: $0

There is no funding requested in this budget category.

G. Consultants/Contracts: $79,000

The budget request in this category is for the outsourcing of 30 cases to Orchid Cellmark. The RSBI-DFS has a previous contract in place with Orchid Cellmark and will continue the contract under this funding at an average cost of $1333 per case. In order to stretch our training dollars and ensure that every analyst gets the annual required DNA training, we plan to issue a contract to have a mixture interpretation class in the lab. A service contract for the two new ABI 3500s for one additional year is also needed.

H. Other: $6415

The requests in this category are:

- Registration for five analysts to attend the American Academy of Forensic Sciences conference plus 1 continuing education workshop at $200 per each for all five analysts
- Registration for four analysts to attend the annual Promega Conference to attend informative sessions and workshops for continuing education requirements
- Ten copies of the new edition of John Butler's "Fundamentals of Forensic DNA Typing." Each analyst will have a copy of the book. The cost is estimated from Amazon.com.
- One institutional subscription to the *Journal of Forensic Sciences* (JFS) so that analysts can have easy access to scientific articles to keep up with the new and emerging technologies in the field of forensic DNA

I. Indirect Costs

There is no funding requested in this budget category.

Total Funding Request: $1,012,549.60.

Questions

1. Are all the resources requested consistent with the stated goals and objectives? Why or why not? Give at least two specific examples of resources and explain why they are needed.
2. What is the most expensive budget component in this application? Briefly summarize it (one to two sentences), and describe the justification provided for it.
3. Based on the concepts described in this chapter, what is missing from this application or what could be improved? Give at least one specific example and explain.

■ ■ ■

■ ■ ■ ──

Case Study 4–2 The Brady Act: Why Action Planning Is Needed

Instructions

Controversies about the Brady Act extended far beyond arguments about the desirability of tougher handgun regulation. Disagreement ensued about who was going to pay to update and automate local criminal records information systems to comply with provisions of the Brady Act. This is a major reason why the National Criminal History Improvement Program (NCHIP) described below was created. NCHIP was an excellent example of "action planning." Without this enabling legislation and funding, problems in gaining state compliance with the new Act could have been insurmountable. Similarly, the Firearm Inquiry Statistics (FIST) Program was needed to monitor implementation of the Act over time. Read the material below, and then answer the questions at the end of this case study.

The Federal Gun Control Act (GCA), 18 U.S.C. 922, prohibits transfer of a firearm to a person who:

- Is under indictment for, or has been convicted of, a crime punishable by imprisonment for more than 1 year
- Is a fugitive from justice
- Is an unlawful user of, or is addicted to, any controlled substance
- Has been adjudicated as a mental defective or committed to a mental institution
- Is an illegal alien or has been admitted to the United States under a nonimmigrant visa
- Was discharged from the U.S. Armed Forces under dishonorable conditions
- Has renounced U.S. Citizenship
- Is subject to a court order restraining him or her from harassing, stalking, or threatening an intimate partner or child
- Has been convicted in any court of a misdemeanor crime of domestic violence.

The GCA categories of prohibited persons are the prevailing minimum for all states. Many states have similar prohibitions and have enacted additional categories of prohibited persons, such as those who have committed alcohol-related or juvenile offenses (Bureau of Justice Statistics, 2006a).

Following 7 years of political battles and NRA opposition, the Brady Act amended the GCA and included interim provisions, 18 U.S.C. 922(s), which were in effect from February 29, 1994, until November 29, 1998.[3] The U.S. Department of Justice developed the National Instant Criminal Background Check System (referred to as NICS) during the

[3]*Brady Handgun Violence Prevention Act* (Brady Act), PL 103-159.

57-month interim period, as authorized by the permanent provisions of the Brady Act, 18 U.S. C. 922(t).

Interim provisions were intended to allow states a reasonable period of time to comply with the new law, which required dramatic changes in state criminal background information systems. The interim provisions of the Act required that licensed firearm dealers request a presale check on all potential handgun purchasers from the Chief Law Enforcement Officer (CLEO) in the jurisdiction where the prospective purchaser resides. The CLEO must make "a reasonable effort" to determine if the purchaser is prohibited from receiving or possessing a handgun. The federal firearms licensee must wait five business days before transferring the handgun to the buyer unless earlier approval is received from the CLEO. The "interim provisions" also permitted states to follow a variety of alternatives to the 5-day waiting period, including issuing firearm permits (e.g., Missouri), performing "instant checks" (e.g., Virginia), or conducting "point-of-sale" checks (e.g., California).

This interim system remained in effect until November 30, 1998, when an instant background check was to become mandatory for purchasers of all firearms. Under the "permanent provisions" of the Brady Act, presale inquiries were to be made through the National Instant Criminal Background Check System (NICS). The background check would determine, based on available records, if an individual was prohibited under the Federal Gun Control Act or state law from receiving or possessing firearms. The Act required the NICS, operated by the FBI, to be established no later than November 1998.

In a close 5-4 decision on June 27, 1997, the U.S. Supreme Court ruled that the federal government cannot require local police to conduct background checks on people who want to buy handguns.[4] Justice Antonin Scalia noted in his opinion that the federal government cannot force states to enact or administer a federal regulatory program (a controversy known as federalism). The 5-day waiting period specified by the Act was ruled constitutional, as long as the states retained discretion to perform the background checks or not.[5]

Under the FBI's NICS program, state criminal history records are provided through each state's central repository and the Inter-state Identification Index. The Index, maintained by the FBI, points instantly to criminal records that states hold. In addition, the FBI provides records of federal offenses, Federally maintained state data, and federal data on nonfelony disqualifications. States responding to NICS inquiries for nonfelony prohibitions provide their records directly.

To help ensure availability of complete and accurate state records, the Brady Act established a grant program, the National Criminal History Improvement Program (NCHIP). The program was designed to assist states in developing or improving existing criminal history record systems and to establish interface with the NICS.

The Firearm Inquiry Statistics Program (FIST) was established under the NCHIP to develop data on the impact of presale firearm checks on the identification of prohibited firearm

---

[4]*Printz, Sheriff/Coroner, Ravalli County, Montana v. United States* 117 S.Ct 2365,138 L. Ed.2d 914 (1997).

[5]For additional information regarding Brady Act design and implementation, go to the Bureau of Alcohol, Tobacco, Firearms, and Explosives (ATF) web site (http://www.atf.gov). Choose "Search" from the menu, and enter the words "Brady Act." You will find a wealth of relevant information about the Brady Act.

purchasers. Data summarizing the number of inquiries, rejections, and reasons for rejections are summarized and released annually by the U.S. Bureau of Justice Statistics.

ATF issued an FAQ (frequently asked questions) sheet addressing 60 specific questions about who is responsible for doing what under the permanent provisions of the Brady law found in section 922(t) of the Gun Control Act.[6] These provisions became effective on November 30, 1998. Ten examples are provided below.

1. *Q. Who must comply with the requirements of the Brady law?*
   A. Federally licensed firearms importers, manufactures, and dealers must comply with the Brady law prior to the transfer of any firearm to a nonlicensed individual.
2. *Q. When did the provisions of the permanent Brady law take effect?*
   A. The permanent Brady law went into effect on November 30, 1998. Accordingly, any transfer occurring on or after November 30, 1998, is subject to the requirements of this law.
3. *Q. Is NICS operated by ATF?*
   A. No. NICS is operated by the Federal Bureau of Investigation (FBI).
4. *Q. Do all NICS checks go through the FBI's NICS Operations Center?*
   A. No. In many states, licensees initiate NICS checks through the State point of contact (POC).
5. *Q. If the State is acting as a point of contact (POC), does that mean that all NICS checks go through the POC rather than the FBI?*
   A. That depends on the state. In some states, the POC conducts background checks for all firearms transactions. In other states, licensees must contact the POC for handgun transactions and the FBI for long gun transactions. In some POC states, NICS checks for pawn redemptions are handled by the FBI.
6. *Q. How does a licensee know whether to contact the FBI or a State point of contact (POC) in order to initiate a NICS check?*
   A. Prior to November 30, 1998, ATF sent an open letter to licensees in each state, providing the licensees with instructions as to how to initiate a NICS check in their state. ATF has alerted FFLs if their State's procedures have changed since this time. Your local ATF office can advise you on the appropriate point of contact for NICS checks or you can check the ATF web page at http://www.atf.gov.
7. *Q. Is there a charge for NICS checks?*
   A. The FBI does not charge a fee for conducting NICS checks. However, states that act as points of contact for NICS checks may charge a fee consistent with state law.
8. *Q. Must licensees enroll with the FBI to get access to NICS?*
   A. Licensees must be enrolled with the FBI before they can initiate NICS checks through the FBI's NICS Operations Center. Licensees who have not received an enrollment package from the FBI should call the FBI NICS Operations Center at 1-877-444-6427 and ask that an enrollment package be sent to them. Licensees in states where a state agency is acting as a point of contact for NICS checks should contact the state for enrollment information.
9. *Q. Does the Brady law apply to the transfer of long guns as well as handguns?*
   A. Yes.

[6]The full text of 60 questions and answers can be found at: http://www.atf.gov/firearms/bradylaw/q_abrady.htm.

10. *Q. Does the Brady law apply to the transfer of antique firearms?*

A. No. Licensees need not comply with the Brady law when transferring a weapon that meets the Gun Control Act's definition of an "antique firearm."

Questions

1. Choose one of the eight instructional episodes about the Brady Act prepared by the ATF: http://www.atf.gov/training/firearms/ffl-learning-theater/
   (a) Discuss how this instructional format illustrates concepts discussed in this chapter (e.g., Developing Mechanisms of Self-Regulation; Managing Resistance and Conflict).
   (b) Analyze how well the answers provided by the ATF address the specific issues raised in the episode you chose. Is anything still unclear? Should any further difficulties in implementing provisions of the Act be anticipated? Why or why not?
2. Read one of the dissenting opinions of the three Supreme Court Justices who opposed the majority decision in *Printz v. United States*. Dissenting and concurring opinions are available at: http://www.law.cornell.edu/supct/html/95-1478.ZS.html
   (a) Identify the judge who wrote the opinion, and summarize his or her arguments in your own words.
   (b) Do you agree or disagree with those arguments? Why or why not? Provide evidence to support your position.

(Adapted from: Bowling, Lauver, Hickman, & Adams, 2003; Bureau of Justice Statistics, 2006b)

■ ■ ■

References

Bowling, M., Lauver, G., Hickman, M. J., & Adams, D. B. (2003). *Background checks for firearm transfers, 2002 (NCJ 200116)*. Washington, DC: U.S. Department of Justice, Office of Justice Programs, Bureau of Justice Statistics.

Bureau of Justice Statistics. (2006a). *Survey of state procedures related to firearm sales, 2005 (NCJ 214645)*. Washington, DC: U.S. Department of Justice, Office of Justice Programs, Bureau of Justice Statistics. Available at: http://www.ojp.usdoj.gov/bjs/pub/pdf/ssprfs05.pdf.

Fisher, R., Ury, W., & Patton, B. (2003). *Getting to yes: Negotiating agreement without giving in*. New York: Random House.

Kettner, P. M., Moroney, R. K., & Martin, L. L. (2008). *Designing and managing programs: An effectiveness-based approach* (3rd ed.). Thousand Oaks, CA: Sage.

Miller, G., Rabin, J., & Hildreth, W. B. (2001). *Performance-based budgeting: An ASPA classic*. Boulder, CO: Westview.

5

Program/Policy Implementation and Monitoring

CHAPTER OUTLINE

- **"Monitoring"** refers to the collection of information to determine to what degree the program or policy design (see Chapter 3) was carried out as planned. How will we know whether the intended target population was reached? Were program/policy activities or provisions actually carried out as planned? Were appropriate staff or responsible authorities selected and trained, and did they carry out their assigned duties?

- **Design monitoring instruments to collect data** (e.g., observations, surveys, interviews). Data is collected to find out what is actually being delivered to clients or targets. The purpose is to identify gaps between the "program/policy on paper" (design) and the "program/policy in action."

- **Fiscal monitoring.** Funding sources require regular financial reports detailing how funds were spent. Once the program or policy is implemented, one may find that adjustments to the budget become necessary.

- **Designate responsibility for data collection, storage, and analysis.** Ensure that there is no ambiguity about what information is to be collected, who is responsible for collecting it, or how it is to be collected, stored, and analyzed.

- **Develop information system capacities.** Information systems may consist of written forms and records that are filed, or fully computerized data entry and storage systems.

- **Develop mechanisms to provide feedback to staff, clients, and stakeholders.** Depending on the results of monitoring analyses, it may be necessary to make adjustments either to what is being done ("the program or policy in action") or to the intended design ("the program or policy on paper").

We need to develop a strategy to observe the program or policy in action. History has taught us that good intentions alone are insufficient: planning and implementing an intervention are two different things. The example below illustrates how the same strategy can be implemented very differently in different locations.

Example 5–1   Is "Weed and Seed" Bearing Fruit?

By 2009, Weed and Seed included more than 184 sites nationwide (Community Capacity Development Office, 2011). Weed and Seed was a federally funded strategy to mobilize and coordinate anti-drug resources in high-crime communities. Four key components were included (Dunworth & Mills, 1999):

1. *Weeding:* Concentrated and enhanced law enforcement efforts to identify, arrest, and prosecute violent offenders, drug traffickers, and other criminals operating in the target areas.

Continued

Example 5-1 Is "Weed and Seed" Bearing Fruit?—Cont'd

2. *Seeding*: Human services, including after-school, weekend, and summer youth activities; adult literacy classes; parental counseling; and neighborhood revitalization efforts to prevent and deter further crime.
3. *Enhanced Coordination*: Coordinated analysis of local problems and developing strategies to address them. The federal oversight responsibility for each participating site rests with the U.S. Attorney's Office for the corresponding district.
4. *Community Policing*: Proactive police/community engagement and problem solving in which police officers are assigned to specified geographic locations. This effort is seen as the bridge between weeding and seeding. By gaining the trust and support of the community, police engage residents and businesses as problem-solving partners in the law enforcement effort (e.g., neighborhood watches, citizen marches and rallies, and graffiti removal).

A national evaluation of eight cities examined program implementation and effects on crime and public safety (Dunworth, Mills, Cordner, & Greene, 1999). Each site had high rates of violent crime related to drug trafficking and drug use. The study included a review of funding applications and other program documents; interviews with key program administrators, senior law enforcement staff, managers of seeding activities, service providers, and community leaders; analyses of automated, incident-level records of crimes and arrests; group interviews with participants in seeding programs; and two surveys of residents in target areas.

Developing appropriate seeding strategies in specific communities proved to be more difficult than anticipated. Seeding efforts (e.g., youth prevention and recreation programs, family support services, community economic development) required participation and commitment from many diverse organizations with many different goals. Community participants discovered that much more time was needed for planning, relationship building, and gaining consensus and commitment. Weeding, in contrast, had a relatively clear mission and was carried out within the more established structures of law enforcement and criminal justice.

Within the target areas of each site, evaluators compared Part 1 crime trends for the year prior to implementation of Weed and Seed and the second year after Weed and Seed began. Five target areas had double-digit percentage decreases: (Stowe Village in Hartford, 46%; Crawford-Roberts in Pittsburgh, 24%; North Manatee, 18%; the Shreveport target area, 11%; and the Central District in Seattle, 10%). One target area (West Las Vegas) had a single-digit decrease (6%), and three target areas experienced increases in Part 1 crime (South Manatee, 2%; Meadows Village in Las Vegas, 9%; and Salt Lake City, 14%).

Because a controlled experimental study was not possible, researchers could not state definitively the extent to which Weed and Seed or other factors contributed to observed changes in crime. Available evidence, however, suggested that Weed and Seed had little effect on crime rates. Crime rates in the surrounding (non-target) areas mirrored increases or decreases in the target areas. For example, Hartford and Pittsburgh achieved the largest Part 1 crime decreases in their target areas, but they also experienced the largest Part 1 crime decreases in non-target areas (i.e., areas where there was no intervention).

Changes in drug arrest rates appeared to be associated with changes in the overall Part 1 crime rates. Among six target areas for which arrest data were available, the four areas reporting decreases in Part 1 crime from the year prior to Weed and Seed through the second year of

> **Example 5–1   Is "Weed and Seed" Bearing Fruit?—Cont'd**
>
> implementation (Hartford, Pittsburgh, North Manatee, and Shreveport) all experienced initial high rates of drug arrests, suggesting an initial period of intense weeding activities followed by declining drug arrest rates. Assuming that levels of law enforcement remained somewhat constant, this trend may reflect some success in reducing drug activity.
>
> Participant interviews and community surveys were also conducted. According to the residents interviewed, the seeding programs provided services that otherwise would not have been available in the target areas. Most of those interviewed indicated that participation in the seeding programs was a positive experience that helped them feel more secure emotionally, physically, or both. Benefits perceived by participants included providing additional structure and discipline in the lives of target area youths, and opportunities and assistance for adults to work toward personal and professional growth.
>
> Community surveys, however, suggested inconsistent effects. Residents in only two areas (Manatee and Pittsburgh) perceived substantial improvements in police effectiveness and decreases in crime severity. Residents in Akron and Seattle perceived slight reductions in drug-related crime; Hartford residents perceived some reduction in violent and gang-related crime. Residents in three areas (Las Vegas, Salt Lake City, and Shreveport) perceived little improvement in general public safety or the severity of specific types of crime.
>
> In sum, the implementation and effectiveness of weeding and seeding activities varied considerably across the eight sites. Pre-existing community features (e.g., community cohesion) likely played a key role in enhancing or weakening Weed and Seed efforts. Important factors included the strength of the existing social and institutional infrastructure (e.g., an established network of community-based organizations and community leaders), the severity of crime problems, geographical advantages favoring economic development, and transience of the population. Finding the appropriate mix and sequence of "weeding" and "seeding" activities for specific communities remains a compelling challenge.

Previously, in the design stage (Chapter 3), we talked about *identifying* "who does what to whom in what order, how much, and how often?" At the monitoring stage, we are concerned with finding out whether the intended design is (or was) properly implemented, or whether it was implemented differently at different sites. Monitoring, as we will see shortly, requires ongoing data collection throughout the life of the program or policy. It is useful to distinguish implementation from monitoring.

■ ■ Implementation ■

The initiation, management, and administration of the action plan (see Chapter 4). Once the program or policy actually begins, we want to minimize discrepancies between what was planned (i.e., the program or policy design) and what was actually done (i.e., the "program or policy in action").

At the monitoring stage, we attempt to find out if the program or policy was implemented properly. *Monitoring* refers to the collection of information to determine to what degree the design or blueprint (the program or policy "on paper") is being carried out as planned. Data (e.g., observations, surveys, interviews) are collected to find out what is actually being delivered to clients (the program or policy in action). Adjustments may then need to be made to revise either the design of the intervention (e.g., either service delivery or policy provisions) or to make what is currently being done conform to the intended design. The example below illustrates monitoring requirements of the Bureau of Justice Assistance (BJA), a major source of federal funding for local and state justice programs.

■ ■ Monitoring ■

An attempt to determine whether program or policy implementation is proceeding as planned. Monitoring is a process that attempts to identify any gaps between the program or policy on paper (design) and the program or policy in action (implementation).

Example 5–2   BJA Monitoring Requirements

BJA grantees are required to submit Progress Reports on project activities and accomplishments. In order for BJA to capture pertinent information on a consistent basis, BJA asks seven questions at the beginning of the Progress Report. These questions provide BJA with sufficient information to monitor grant implementation and goal achievement. The seven questions are:

1. What were your accomplishments within this reporting period?
2. What goals were accomplished, as they relate to your grant application?
3. What problems/barriers did you encounter, if any, within the reporting period that prevented you from reaching your goals or milestones?
4. Is there any assistance that BJA can provide to address any problems/barriers identified in question #3 above? (Please answer YES or NO only.)
5. Are you on track to fiscally and programmatically complete your program as outlined in your grant application? (Please answer YES or NO. If no, please explain.)
6. What major activities are planned for the next 6 months?
7. Based on your knowledge of the criminal justice field, are there any innovative programs/accomplishments that you would like to share with BJA?

(Bureau of Justice Assistance, 2008)

Outline the Major Questions for Monitoring

Monitoring relates directly back to the design stage (Chapter 3). How do we measure whether the critical elements of program or policy design have been implemented properly? We can specify all the key questions for monitoring in terms of their corresponding program or policy design features (see Figures 5–1 to 5–3).

We can illustrate the correspondence between program or policy design and monitoring by referring to the chart in Figure 5–4, and we can easily see what kinds of questions we

- Were appropriate targets selected? What were the characteristics of the actual persons targeted by the program or policy?
- Did the program or policy meet its specified criteria in terms of client eligibility (e.g., age, sex, income, region, etc.) and numbers to be served?
- Were proper target recruiting, referral, screening, and intake procedures followed? How were target selection decisions made?

FIGURE 5–1 Target population.

- *Who did what to whom in what order, how much, and how often?* We need some unit of measuring what was done. In a drug treatment program, for example, one way of measuring services delivered to clients is to record the total hours of counseling that were actually delivered to clients. We could also measure the number of clients admitted, attendance at regular program sessions (e.g., group meetings), and the number of clients who successfully completed a program. For three-strikes laws, in addition to describing the rules for charging and processing suspects, we could count the number of people charged and convicted.
- *Were there variations in how program services or policy provisions were delivered?* In a program, for example, did one client receive different amounts or types of services than another (e.g., frequency or quality of treatment)? Was there more than one site or location where a program or policy was carried out, and if so, were services administered consistently across different sites? Within a state, for example, were courts in some cities or counties more active than others in charging under three-strikes provisions?

FIGURE 5–2 Program components or policy provisions.

- *For a program:* Were proper staff selected and trained? Did they fit the specified job descriptions? Did staff understand their duties and perform them as expected? Did different program staff provide services in a different manner?
- *For a policy:* Were the individuals responsible for carrying out a policy clearly identified? Did they understand the policy and their specific responsibilities? Were proper procedures for implementing a specific policy consistently followed by the designated authorities? Did different policy authorities implement the same rule differently?

FIGURE 5–3 Program staff or individuals designated to implement the policy.

need to ask. In Column 1, we summarize all the key design features in terms of targets, staff or responsible authority, and program components or policy provisions. We should have all this information available from our previous assessment of program or policy design (Chapter 3). Then, as Column 2 indicates, we need some method of collecting data (to be discussed shortly) to find out whether intended design features were properly implemented. In Column 3, we report the results of monitoring: how was the program or policy actually implemented? Finally, in Column 4, we summarize any gaps detected between program or policy design and implementation (compare Column 1 with Column 3). Information collected from monitoring analysis is vital for modifying the program or policy to correct any implementation gaps detected.

	1. *What was intended?* (i.e., the program or policy on paper, the design of the program or policy)	2. *How was monitoring done?* (i.e., which of the four data collection methods were used?)	3. *What were the results of monitoring?* (i.e., how was the program or policy actually implemented?)	4. *What gaps were found* between the program or policy on paper (design) and the program or policy in action (implementation)?
Targets (e.g., eligibility, numbers to be served, access, screening, intake)				
Program Staff or Individuals Responsible for Implementing the Program or Policy (e.g., selection, training, duties)				
Program Components or Policy Provisions (e.g., specific goods, services, opportunities, or interventions to be delivered)				

FIGURE 5–4 Monitoring analysis.

Instruments to Collect Monitoring Data

There are four major data-collection techniques for monitoring (Rossi, Lipsey, & Freeman, 2003): (1) Observational Data, (2) Service Records (documents), (3) Service Provider Data (staff), and (4) Participant Data (targets). Wherever possible, it is best to use more than one technique, and, depending on the time and resources available, as many as possible. Each has its advantages and limitations.

Observational Data

Observational data may provide a rich and detailed source of information about program activities and policy provisions. By observational data, we mean that evaluators and/or trained observers actually participate in or observe the program or policy in operation. For example, in the classic Minneapolis Domestic Violence Experiment (Sherman & Berk, 1984), trained observers rode along in police cars to observe how police handled domestic violence calls, and to determine whether they followed agreed-upon procedures for administering one of three interventions (arrest, mediation, or separation). Good observational data, however, is rarely obtained simply by "hanging out" at the program or policy site. Observers must be trained in how to make observations and how to record their observations. We need some systematic method for making and recording observations. Three main observational techniques are possible: (1) the narrative method, (2) the data guide method, and (3) the structured rating scheme (Sherman & Berk, 1984).

When using the *narrative method,* an observer records events in detail, in the order in which they occur. This is very much like a diary. It is the least structured of the three observational methods, but it may provide rich detail on implementation. The observer describes what services were provided, how the clients reacted, how the staff acted, and so on.

In the *data guide method,* the evaluator or change agent gives observers specific questions that they are required to answer from their observations. This technique is more structured than the narrative method, but less structured than the structured rating scheme. For example, observers may go out with police to observe DUI stops. Observers are given a list of questions that they attempt to answer for each stop:

- How did police officers select the vehicle for a DUI check?
- How many people were in the car?
- What kind of car was it (model, year)?
- Describe the driver (age, sex, race).
- Was the suspect: respectful? cooperative?
- Was the officer respectful? Did the officer explain the purpose of the stop?
- What police action was taken (e.g., sobriety test; breathalyzer; warning; other; none)?
- Did anything unusual or significant happen during this stop?

The structured rating scheme is the most constrained of the three observational methods. We can ask observers to rate some kind of behavior on a standardized scale or checklist. Using the same example as above, where observers go out on police DUI stops, the observer may be given a checklist that he or she completes for every police stop. The checklist may contain items such as those shown in Figure 5–5.

In general, the major advantage of observational methods lies in the firsthand description of program activities that observers can provide. The major problem with these techniques is that the presence of observers may actually alter the behavior of program personnel or participants. Would police officers, for example, be more guarded in their speech and actions when they know a civilian observer is watching them? Another problem is that observers may not report or record information consistently or accurately. The less structured the observational scheme is (e.g., the narrative method), the greater the concerns with observer reliability and subjectivity.

Service Record Data

Service record data refers to written, typed, or computerized records that are kept by staff. Many programs require staff to collect certain information on program clients, service delivery, and staff duties. One simple example is program attendance data: staff may be

---

Name of observer: _____   Date and time of
Type of vehicle: _____   DUI stop: _____

Observer Instructions: Rate the behavior of the suspect and the police officer on the five-point scales provided below. Circle the number that best fits your perception of what happened.

1. The suspect was: 1   2   3   4   5
                                 polite   abusive

2. The police officer was: 1   2   3   4   5
                                 polite   abusive

3. The police instructions were: 1   2   3   4   5
                                 clear   vague

4. Action taken (check one):
_____ Field sobriety test   _____ Breathalyzer
_____ Warning   _____ No action taken
_____ Other (Please specify: _____)

FIGURE 5–5 Observer checklist for DUI stops.

required to record whether clients are absent or present for scheduled meetings, or they may be required to record the total number of hours each client participates in the program. The first author once worked at a federal forensic prison in Canada. This facility provided psychological assessments for the courts and treatment services for convicted offenders. Because the facility was an accredited hospital, as well as a prison, medical records had to be kept. Staff (e.g., psychiatric nurses, psychologists, psychiatrists, and research staff) were required to make an entry in a medical records binder each and every time they visited a prisoner, describing the purpose of the visit, the length of the visit, what happened, the client's state of mind, and what (if any) action was taken with that client. In general, for many programs, we could ask program staff to make regular entries in a logbook describing what they did with each client, how much time they spent on different activities, and so on. These records may provide a good source of monitoring information, depending upon their complexity and reliability.

Service record data have at least two advantages: such data is (1) inexpensive, and (2) easily obtainable. However, service record data also present two common disadvantages: (1) program records may not contain sufficient information needed to monitor clients and the services provided adequately, and (2) staff may not record this information consistently, accurately, or completely. There are three possible solutions to these problems: (1) seek participation by staff in developing monitoring instruments, (2) train staff in how to use these instruments, and (3) conduct regular quality-control checks to make sure that records are being kept properly. There are three key guidelines for using service record data:

1. It is better to gather a few items of data consistently and reliably than to gather a lot of data poorly.
2. Recording forms should be structured as checklists whenever possible to simplify usage by program staff.

3. Service records should be checked immediately after completion for consistency and accuracy. Checks should be conducted on a regular basis, and corrective feedback should be given to staff as needed.

Service Provider Data

Service provider data refers to information that the evaluator or change agent obtains from program or agency staff members directly. As opposed to service records, for example, we could ask staff about the specific activities and services being provided. We could ask them whether client participation was high/low, how much time was spent on different activities, how clients responded, and so on. We could use relatively informal or more structured interviews to obtain staff perceptions, or we could use questionnaires or surveys. The major advantage of this technique is that program or agency personnel have regular involvement in the intervention, and they can often provide detailed, firsthand experience and knowledge. The major problem is potential subjectivity: program staff or policy authorities may answer questions so as to make themselves or the program/policy look good. Staff may also dislike the extra time or work required by this method (e.g., more paperwork), so the researcher or change agent must make sure that the information provided by staff is not incomplete or inaccurate.

Participant Data

Participant data refers to information that the evaluator or change agent obtains from clients or targets directly. Too often, client perceptions of interventions are ignored. It is important to get clients' perceptions not only of what services were actually delivered, but often their degree of satisfaction with program services or policy provisions. In asking about services provided by a D.A.R.E. (Drug Awareness Resistance Education) program, for example, we might ask participants whether the information they received was understood, and whether the information was utilized (e.g., were students less likely to use drugs as a result of participating in the program?). Evidence has suggested that information provided by D.A.R.E. programs may be well understood but rarely utilized (Gottfredson, 1998; Ringwalt et al., 1994).

As was the case with measuring staff perceptions of program services, we can assess client perceptions by using questionnaires and/or interviews. The advantages of obtaining client perceptions are that clients have abundant firsthand experience with program or policy services, and they are the only ones who can provide the perspective of the intended targets of change. Disadvantages to be considered are possible subjectivity (clients or targets may want to make the intervention look either "good" or "bad," depending on their personal experience), and their possible mistrust of unfamiliar evaluators or "outsiders." It takes some skill to get valid responses from participants, but these problems are by no means insurmountable.

Fiscal Monitoring

An additional type of monitoring data is always required by funding sources: regular (usually quarterly or semi-annually) financial reports detailing how funds were spent during the project, program, or policy implementation. It is necessary to have a sound accounting and financial reporting system in place prior to implementation of the intervention (see Section "Resource Planning," Chapter 4), and it is necessary to comply fully with the reporting requirements of the funding agency. An example of federal accounting requirements is provided below.

Example 5–3   Standards for Financial Management Systems: Excerpts from the Office of Justice Programs Financial Guide

All recipients and subrecipients are required to establish and maintain adequate accounting systems and financial records and to accurately account for funds awarded to them. As a recipient, you must have a financial management system in place that is able to record and report on the receipt, obligation, and expenditure of grant funds. You should keep detailed accounting records and documentation to track all of the following information:

- Federal funds awarded
- Federal funds drawn down
- Matching funds of State, local, and private organizations, when applicable
- Program income
- Subawards (amount, purpose, award conditions, and current status)
- Contracts expensed against the award
- Expenditures

Please consult Title 28 CFR Part 66 and Title 28 CFR Part 70 for more information.

ACCOUNTING SYSTEM
- An adequate accounting system can be used to generate reports required by award and Federal regulations. Your system must support all of the following:
  - Financial reporting that is accurate, current, complete, and compliant with all financial reporting requirements of your award or subaward
  - If you are a recipient, establishment of reasonable procedures to ensure the receipt of reports on subrecipients' cash balances and cash disbursements in sufficient time to enable them to prepare complete and accurate cash transactions reports to the awarding agency
  - Accounting systems should be able to account for award funds separately (no commingling of funds).
- An adequate accounting system allows you to maintain documentation to support all receipts and expenditures and obligations of Federal funds.
- An adequate accounting system collects and reports financial data for planning, controlling, measuring, and evaluating direct and indirect costs. Your system should help you capture all relevant expenses to make sure that you obtain approval from your cognizant Federal agency for all indirect costs.

Example 5–3   Standards for Financial Management Systems—Cont'd

RECIPIENT AND SUBRECIPIENT ACCOUNTING RESPONSIBILITIES

1. Reviewing Financial Operations
  - Direct recipients should be familiar with, and periodically monitor, their subrecipients' financial operations, records, systems, and procedures.
  - As a recipient, you should direct particular attention to the subrecipient's maintenance of current financial data.
  - Please refer to *Chapter 19* for additional information about subrecipient monitoring.

2. Recording Financial Activities
  - The recipient should record in its books in summary form the subrecipient's award or contract obligation, as well as cash advances and other financial activities.
  - The recipient should record on its books the expenditures of its subrecipients. Alternatively the subrecipient may file report forms for tracking of its financial activities.
  - Non-Federal contributions applied to programs or projects by subrecipients should likewise be recorded, as should any program income resulting from program operations.

3. Budgeting and Budget Review
  - The recipient should ensure that each subrecipient prepares an adequate budget on which its award commitment will be based.
  - The detail of each project budget should be kept on file by the recipient.

4. Accounting for Non-Federal Contributions
  - Non-Federal contributions may include in-kind services (donated services such as volunteered time) or cash.
  - Recipients should ensure that the requirements, limitations, and regulations pertinent to non-Federal contributions are applied.

5. Ensuring that Subrecipients Meet Audit Requirements
  - Recipients must ensure that subrecipients have met the necessary audit requirements contained in this *Guide* (see Chapter 24).

6. Reporting Irregularities
  - Recipients and their subrecipients are responsible for promptly notifying the awarding agency and the Federal cognizant audit agency of any illegal acts, irregularities, and/or proposed or actual actions.
  - Illegal acts and irregularities include conflicts of interest, falsification of records or reports, and misappropriation of funds or other assets.
  - Please notify the appropriate OJP Bureau or Program Office of any irregularities that occur.

7. Avoiding Business with Debarred and Suspended Organizations
  - Recipients and subrecipients must not award or permit any award at any level to any party which is debarred or suspended from participation in Federal assistance programs.
  - For details regarding debarment procedures, see *Title 28 CFR Part 67, "Government-wide Debarment and Suspension."*

8. Bonding
  - The awarding agency may require adequate fidelity bond coverage where a recipient lacks sufficient coverage to protect the Federal Government interest (see *Title 2 CFR Part 215, Subpart C, paragraph 21(c)*).

(Office of Justice Programs, 2011)

Making Adjustments to the Resource Plan

Once the program or policy is implemented, one may find that adjustments to the budget become necessary because resources prove inadequate, or potential funding providers cannot fully fund the proposed budget. In the first instance, program expenditures after implementation may begin to get too high (e.g., beyond the limit of available funds), necessitating cutbacks on the program's activities and/or its objectives. Better to cut back now than to find out later that we simply didn't have the necessary resources to implement our intended program design. If the program fails to achieve its stated objectives, nobody is interested in hearing the excuse that "we just didn't have enough resources"; that is tantamount to saying: "we didn't know what we were doing when we did our budget." Such excuses do not inspire confidence. In the second instance, a potential funding source may receive the application for funding, favorably review it, and then ask the proposal writer to cut program or policy expenses by, say, 2-30%. Or worse, the funding agency may run into fiscal difficulties after the intervention has already begun, and ask the grantee to cut costs by 25-30%.

As a result, the *change agent* and/or members of the *action system* (e.g., the program director) must be ready to make adjustments (see Chapter 1 for discussion of different types of stakeholders). Four options for adjusting resources are possible should available resources prove inadequate to implement the intended program or policy design (see Figure 5–6).

Designate Responsibility to Collect, Store, and Analyze Data

We emphasize that monitoring requires collecting information. This usually means more work for program or agency staff, on top of their service delivery duties. Such information is indispensable, however, and no program or agency can survive or grow without it. For

---

1. *Try to increase funding to cover costs:* Multiple funding sources may be required to fund the program's expenses. Maybe more than one grant will be needed. Sometimes funding providers will ask the agency applying for funds to match the provider's contribution, with the requirement that no award will be made until the applying agency comes up with matching funds.

2. *Redefine target selection and/or eligibility criteria:* This might involve restricting the eligibility of clients (e.g., to those most in need) or lowering the number of clients to be served (e.g., perhaps only 30 high-risk youths can be effectively served by an after-school delinquency prevention program, rather than the originally intended 50).

3. *Reduce or modify program objectives* (e.g., reduce the number of objectives): Rather than provide substance abuse counseling, life skills training, and vocational education and job preparation, limit the program's objectives to one goal, such as employment.

4. *Modify the program design:* Eliminate one or more program components, beginning with the least essential components of the program, or shorten the length of the program.

FIGURE 5–6 Making adjustments to the resource plan: four options.

example, all programs need to record some basic information for accountability purposes. Examples might include the number of contacts made with clients in an intensive supervision probation program, the number of hours of participation in an after-school delinquency prevention program, and weekly attendance at group counseling sessions in a substance abuse program.

In the authors' work with nonprofit groups and criminal justice agencies, we have often found that funding agencies or program supervisors do not always clearly communicate or emphasize the information reporting requirements for programs, and we have found that staff who have been assigned the responsibility for collecting monitoring data often lack the training, skills, and time needed to fulfill such tasks. These are not excuses. The program manager or director bears full responsibility to make sure that certain information is recorded consistently and accurately. Expect that stakeholders will want regular reports on the numbers and characteristics of clients served, their level of need, their progress and participation in the program, and, eventually, their outcomes.

Someone must take responsibility to make sure the job gets done. If the program manager assigns responsibility to staff to undertake these tasks, he or she is also responsible to make sure that it gets done. If there is any ambiguity at all about what information is to be collected, who is responsible for collecting it, or how it is to be collected, recorded, and stored, the program manager must make sure such ambiguities are cleared up before the program or policy begins operations. If such gaps are detected afterwards, they must be filled. The risk of not taking such "mundane" considerations seriously is the potential death of the program or policy when those funding it or authorizing it lose faith in it.

Develop Information System Capacities

A good information system can serve several purposes. First and foremost, a good information system can demonstrate accountability to funding agents, the community, and other stakeholders who may provide either critical support or resistance. A good information system is also useful for planning: it allows program managers or policy authorities to see how well plans are going and what problems emerge, and make decisions about adjustments. A useful information system allows for continuous monitoring over time: it is sensitive to both intended and unintended changes in program or policy design. Five guidelines should facilitate the development of a useful information system.

■ ■ Information Systems ■

Information systems are ongoing methods of collecting data about clients, staff, and program or policy activities. They may consist of written forms and records that are filed, or fully computerized data entry and storage systems.

First, it is vital to gain staff acceptance. Extra paperwork or online data entry is unwelcome unless you can show that it provides meaningful and useful information. For example, staff may be more receptive to doing the work if they find out that they receive useful feedback about client performance, program services, and their own performance.

Cost is another consideration: even printing new forms can be expensive for a small, nonprofit agency. Certainly purchasing new computers or setting up a coordinated computer network can get very expensive. The bigger the agency, and the greater the number of clients, however, the greater the likelihood that more sophisticated information storage systems are needed. Greater needs are also implied by detailed and regular client assessment and reassessment procedures (e.g., risk and needs classifications of ex-offenders), and sophisticated, multiple services provided to a diverse clientele.

We should also consider compatibility: what information is already being collected? Can current information systems be modified somewhat, rather than designing a brand-new information system? Is there a need to share information with other agencies?

Safeguarding of information is important. In a delinquency prevention program, for example, staff need to protect the identity of the juvenile. To assess a juvenile's needs adequately, however, the program needs sensitive information about the juvenile's previous criminal record and his or her current school performance. Strict procedures must be developed for handling, using, and storing such information.

In general, training of staff is essential if good information is to be collected. Never just give someone an overview of an online system or hand over a package of forms and explain, "instructions are enclosed." Make sure that staff members understand what is being asked of them and why. Consider these five guidelines as you read Case Study 5–3.

Develop Mechanisms to Provide Feedback to Stakeholders

Finally, make plans to use monitoring information. The change agent should identify the appropriate stakeholders (e.g., program clients, staff, other agencies, legislators, funding agencies, community representatives), and schedule individual and/or group meetings to communicate results. Some reporting, particularly to funding agencies, will come in the form of program reports or research reports. Wherever gaps are detected, corrective action should be discussed and implemented. The bottom line is that any effective organization, private, public, or nonprofit, requires monitoring information on a regular basis to figure out how well it is doing. Can you imagine any effective business that only examined its sales once a year? A stock market that reports transactions only once a month? A television network that examines ratings only at the end of the season? Failure to monitor program or policy performance is not good business. In extreme cases, such failure can be fatal to the program or policy.

Conclusion

Monitoring is a process that attempts to identify any gaps between the program or policy on paper (design) and the program or policy in action (implementation). We can specify all the key questions for monitoring in terms of corresponding program or policy design features: what was intended in terms of targets, staff, and program/policy services? Second, how do we collect data to determine the degree to which these design features are actually being implemented? Third, what gaps exist (if any) between the program or policy on paper, and the program or policy in action? Where gaps are found, adjustments must be made: either the design (the program or policy on paper) must change, or the way the program or policy is being implemented (the program or policy in action) must change.

We emphasize that the purpose of monitoring is not simply to ensure compliance with the original program or policy design. There is always some drift between the original design and actual implementation of any program or policy. Over time, as conditions in the environment change, and as unanticipated difficulties emerge, modifications to the original design are inevitably made. Leadership changes, staff persons come and go, and services are altered. Sometimes these changes are necessary and for the better. We discuss the need for innovations to learn continually and adapt more fully in Chapter 7. What we are seeking, after all, is better programs and policies, not blind obedience to a piece of paper. If monitoring is timely and consistent, we can observe these changes in program or policy design and make explicit, intentional decisions about whether to adopt certain changes.

Consider this example. A residential drug treatment program's funding from the county is in jeopardy because it is serving too few clients with serious drug abuse problems. Monitoring data has indicated that the staff persons responsible for client intake have been turning away seriously addicted clients because they are too disruptive. What actions should be taken? Different options are possible. First, less stringent client eligibility criteria might be adopted to maintain funding levels. Alternatively, the program may seek funding from a different sponsor that will be more sympathetic to their existing client selection and treatment procedures. In the first case, changes in client selection (e.g., more clients with more serious drug abuse problems) will also necessitate changes in program design (e.g., type of counseling and total hours of counseling needed for seriously addicted clients). In the second case, changes in program funding may affect the program's entire mission and goals. We emphasize: any deviations from the original program or policy design should be consciously intended, explicit, and visible. Monitoring facilitates deliberate decisions about program or policy design, and helps prevent unintended or invisible "drift."

Monitoring provides essential, continuous information that can be used to satisfy accountability requirements, improve program services or policy implementation on a regular basis, and move toward desired outcomes. As we will see in the next chapter, thorough monitoring should precede and accompany any valid evaluation of a program or policy. Though the two are linked, monitoring more closely emphasizes process; evaluation emphasizes outcome.

Discussion Questions

1. **(a)** What is meant by the term "monitoring"? (b) What is the purpose of monitoring?
2. What questions do we need to ask about a program or policy at the monitoring stage? Be specific, and give examples to illustrate your answer.
3. Describe each of the four methods that can be used to collect data for monitoring. Discuss the strengths and weaknesses of each.
   (a) Observational methods
   (b) Service records
   (c) Service provider data
   (d) Program participant data
4. What options are possible when resources prove to be inadequate?
5. What are the purposes of an information system? Describe three major guidelines for developing such a system.

EXERCISE 5–1

Read the SEARCH report *Drug Court Monitoring, Evaluation, and Management Information Systems* (SEARCH, The National Consortium for Justice Information and Statistics, 2003a) or read a different one assigned by your instructor. Complete a monitoring analysis by using the Monitoring Analysis Chart as a guide (see Figure 5–1).

■ ■ ■ ▬▬

Case Study 5–1 Program Monitoring: The Correctional Program Assessment Inventory (CPAI)

Professors Don Andrews and Paul Gendreau have inquired extensively into the characteristics of effective correctional treatment programs and how those characteristics can be shaped to improve treatment outcomes. This approach is based upon empirical evidence that rehabilitation *is* sometimes effective, at least with certain offenders under certain circumstances. Following a review of relevant outcome literature, and using a technique called meta-analysis, they examined the average "effect size" produced by different programs with different characteristics. They wanted to know what the characteristics of "effective" programs are (i.e., programs that have produced larger than average decreases in reoffending). Their argument is simple but convincing: there are identifiable characteristics of effective programs that can be assessed and adjusted so as to improve the achievement of program outcomes (e.g., reduction of recidivism). According to Andrews et al., effective programs evidence the principles of risk, need, and responsivity (Andrews et al., 1990; Cullen & Gendreau, 2000).

1. *Risk:* Effective programs clearly differentiate between low-risk and high-risk clients. The largest effects on recidivism are likely to be achieved by targeting high-risk rather than low-risk offenders. High-risk cases should receive high levels of intervention and services; low-risk cases should receive minimal intervention.

2. *Needs:* Criminogenic needs are dynamic (i.e., changing) risk factors that are predictive of recidivism (e.g., antisocial cognitions and emotional states, association with antisocial peers, substance abuse, weak self-control, and problem-solving skills). Programs that effectively target and reduce such individual needs accomplish larger decreases in reoffending.

3. *Responsivity:* Programs that *appropriately* target the specific needs and learning styles of their clients are more effective. For example, clients who are interpersonally and cognitively immature require more structured services, but more mature clients benefit from more flexible approaches. Andrews et al. argue that the most effective styles of treatment have been cognitive-behavioral and social learning strategies that focus on skill development in a variety of areas. Conversely, programs that incorrectly target the criminogenic needs of their clients may actually increase rather than decrease re-offending.

The Correctional Program Assessment Inventory (CPAI) was designed to assess, in a fairly structured and objective manner, the degree to which a program has been adequately designed and implemented. It is sensitive to the three principles of risk, need, and responsivity derived from empirical research. The instrument has demonstrated its usefulness in a wide variety of correctional settings (Andrews, 1995; Gendreau & Andrews, 1994). The CPAI assesses a specific program by tabulating the presence, number, and variety of the best-validated elements of effective correctional programs. There are six primary sections of the CPAI:

1. *Program implementation:* This section assesses the qualifications and involvement of the program director, the extent to which the treatment literature was considered in the program design, and whether the program is consistent with existing values in the community, meets a local need, and is perceived to be cost-effective.

2. *Client pre-service assessment:* This section examines the program's offender selection and assessment processes to ascertain the extent to which clients are appropriate for the services provided. It also addresses the methods for assessing risk, need, and responsivity factors.

3. *Characteristics of the program:* This section examines whether the program is targeting criminogenic attitudes and behaviors, the specific treatment modalities employed, the use of rewards and punishments, and the methods used to prepare the offender for release from the program.

4. *Characteristics and practices of the staff:* This section identifies the qualifications, experience, stability, training, and involvement of the program staff.

5. *Evaluation:* This section centers on the types of feedback, assessment, and evaluations used to monitor how well the program is functioning.

6. *Miscellaneous:* This final section of the CPAI includes miscellaneous items pertaining to levels of funding and community support for the program.

Each section of the CPAI consists of 6-26 items for a total of 77 items designed to operationalize the principles of effective intervention. The number of items in each section represents the weight given to that particular section relative to the other sections of the instrument. Each item is scored as "1" or "0." To receive a "1" programs must demonstrate that they meet the specified criteria (e.g., the director is involved in some aspect of direct service delivery to clients; client risk of recidivism is assessed through a standardized, quantifiable measure).

Based on the number of points earned, each section is scored as either "very satisfactory" (70-100%); "satisfactory" (60-69%); "satisfactory, but needs improvement" (50-59%); or "unsatisfactory" (less than 50%). The scores from all six areas are totaled and the same scale is used for the overall assessment score. Some items may be considered "not applicable," in which case they are not included in the scoring. Data for the CPAI are gathered through structured interviews with program staff at each of the sites. Other sources of information include the examination of program documentation, the review of representative case files, and some observation of program activities. As you read the example below, think of the basic elements of program design and monitoring discussed in Chapters 3 and 5, and note how the CPAI assesses critical features of program design.

Example: The MonDay Community Correctional Institution

The MonDay Community Correctional Institution (MonDay), located in Dayton, Ohio, is a state-funded, community-based facility for both male and female felony offenders. Offenders are sentenced to MonDay in lieu of prison for a period not to exceed 6 months. In October 1997, MonDay was awarded a federal grant for the purpose of implementing a Residential Substance Abuse Treatment Program (RSAT). Thirty beds (20 male and 10 female) were designated as RSAT beds for offenders identified as needing long-term residential treatment. In conjunction with the RSAT grant, MonDay developed a Therapeutic Community (TC) that was fully implemented by January 1, 1998. The University of Cincinnati conducted a process evaluation that included a CPAI assessment (Fulton, Latessa, & Pealer, 2001).

The average overall CPAI score for 150 programs across the United States was 54.4; MonDay's RSAT program scored a commendable 74.2%. The following areas were identified as program strengths:

- Both the program director and the clinical director have extensive experience working with offender populations and the requisite educational background. Both have been intricately involved in all aspects of program development. The program development process was extremely thorough and included a comprehensive literature review, a formal pilot period, and a needs assessment that identified many offenders in need of long-term residential treatment.
- A comprehensive screening and assessment process that includes the Level of Service Inventory (LSI-R), the Adult Substance Use Survey (ASUS), and a social history interview facilitates the identification of appropriate clients for the RSAT program. Combined, these instruments provide MonDay with a quantifiable measure of client risk and need and a detailed assessment of the offender's substance abuse history.
- The treatment and services offered by MonDay's RSAT program are designed to target criminogenic needs.
- The program is theoretically based: the TC model is rooted in a social learning approach that provides opportunities for modeling and behavioral rehearsal techniques that engender self-efficacy; and the specific treatment groups provided within the TC (e.g., chemical dependency education, relapse prevention, criminal thinking errors, anger management, problem solving) incorporate a cognitive behavioral approach that aims to challenge antisocial attitudes and develop self-control procedures.

- Close offender monitoring and detailed treatment manuals contribute to the consistency in services and help maintain program integrity.
- Treatment is individualized for the RSAT participants with the duration, intensity, and nature of treatment varying according to the level of client risk and need.
- The RSAT staff are well qualified with appropriate educational backgrounds and licensures. Turnover is low, and staff are involved in program development and modifications.
- MonDay has several mechanisms in place to monitor how well the program is functioning. First, ongoing quality assurance mechanisms include file reviews, group observation, and client satisfaction surveys. Second, client progress in treatment is monitored during treatment team meetings and through a reassessment of client risk using the LSI-R. Third, MonDay is participating in an outcome evaluation of RSAT that incorporates a quasi-experimental design.

The following areas were identified as needing improvement:

- The clinical director is not systematically involved in the delivery of direct services to offenders (e.g., conducting groups, assessing offenders, individual counseling). This is recommended as a means of staying abreast of the challenges faced by staff and clients and the skill level and resources necessary for the effective delivery of services.
- Information regarding responsivity factors, or personal characteristics that may interfere with treatment, were not available to treatment staff for consideration in treatment planning. Assessing and disseminating this type of information facilitates improved treatment matching (e.g., between client and program; between client and staff).
- The MonDay program utilized both rewards and punishments in response to client behavior. These rewards and punishments, however, could be used more systematically to ensure achievement of the recommended ratio of at least four rewards to one punishment and to promote consistency and immediacy in the administration of punishment.
- MonDay has developed specific program completion criteria to guide successful terminations that are based on the acquisition and demonstration of prosocial attitudes, skills, and behaviors. The 180-day maximum stay mandated by the state, however, negates the ability of the program to keep clients who could benefit from a longer stay.
- MonDay does not systematically involve family members or significant others in the offender's treatment.
- Because of the number of different county probation departments responsible for post-release supervision, there is inconsistency in the extent to which aftercare and/or booster sessions are provided to MonDay clients.
- Staff training is accomplished primarily through a 40-hr. on-the-job orientation. It is recommended that program staff receive 3-6 months of formal training in theory and practice of interventions employed by the program.
- Although the clinical staff receives group supervision, it is recommended that individualized clinical supervision be provided on a routine basis for the purpose of discussing problem cases and enhancing clinical skills.

CPAI Results of MonDay Correctional Institution Compared to National Average Scores

A CPAI assessment provides valuable data for programs to articulate what they are about: for example, who is served, with what intent, in what ways, and with what intermediate and long-term changes expected. Similar to the process of "evaluability assessment" (Rutman, 1984; Wholey, 1994), examination and clarification of program goals and structure can provide valuable learning opportunities for program staff and directors, and can inform useful and necessary program adjustments prior to undertaking formal outcome evaluation (see Chapter 6).

What Andrews, Gendreau, and their colleagues prescribe for correctional programs may be applicable to a wider variety of interventions: drug treatment programs, delinquency prevention programs, counseling programs for domestic violence offenders, and so on. Their approach is based on sound principles of program development, and it utilizes a scientific approach that reduces the subjectivity of judgments about adequate program functioning.

Question

1. Describe how the CPAI assesses basic dimensions of program design and monitoring. Using Figure 5–1 ("Monitoring Analysis") as a guide, briefly describe one example for each of the cells in Column 1 ("what was intended": clients, staff, and program services) and Column 4 ("gaps": clients, staff, and program services).

Case Study 5–2 Hot Spots Policing: Implementation Issues

In this invited essay, Professor Maguire (2010) responds to a policy proposal written by three well-known criminologists. Mastrofski, Weisburd, and Braga (2010) proposed that U.S. police agencies should be fundamentally restructured around the idea of hot spots policing and that a national research effort should evaluate the effectiveness of the proposed reforms. Drawing on theories of organization and innovation in his critique, Professor Maguire raises questions about the capacity of American police to implement and sustain the proposed reforms with the intended fidelity and dosage. He concludes that any national research agenda on hot spots policing should pay at least as much attention to implementation and sustainability as to effectiveness.[1]

Taking Implementation Seriously: A Response to Mastrofski, Weisburd, and Braga

Mastrofski, Weisburd, and Braga (hereafter "the authors") propose an ambitious plan for the adoption and evaluation of hot spots policing in American police agencies. Their proposal is logical, rooted firmly in scientific evidence, and well-argued. I agree for the most part with its fundamental premise. At the same time I share some of the concerns raised about hotspots policing in a recent critique by Rosenbaum (2006). Given page limits, I don't present a comprehensive critique, nor do I repeat most of the concerns already raised by Rosenbaum. Instead I focus on just one issue: the capacity of police agencies to implement and sustain the proposed reforms with the intended fidelity and dosage. Paying more serious attention to implementation issues will strengthen an otherwise sound proposal.

The study of innovation in organizations provides some useful insights for evaluating the authors' proposal. Innovation theorists have found it necessary to draw a distinction

---

[1]Description from the author's web site at: http://www.edmaguire.net/article_detail/73.

between different classes or categories of innovations. For example, more than three decades ago, Downs and Mohr (1976, p. 701), in seeking to explain a pattern of disparate findings in innovation research, concluded that: "the most straightforward way of accounting for this empirical instability and theoretical confusion is to reject the notion that a unitary theory of innovation exists and postulate the existence of distinct types of innovations whose adoption can best be explained by a number of correspondingly distinct theories." Consistent with innovation research more generally, research on police innovation has drawn distinctions between different categories of innovations. For instance, Moore, Sparrow, and Spelman (1997), drawing on Damanpour (1991), classified innovations in policing into four categories: strategic, administrative, technological, and programmatic. King (2000) used a similar scheme containing five categories: radical, management technical, line technical, administrative, and programmatic.[2]

Regardless of the specific typology used, thinking of different categories of innovation is vital for at least two reasons. First, some innovations are easier to adopt than others. Those that can be purchased or implemented in a canned way are more "adoptable" than those that lack specificity or require significant adaptation or tailoring to local circumstances. For example, getting agencies to purchase a new type of firearm or software is likely to be easier than implementing a strategic or radical innovation like hot spots policing whose adoption would "fundamentally restructure urban policing" (to use the authors' words).[3] Second, understanding the differences between types of innovation focuses us more sharply on the explanatory variables most likely to influence the adoption of those innovations. The authors have clearly proposed a "radical" (King, 2000) or "strategic" (Moore et al., 1997) innovation—one that would significantly alter the way police work is carried out, managed, and structured. Given the ambitious and far reaching nature of the proposal, there are reasons to question whether the proposed innovation can (or will) be adopted with the prescribed levels of fidelity and dosage. It would be useful to test hypotheses about which social forces or explanatory variables regulate the nature and extent with which strategic innovations get adopted. The proposal pays short shrift to adoptability concerns.

We don't need to look back very far into the history of policing to find another radical or strategic reform movement—problem-oriented policing—with far reaching implications for how police work is done. In fact, the authors of this proposal have all contributed key insights to the literature on problem-oriented policing (POP). Several recent studies have cast doubt on the extent to which problem-oriented policing has been implemented in ways consistent with Goldstein (1990) early reform prescriptions. For instance, Cordner and Biebel's (2005, p. 155) research in the San Diego Police Department, an agency widely acclaimed as a worldwide leader in the implementation of problem-oriented policing, found that non-specialist officers only "tended to engage in small-scale problem-solving with little formal analysis or assessment." Cordner and Biebel (2005) concluded that it is time to draw

[2]King (2000) treated the four categories used by Moore and his colleagues as a point of departure for his own research on police innovation. King chose the term "radical" as a substitute for "strategic." He also split the "technological" category into two categories: line technical and management technical.

[3]King (2000, p. 310) characterizes line-technical innovations as those that would be used primarily by street officers as opposed to other people in police organizations. King argues that line-technical innovations that "are perceived by line police officers to enhance their law enforcement image will be more readily adopted than technical innovations that do not enhance the law enforcement image."

a distinction between the everyday "problem-solving" carried out by officers, and the more intensive forms of "problem-oriented policing" envisioned by reformers. Bichler and Gaines (2005) examined the extent to which officers are effective in identifying the problems in their assigned geographic areas. They found "little consistency between focus groups of officers working in the same district" in a medium-sized southern police department (Bichler & Gaines, 2005, p. 68). Taken together, this recent wave of research paints a glum picture of a reform movement in which the reality of what is practiced on the streets looks very different from what the original architects of the reform envisioned. While problem-oriented policing is practiced with fidelity by some officers and some specialized units some of the time, to our knowledge it is not practiced routinely by generalist police officers in any agency.

A recent reflection on the current state of problem-oriented policing by two of the proposal's authors concluded that shallow problem-solving efforts with "weak analyses, mostly traditional responses, and limited assessments" are the norm (Braga & Weisburd, 2006, p. 149). Yet, they also concluded optimistically that even shallow implementation of problem-oriented policing still produces crime prevention benefits. They urge problem-oriented policing reformers to abandon their quest for the ideal and "embrace the reality of . . . ad hoc shallow problem-solving efforts" (Braga & Weisburd, 2006, p. 149). It is not difficult to imagine researchers reaching a similar conclusion about hot spots policing a decade or two from now.

Radical or strategic reform efforts in policing, including team policing, community policing, and problem-oriented policing, all seem to have encountered a seemingly insurmountable set of constraints in their quest to alter the core technologies of policing. The current proposal pays insufficient attention to these constraints. Some of the "usual suspects" among these constraints include culture, structure, environment, history and tradition. Strategic reform efforts in policing often seem to clash with widely held beliefs among both officers and key stakeholders about how the job of policing should be done. The history of police reform is littered with well-intentioned and potentially effective reforms that paid insufficient attention to implementation constraints.

The Role of Implementation in Evidence-Based Criminology

All three of the proposal's authors are affiliated with the Center for Evidence Based Crime Policy at George Mason University and their proposal is consistent with the emerging evidence-based criminology (EBC) movement. EBC holds significant promise for expanding the policy reach and the relevance of criminology. Evidence-based criminology tends to treat criminal justice organizations as a black-box. The implicit assumption seems to be that if there is sufficient evidence that a program or policy "works," organizations will embrace it, support it, and implement it. This viewpoint is consistent with a rational choice model of innovation adoption in organizations. However, four decades of research in the organizational sciences (including public administration) fail to find strong support for rational choice theories of organizational behavior. Since the late 1960s, organizational scholars have invested substantial effort in specifying and testing theories that seek to explain the seemingly irrational behaviors of organizations. Irrationality is a particular concern among public sector organizations, which are often able to persist in spite of compelling evidence of their ineffectiveness and inefficiency (Meyer & Zucker, 1989). The unfortunate reality is that evidence about what works is an insufficient motivator to compel people and organizations to do things differently. Implementation is currently the Achilles heel of the evidence-based criminology movement. Consider evidence-based medicine (EBM), an older and more mature evidence-based policy movement than EBC. In spite of all the progress made by EBM, many physicians continue to prescribe treatments that have been shown to harm (and sometimes kill) their patients. One study concluded that "there is sufficient evidence to suggest that most clinicians' practices do not reflect the principles of evidence-based medicine but rather are based upon tradition, their most recent experience, what they learned years ago in medical school or what they have heard from their friends. The average physician is said to read scientific journals approximately 2 h a week and most are likely overwhelmed by the volume of material confronting them" (Eisenberg, 2000). Another study noted that the "lag between the discovery of more efficacious forms of treatment and their incorporation into routine patient care is unnecessarily long, in the range of about 15-20 years. Even then, adherence of clinical practice to the evidence is highly uneven" (Institute of Medicine, 2001). Although evidence-based medicine has attended to implementation issues much more seriously than evidence-based criminology, the medical field continues to evidence a substantial gap between knowledge and practice.

Conclusion

The authors articulate a clear argument for launching a national effort to support the adoption and evaluation of hot spots policing in American police agencies. The argument is based firmly in the evidence-based criminology tradition with its reliance on randomized trials "to assess the overall impacts of hot spots policing on crime." Although five randomized trials have already evaluated the effectiveness of hot spots policing, little (if any) scientific progress has been made in illuminating implementation issues. The current proposal would add to the existing collection of effectiveness studies but there is no indication that it would focus any systematic attention on implementation issues.

Organizations vary widely in their capacity to adopt innovation, and innovations vary widely in the extent to which they are easily adoptable by organizations. The authors propose the adoption of a particularly complex strategic innovation—one that will fundamentally alter the way police agencies do their work. While accumulating further research evidence on the effectiveness of the proposed innovation is certainly sensible, the time has come for evidence-based criminology to pay more attention to implementation issues. Evidence-based medicine researchers have discovered a lengthy "implementation gap"—the period of time between which scientific evidence becomes available and clinical practice begins to change in response to that evidence (Dopson, Locock, Gabbay, Ferlie, & Fitzgerald, 2003; Institute of Medicine, 2001). Evidence-based criminology has focused so intently on accumulating high-quality research evidence on the effectiveness of interventions that insufficient attention has been paid to understanding the agencies charged with implementing those interventions. As a result, little is known about the implementation gap in criminal justice.

The authors can improve the relevance and policy reach of their proposal by designing a systematic research agenda to explore the capacity of American police organizations to adopt hot spots policing. More generally, evidence-based criminology can benefit from blending insights from criminology and organizational science in an effort to understand not only whether interventions reduce crime, but whether agencies are capable of implementing and sustaining those interventions.

Questions

1. Which implementation issues does Maguire discuss in regard to concepts discussed in Chapter 5: (a) target population, (b) policy provisions, and (c) individuals designated to implement the policy? Give specific examples to illustrate your answers.

2. What types of monitoring data might be useful to address the kinds of questions Maguire has raised? Give two specific examples. In your examples, explain what kinds of data could be used to monitor hot spots policing.

3. In his essay, Maguire argues: "Evidence-based criminology has focused so intently on accumulating high-quality research evidence on the effectiveness of interventions that insufficient attention has been paid to understanding the agencies charged with implementing those interventions." Do you agree or disagree with this statement? Why? Give evidence and examples from the case study to support your answer.

Case Study 5–3 Why Drug Courts Need Good Information Systems

Drug courts are a growing phenomenon. Drug courts represent a unique, information-intensive approach to managing drug-related cases. Drug courts were developed to reduce substance abuse and recidivism through techniques such as treatment, judicial supervision, and graduated sanctions.

Typically, each drug court team—judge, drug treatment providers, court coordinator, prosecutor, defense attorney, and other integral players such as probation and pretrial services—carefully monitors and continually reports on the nonviolent defendant's journey to a drug-free life. For example, most drug courts require participants to obtain a General Educational Development (GED) diploma, to keep a job, and to pay current financial obligations, including drug court fees and child support (where applicable).

As team members track participants' compliance with program requirements, the "total progress picture" must be available quickly and accurately so drug court team members can manage the participants effectively. The drug court team must be able to analyze and summarize these progress pictures to provide the data that drug courts need to monitor their day-to-day operations, evaluate their processes and impact, and demonstrate the costs and benefits of their programs to their communities.

Unfortunately, most programs began without the benefit of rigorous evaluation plans or automated management information systems (MIS). In recognition of this gap, the Drug Courts Program Office (DCPO) established initiatives to quantify the courts' needs for information technology and evaluation training and technical assistance, and to develop training and technical assistance solutions to address drug court priority needs.

More than 75% of the drug courts in the United States participated in a national survey designed to help those dealing with large drug caseloads assess their needs for enhanced information-gathering tools. The survey queried the entire population of known drug courts in the United States. Survey responses were received from 257 of the 340 (76%) drug courts that were operational at the time of the survey. The major findings were summarized in 10 key points:

1. Although there was widespread access to personal computers, vital data were not generally entered into automated systems, and there was not widespread, appropriately shared access to data among drug court team members. Less than one-quarter of courts surveyed use automation to help judges interact with their caseload of defendants.

2. A strong relationship existed between automation and the time it took for the judge to receive results of a failed drug test. The critical factor was the importance that the drug court places on the value of information.

3. An overwhelming majority of the drug courts surveyed expressed their willingness to use every technical assistance option offered to acquire the proper automation, maintain the technology, and obtain the education needed to generate regular productivity reports.

4. A lack of funding was the number-one reason drug courts did not acquire the additional automation needed and the training and technical assistance to improve the administration of drug court justice.

5. In addition to funding barriers, drug courts also listed difficulty with linking to other systems as a prime barrier to automation.

6. The largest drug courts—those with 200 or more participants—were highly automated with good MIS support. The majority of courts (the smaller ones), however, lacked such resources.

7. Drug courts clearly specified that they needed technical assistance with all aspects of automation—including help with initial steps, such as developing needs assessments and technology plans and preparing funding proposals for stakeholders.

8. Surveyed drug courts expressed a desire for additional education and training to deal specifically with evaluation and management information systems. Targeted workshops and videotaped training sessions dedicated to monitoring, evaluation, and MIS development rated highly among surveyed courts.

9. Difficulty with data entry and sharing were not a result of drug court indifference to the need to provide regular evaluation information. Indeed, fewer than half of the drug courts surveyed rated their current systems as good or very good at providing information for evaluations.

10. Less than 15% of all surveyed courts reported that they had completed the necessary automation required to produce reports needed for overall program evaluation.

The results of the survey clearly showed that the automated support being provided to the drug courts by existing computer systems is inadequate. Without technology, it is difficult for drug courts to link the information about their results with the goals of the court. It is also difficult to produce the reports and evaluations needed to persuade stakeholders to allot more funding for technology.

Questions

1. Describe the information needs of different stakeholders for drug courts. How well do current information systems satisfy those needs?

2. What improvements might be needed? Review the guidelines for developing useful information systems discussed in Chapter 5, and discuss how they apply to this case study:

- Staff acceptance
- Cost
- Compatibility
- Safeguarding of information
- Staff training

(Adapted from: SEARCH, The National Consortium for Justice Information and Statistics, 2003)

■ ■ ■

References

Andrews, D. A. (1995). Assessing program elements for risk reduction: The correctional program assessment inventory (CPAI). In *Paper presented at the "Research to Results" conference, sponsored by IARCA, Ottawa, Canada, October 11-14, 1995.*

Andrews, D. A., Zinger, I., Hoge, R. D., Bonta, J., Gendreau, P., & Cullen, F. T. (1990). Does correctional treatment work? A clinically relevant and psychologically informed meta-analysis. *Criminology, 28,* 369–404.

Bichler, G., & Gaines, L. (2005). An examination of police officers' insights into problem identification and problem solving. *Crime and Delinquency, 51,* 53–74.

Braga, A., & Weisburd, D. (2006). Problem-oriented policing: The disconnect between principles and practice. In D. Weisburd & A. Braga (Eds.), *Police innovation: Contrasting perspectives* (pp. 133–152). Cambridge: Cambridge University Press.

Bureau of Justice Assistance. (2008). *GMS progress report module update: New questions added in January 2007.* Retrieved http://www.ojp.usdoj.gov/BJA/grant/ProgressReport.html; from the BJS web site at: http://www.ojp.usdoj.gov/BJA/grant/ProgressReport.html.

Community Capacity Development Office. (2011). *Weed and seed data center.* U.S. Department of Justice, Office of Justice Programs. Retrieved August 25, 2011, from the Weed and Seed Data Center at: http://www.weedandseed.info/.

Cordner, G., & Biebel, E. P. (2005). Problem-oriented policing in practice. *Criminology & Public Policy, 4,* 155–180.

Cullen, F., & Gendreau, P. (2000). Assessing correctional rehabilitation: Policy, practice and prospects. In J. Horney (Ed.), *Criminal Justice 2000.* Vol. 3(pp. 109–175). Washington, DC: U.S. Department of Justice, Office of Justice Programs, National Institute of Justice (NCJ-182410). Retrieved August 28, 2011, from the NCJRS web site at: http://www.ncjrs.gov/criminal_justice2000/vol_3/03d.pdf.

Damanpour, F. (1991). Organizational innovation: A meta-analysis of effects of determinants and moderators. *Academy of Management Journal, 34,* 555–590.

Dopson, S., Locock, L., Gabbay, J., Ferlie, E., & Fitzgerald, L. (2003). Evidence based medicine and the implementation gap. *Health: An Interdisciplinary Journal for the Social Study of Health, Illness, and Medicine, 7*(3), 311–330.

Downs, G. W., Jr., & Mohr, L. B. (1976). Conceptual issues in the study of innovation. *Administrative Science Quarterly, 21,* 700–714.

Dunworth, T., & Mills, G. (1999). *National evaluation of weed and seed (NCJ-175685)*. Washington, DC: U.S. Department of Justice, National Institute of Justice.

Dunworth, T., Mills, G., Cordner, G., & Greene, J. (1999). *National evaluation of weed and seed: Cross-site analysis (NCJ-176358)*. Washington, DC: U.S. Department of Justice, National Institute of Justice.

Eisenberg, J. M. (2000). Quality research for quality healthcare: The data connection. *Health Services Research, 35*, 12–17.

Fulton, B., Latessa, E., & Pealer, J. (2001). *MonDay community correctional institution: RSAT process evaluation, final report.* Retrieved August 28, 2011, from the NCJRS web site at: http://www.ncjrs.gov/pdffiles1/nij/grants/188871.pdf.

Gendreau, P., & Andrews, D. A. (1994). *Correctional program assessment inventory* (4th ed). St. John, New Brunswick: University of New Brunswick. A shorter version called the Correctional Program Checklist (CPC) has also been developed by researchers at the University of Cincinnati: http://www.uc.edu/corrections/training.html.

Goldstein, H. (1990). *Problem-oriented policing.* New York: McGraw-Hill.

Gottfredson, D. C. (1998). School-based crime prevention. (Chapter 5). In L. W. Sherman, D. C. Gottfredson, D. MacKenzie, J. Eck, P. Reuter & S. Bushway (Eds.), *What works, what doesn't, what's promising: A report to the United States Congress.* Prepared for the National Institute of Justice [Online]. Retrieved August 28, 2011, from the NCJRS web site at: https://www.ncjrs.gov/works/.

Institute of Medicine. (2001). *Crossing the quality chasm: A new health system for the 21st century.* Washington, DC: National Academy Press.

King, W. R. (2000). Measuring police innovation: Issues and measurement. *Policing: An International Journal of Police Strategies and Management, 23*, 303–317.

Maguire, E. R. (2010). Taking implementation seriously: A response to Mastrofski, Weisburd, and Braga. In N. A. Frost, J. D. Freilich & T. R. Clear (Eds.), *Contemporary issues in criminal justice policy: Papers from the American society of criminology conference* (pp. 265–270). Belmont, CA: Wadsworth.

Mastrofski, S. D., Weisburd, D., & Braga, A. A. (2010). Rethinking policing: The policy implications of hot spots of crime. In N. A. Frost, J. D. Freilich & T. R. Clear (Eds.), *Contemporary issues in criminal justice policy: Papers from the American society of criminology conference* (pp. 265–270). Belmont, CA: Wadsworth.

Meyer, M. W., & Zucker, L. G. (1989). *Permanently failing organizations.* Newbury Park, CA: Sage Publications.

Moore, M. H., Sparrow, M., & Spelman, W. (1997). Innovations in policing: From production lines to job shops. In A. A. Altshuler & R. D. Behn (Eds.), *Innovation in American government* (pp. 274–298). Washington, DC: Brookings Institution Press.

Office of Justice Programs. (2011). *2011 Financial Guide.* U.S. Department of Justice, Office of Justice Programs, Office of the Comptroller. Washington, DC: U.S. Government Printing Office. Retrieved August 28, 2011, from the OJP web site at: http://www.ojp.usdoj.gov/financialguide/PDFs/OCFO_2011FinancialGuide.pdf.

Ringwalt, C. L., Greene, J. M., Ennett, S. T., Iachan, R., Clayton, R. R., & Leukefeld, C. G. (1994). *Past and future directions of the D.A.R.E. program: An evaluation review.* Draft Final Report, September 1994. Washington, DC: U.S. Department of Justice, Office of Justice Programs, National Institute of Justice. Retrieved August 28, 2011, from the NCJRS web site at: http://www.nij.gov/pubs-sum/152055.htm.

Rosenbaum, D. P. (2006). The limits of hot spots policing. In D. Weisburd & A. Braga (Eds.), *Police innovation: Contrasting perspectives* (pp. 245–266). Cambridge: Cambridge University Press.

Rossi, P. H., Lipsey, M. W., & Freeman, H. E. (2003). *Evaluation: A systematic approach* (7th ed). Thousand Oaks, CA: Sage.

Rutman, L. (1984). *Planning useful evaluations: Evaluability assessment.* Beverly Hills, CA: Sage.

SEARCH, The National Consortium for Justice Information and Statistics, (2003). *Drug court monitoring, evaluation, and management information systems: National scope needs assessment (NCJ 195077)*. Washington, DC: U.S. Department of Justice, Office of Justice Programs, Bureau of Justice Assistance. Retrieved February 26, 2008, from the NCJRS web site at: https://www.ncjrs.gov/pdffiles1/bja/195077.pdf.

Sherman, L. W., & Berk, R. A. (1984). The specific deterrent effects of arrest for domestic assault. *American Sociological Review, 49*, 261–272.

Wholey, J. S. (1994). Assessing the feasibility and likely usefulness of evaluation. In J. S. Wholey, H. P. Hatry & K. E. Newcomer (Eds.), *Handbook of practical evaluation* (pp. 15–39). San Francisco: Jossey-Bass.

6

Evaluating Outcomes

CHAPTER OUTLINE

- **The evidence-based paradigm.** Recently, we have seen widespread adoption of a new normative value: that criminal and juvenile justice systems should implement programs that have been proven through rigorous evaluation research to be effective.

- **Types of evaluation.** Impact, performance, and efficiency. Is the program or policy achieving its objectives, how do outcomes change over time, and is it worth the investment of resources devoted to its implementation? Impact evaluations depend on methods that enable us to attribute observed outcomes to the intervention, rather than other potential influences. Additionally, meta-analysis combines the results of many individual evaluation studies to determine if different intervention approaches or practices work better than others.

- **Three prerequisites for evaluation must be met.** (1) Objectives must be clearly defined and measurable, (2) the intervention must be sufficiently well designed, and (3) the intervention must be well implemented.

- **Evaluability assessment and logic modeling.** These are two methods for examining the components of a program in preparation for evaluation. Both methods also help clarify program and policy designs.

- **Outcome measures should be derived from an intervention's objectives.** Good outcome measures are *valid* and *reliable*.

- **Identify potential confounding factors** (factors other than the intervention that may have biased observed outcomes). Common confounding factors include biased selection, biased attrition, and history. There are three major techniques for minimizing confounding effects: (1) random assignment, (2) nonequivalent comparison groups, and (3) propensity score analysis.

- **Specify the research design to be used.** Examples include: the simple pre-post design; the pre-post design with a control group; the pre-post design with multiple pretests; the longitudinal design with treatment and control groups; the cohort design; and time series analysis.

- **Identify users and uses of evaluation results.** Who is the intended audience, and how can results be effectively and efficiently communicated? How will the results be used?

Now the time has come to measure the impact of the intervention: Has the program or policy achieved its intended effect(s)? How can we tell? The goal at this stage is to develop a research design for measuring program or policy outcomes (a specific, intended change in the problem, defined by objectives). Did the program or policy achieve its intended objectives? Why or why not?

In spite of how obvious the need for evaluation may seem, many programs and policies have never been evaluated. Cost is often given as a reason for not conducting evaluations, but we must also recognize that evaluation can be threatening to stakeholders because their public image, political power, and/or agency budget is linked to the success or failure of a specific program or policy. Sometimes not evaluating is an effective means of avoiding accountability.

Increasingly, however, funding agencies are demanding accountability for outcomes. Grants made to public and private agencies by federal agencies such as the National Institute of Justice typically require an evaluation component, and often an independent researcher must do the evaluation. In the fields of health and mental health, managed care agencies carefully measure outcomes and costs in order to ensure that the money they manage is being used effectively. This kind of thinking is making its way into the criminal justice system.

Remember, when we construct objectives, we identify a result and a criterion (standard for measurement) for each objective (Chapter 3). These objectives become the focus of evaluation.

The Evidence-Based Paradigm

Recently, we have seen widespread adoption of a new normative value: that criminal and juvenile justice systems should implement programs that have been proven through rigorous evaluation research to be effective. This process of replicating proven program designs implies that existing programs that are ineffective are being replaced by programs that have been tested and found to work. The term "evidence-based" is now part of the language of policymaking, and several organizations are working hard to promote the use of these proven program designs, particularly in the areas of juvenile justice and behavioral health. These sources include:

- *National Center for Mental Health and Juvenile Justice* (NCMHJJ): Evidence-based practices are defined as interventions that involve standardized treatment and that have been shown through controlled evaluation research to produce improved outcomes across multiple research groups. Evidence-based practices suggested by NCMHJJ include: Multisystemic Therapy (MST), Brief Strategic Family Therapy (BSFT), and Therapeutic Foster care (see http://www.ncmhjj.com).
- *Blueprints for Violence Prevention* (BVP): BVP, a project developed by the University of Colorado at Boulder, with funding from the Colorado Division of Criminal Justice, Centers for Disease Control and Prevention, the Pennsylvania Commission on Crime and Delinquency, and Office of Juvenile Justice and Delinquency Prevention (OJJDP), has researched programs that are considered "model programs" as well as "promising programs" based on the following criteria: evidence of deterrent effect with a strong research design, sustained effects, and multiple-site replication. Programs identified by BVP include Multisystemic Therapy (MST), Functional Family Therapy (FFT), and Aggression Replacement Therapy (ART) (see http://www.colorado.edu/cspv/blueprints).
- *OJJDP: The Model Programs Guide* (MPG): This guide was developed by OJJDP to assist practitioners and communities in implementing evidence-based prevention and

implementation programs. OJJDP uses a rating system based on the evaluation of the literature of specific prevention and intervention programs based on four criteria: the conceptual framework of the program; program fidelity; the evaluation design; and empirical evidence demonstrating the prevention or reduction of problem behavior, the reduction of risk factors related to problem behavior, or the enhancement of protective factors related to problem behavior. Model programs include: Cognitive Behavioral Treatment (CBT), Functional Family Therapy (FFT), and Wraparound Case Management (see http://dsgonline.com/mpg2.5/mpg_index.htm).

Types of Evaluation

Before we define what kind of evaluation data to collect, it is important to know about different approaches to evaluation. First, we need to be clear about the kinds of evaluative questions we are going to ask before designing the evaluation. If we want to know if a policy is achieving its objectives, an impact evaluation is needed. Evaluations of programs and policies typically take one of three major approaches: (1) impact assessment, (2) continuous evaluation, or (3) efficiency analysis.

Note that we do not intend (or pretend) in this chapter to cover evaluation methods in all their complexity (Berk & Rossi, 1998; Patton, 1996; Rossi, Lipsey, & Freeman, 2003; Wholey, Hatry, & Newcomer, 1994). We do intend that readers should become familiar with some basic concepts necessary to understand evaluation. We will not attempt to teach students or practitioners how to design their own measures in this book; that is a task for a good course in research methods.

Impact Evaluation

The most common type of evaluation, and the type we focus on mainly in this chapter, is an *impact evaluation*. To assess impact, we want to compare *actual* outcomes to *desired* outcomes (objectives). In order to do this, we will need valid measures of the desired outcomes and information about the status of clients on these measures prior to their exposure to the intervention. For example, the fact that a high proportion of clients of a delinquency prevention program end the program with high self-esteem is meaningless if they started the program with high self-esteem. It is not sufficient to know simply that a change occurred: we need to determine whether the program or policy in question caused the observed change. We need to know that this change wouldn't have happened without the intervention. To know this, we will also need information on similar types of persons who were not exposed to the intervention. If the same change occurred in this second group, then we are unable to attribute the change to the intervention.

We may also be interested in long-term effects of a program. Recidivism, for example, is not something we measure prior to the program, but is likely to be influenced by changes that the program is designed to bring about, such as increased attachments to others, improved anger control, or academic achievement. In order to assess the impact of a program on a long-term outcome, we need a comparison group of persons that did not receive the program. If recidivism among those who attended the program is no different from the comparison group, and the two groups are identical in terms of those characteristics believed to be associated with recidivism, then we have evidence that the program does not work.

Performance Evaluation: Outcome-Based Information Systems

One weakness of many impact evaluations is that their results are limited to a specific point in time. Programs, in particular, are constantly changing in terms of their staff, clients, services, and goals. Staff turnover, intervention fads, changes in the political environment, and changes in the characteristics of incoming clients can all produce changes in program outcomes. The results of even the best-designed impact evaluation gradually become obsolete. *Performance evaluation* offers an alternative: why not collect and analyze outcome information on all clients on a permanent basis? This way, stakeholders could learn from the outcome data, make adjustments, and see the consequences of their responses over time. The growth of computerized information systems within criminal justice is making this approach increasingly viable and useful.

This incremental learning process incorporates much of what we talked about in the last chapter with regard to monitoring, but the focus is on improving outcomes rather than assessing the adequacy of implementation. Moreover, this interactive approach to evaluation incorporates the concept of "action research" that was introduced by Kurt Lewin (see Chapter 2). In terms of design, an outcome-based information system is a *multiple cohort design* (see Section "Specify the Research Design" in this chapter) in which the outcomes for each cohort (a specific group of clients) can be compared as a trend over time.

Let's add one more step to this idea: such a system of learning is even stronger when outcome information is monitored for an entire system of programs. For example, a city or state could monitor specific outcome data on all programs that serve a specific population of clients, such as drug offenders or juvenile delinquents. The comparison group is not made up of clients who receive no services but very similar clients (a matched comparison group) who receive different services.

With this information, comparisons of programs over time generate more information about why certain outcomes are being produced. If an intervention is showing positive gains, consideration should be given to conducting an evaluation using an experimental design. Computerized information systems are increasingly common within criminal justice. Although the focus of such systems is typically on management needs—for example, personnel, finance, and case control—client-specific outcome information can easily be added to enhance the capacity of the organization to assess a program or policy's success.

Efficiency Evaluations

Lastly, we may want to know how efficient a given program or policy is. Two types of analyses are useful for this purpose: cost-benefit and cost-effectiveness analyses. In *cost-benefit analysis,* we ask if the amount of change that is being produced (the benefit) is worth the cost (usually in monetary terms). *Cost-effectiveness analyses,* in contrast, express outcomes in substantive terms so as to compare programs and policies that produce similar outcomes. In this case we are viewing programs or policies as competitors, using both cost and outcomes as criteria for judging relative benefit.

For example, let's look at a 3-month school-based curriculum for teaching problem-solving skills to eighth graders determined to be at high risk for delinquency. If desired changes are taking place, then various measures of benefit can be established (e.g., a unit increase in problem-solving skills as measured by a standardized test; the number of children who avoid any subsequent arrest up to age 18). The costs, some of which may be less obvious than others, must now be accurately measured. For example, how much money did it cost to buy course materials (notebooks, videos, etc.) and train classroom teachers to administer the curriculum? Was there a cost in terms of what students *didn't* get (e.g., a reduction in mathematics or science training to free up space for the problem-solving skills curriculum)? We may then compare the difference between total dollars saved by preventing each arrest (e.g., costs of arresting, processing, charging, and supervising each adjudicated delinquent), and dollars expended on operating the problem-solving skills curriculum. In other words, we calculate ratios of costs to benefits. A moderate gain at a low cost may often signal a more worthwhile program than a slightly higher gain at a much more substantial cost. A cost-effectiveness analysis of the same program might estimate the total dollars spent to convert a cohort of delinquents into nondelinquents, and then compare this approach with others that attempt to produce similar outcomes (e.g., secure detention). We can then judge which program is most efficient in producing desired outcomes.

We can also compare actual costs against projected costs: an "efficient" program might be one that came in on budget or under budget, but produced a tangible benefit. In many cases, the costs of achieving the same level of benefit can be compared across different programs, policies, or even settings. Efficiency analyses, therefore, can provide valuable information to assist stakeholders and policymakers in making choices from among competing programs, policies, and projects.

Exactly how specific costs and benefits should be defined, however, is a matter of some controversy, and procedures for conducting efficiency analyses tend to be quite complex. For all three types of evaluation, we expect our readers to be aware of why, how, and where such analyses are used, but their actual conduct requires sophisticated training and expertise. This is particularly true of efficiency analyses (Stokey & Zeckhauser, 1978; Thompson, 1980).

Meta-Analysis

Although an impact evaluation can tell us about the success or failure of a particular program, we can't be sure what components of the program are causing the observed outcomes. Most programs provide several discrete activities, such as group counseling, recreation, behavioral contracting, and education. How can we be sure which of these activities or which combination of activities is causing success? Of course, programs are more than activities: there are other clients attending the program, the staff, the facility, and the management of the organization providing the program. All of these program characteristics can affect a client's experience in a program, and consequently affect program outcomes.

In order to discover whether certain treatment approaches work, researchers like Mark Lipsey (Lipsey & Wilson, 1993) and Paul Gendreau (Gendreau & Little, 1996) have made use of a statistical method that allows us to examine alternative causes of program outcomes. By selecting only those evaluations that are well designed, meaning that the study used an experimental or suitable quasi-experimental design, meta-analysis involves calculating the size of the difference between those who received the intervention and those who did not in each study, called an "effect size," and then combining these effect sizes across different studies into one measure of the impact of the treatment approach (Lipsey & Wilson, 2001).

To date, meta-analyses have found that behavioral and cognitive-behavioral methods are more effective for delinquent youths than various types of client-centered, nondirective therapies (Lipsey & Wilson, 2001). For adult correctional treatment, cognitive-behavioral and behavioral approaches work better than other treatments. Intensive prison drug treatment appears to be effective, especially when combined with community aftercare. Education, vocational training, and prison labor programs have modest effects. The effects of sex offender treatment are uncertain. Findings of meta-analyses, we caution, are often limited by methodological weaknesses of the studies analyzed (e.g., selection bias), a lack of detailed information about the subjects and the treatment, and/or questionable implementation or program fidelity (Gaes, Flanagan, Motiuk, & Stewart, 1999; Welsh & Zajac, 2004).

Three Prerequisites for Evaluation

Before actually evaluating a program or policy, three main criteria (prerequisites) must be satisfied. These prerequisites are defined in Figure 6–1. If any one of these prerequisites is not met, any attempt at evaluation is likely to be unsuccessful, and the results will be unconvincing. Indeed, an entire methodology called "evaluability assessment"

---

1. Program or policy objectives must have been clearly specified, and those objectives must be measurable (see Chapter 3).
2. The intervention must have been well designed (see Chapter 3). Its logic should be meaningful and easy to comprehend.
3. The intervention must have been well implemented so that there is no question that its critical elements (activities) have been delivered to clients as planned. Remember, this is why you do monitoring: to find out whether the "program or policy in action" matches the "program or policy on paper" (see Chapter 5).

FIGURE 6–1 Three prerequisites for evaluation.

(Rossi, Lipsey, & Freeman, 2003a; Rutman, 1984; Wholey, Hatry, & Newcomer, 1994b) has been developed to address these critical concerns.

Evaluability Assessment

Under those circumstances in which we are intending to evaluate an existing intervention, it is often advisable to first examine the program or policy to determine what aspects of the intervention can be measured. It may be that a program has clearly articulated goals but has not completed the task of creating measurable objectives. If one program goal is to see an improvement in offenders' perceptions of their opportunities for the future, how will the program know if these perceptions have changed? It may also be the case that different program staff members have different opinions regarding the program's goals. To the extent that these differences exist, the evaluation may be targeting the wrong objectives.

An evaluability assessment is a method for uncovering actual program components and isolating those elements that can be measured (Wholey, 1994). This evaluable model of the program is the program that is tested in the evaluation. Any program elements that cannot be measured are put aside. The assessment typically involves reading written documents that describe the program, interviewing administrators and line staff members, reading case files, and even interviewing program clients. Each of these sources of information is queried as to program goals and objectives, program activities, impact models, program resources, planning mechanisms, and areas in which change is needed. The result of the evaluability study is a single program model that is then reviewed by program administrators and staff for accuracy. The model often forces program personnel to confront their differences and for the first time achieve consensus regarding important facets of their program.

Logic Modeling

You will recall from Chapter 2 that an *impact model* links an intervention to the causes of a problem, and the cause of the problem to the problem itself (see Figure 6–2). The logic of the model is that the intervention will change the causes of the problem in order to affect the problem. When we evaluate interventions, it is often useful to map out the logic of the program or policy. These maps, which are actually drawn on a page, are called *logic models*. Logic models are a concise way to see how a program is designed.

The logic model summarizes the main components of the program and shows how the activities of the program are related both to the program's objectives and to measurable outcomes. An example of a logic model is shown in Figure 6–3 (Forgatch, Patterson, & DeGarmo, 2005; Guevara & Solomon, 2009; Mihalic, 2004). A logic model can be used to communicate effectively with stakeholders the intent of the program or policy and its underlying strategy, and it can provide a framework for designing an evaluation. It makes clear the outcomes that should and can be measured in order to test the effectiveness of the intervention.

LOGIC MODEL

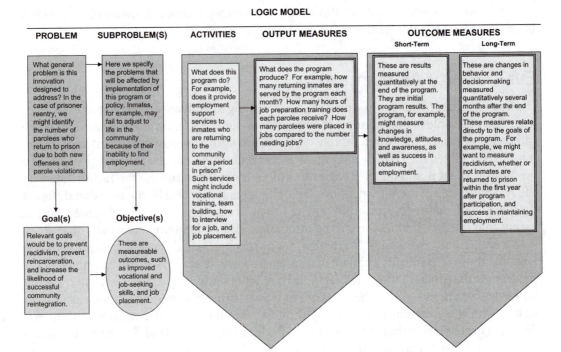

FIGURE 6–2 Logic model.

In each of the diagrams below:
"X" represents the intervention or "treatment"
"O" represents the observation or measure
"PRE" refers to a pre-intervention observation
"POST" refers to a post-treatment observation

FIGURE 6–3 Legend for diagrams of research designs.

Why Develop a Logic Model?

Logic models have numerous uses and benefits. A logic model can be used for at least four different purposes:

1. *Strategic and Program Planning*—Developing a logic model is a form of strategic planning. The process forces you to identify your vision, the rationale behind your program, and how your program will work. This process is also a good way to get a variety of program stakeholders involved in program planning and to build consensus on the program's design and operations.

2. *Effective Communications*—Logic models allow you to provide a snapshot view of your program and intended outcomes to funders, staff, policymakers, the media, or

other colleagues. They are particularly useful for funding proposals as a way to show that what you are doing is strategic, and that you have a plan for being accountable.

3. *Evaluation Planning*—A logic model provides the basic framework for an evaluation. It identifies the outcomes you are aiming for—based on your program's design—and puts those outcomes in measurable terms.

4. *Continuous Learning and Improvement*—A completed logic model provides a point of reference against which progress toward achievement of desired outcomes can be measured on an ongoing basis.

Implementation Assessment

A second assessment is often conducted prior to the evaluation study itself in order to be sure that the program or policy being evaluated has been implemented with fidelity to the design, that is, that their activities and practices conform with the design, that dosage levels are appropriate, that the staff are competent to deliver services, or that decision makers are trained regarding procedures and provisions of a policy (the template for this logic model was retrieved March 1, 2008, from the OJJDP web site at: http://ojjdp.ncjrs. org/grantees/pm/logic_models.html). We are mainly interested in the impact of an intervention that has been designed well. If during or following implementation aspects of the program or policy are changed, it will be impossible to make sense of outcomes that are measured and analyzed. It is critical, then, that evaluators ensure that the program or policy has been implemented well.

Developing Outcome Measures

To develop outcome measures, refer back to the intervention's objectives. How will we adequately measure these objectives? Remember that an adequate objective contains four components (see Chapter 3): time frame, target population, a key result, and a criterion for measurement. We are trying to determine whether a specific intervention (program or policy) produces an intended change in the problem. Recall from Chapter 3 that an impact model specifies such a prediction or hypothesis.

Establishing the impact of a program amounts to establishing causality. In other words, we want to determine whether the intervention produces a specific effect, an intended change in the problem. To do so, we need adequate measures, and an adequate research design.

The *validity* of a measure refers to the degree to which any measure or procedure succeeds in doing (measuring) what it purports to do. Most experts refer to this type of validity as *construct validity*. In other words, how can you tell whether your measure actually assesses the construct or concept that it is supposed to assess?

For example, we might be using a measure of self-esteem, such as the Rosenberg Self-Esteem Scale (Rosenberg, 1965), or we might be using a measure of self-reported drug use, such as the National Survey on Drug Use and Health (available at http://www.oas .samhsa.gov/nhsda.htm). The question is: How accurate is each measure? Is it a good indicator of the construct you are trying to measure? These questions are often investigated through research that attempts to demonstrate that the measure relates to some known indicator of the same concept. We might measure a student's self-esteem, and then correlate self-ratings with ratings from that student's friends and family members. We want to see if there is a relationship between our measure and some other indicator of the same concept. Or, we might validate self-reported drug use with actual drug-testing technology to determine if self-reports are under- or over-inflated. Wherever possible, we try to use existing measures for which previous research has indicated reasonable evidence of validity.

The *reliability* of a measure refers to its consistency. For example, what is the probability of obtaining the same results upon repeated use of the same measuring instrument (i.e., test-retest reliability)? We want to be sure that the measure is somewhat consistent over time, and that results don't vary dramatically from one time to the next. For example, self-esteem is seen as a relatively stable personality trait. Any reliable measure should not yield wildly disparate results about a person's self-esteem from 1 week to the next. Attempts to establish reliability of a self-report measure such as self-esteem usually examine, through research, the internal consistency of the items in a measure (i.e., do items correlate with one another), or relationships between scores obtained from two or more separate administrations of the same test.

Identifying Potential Confounding Factors

Establishing the impact of a program, as we noted above, amounts to an attempt to establish causality. Did the intervention produce an observed change in the problem? Before we look at a few basic research designs, we need to discuss *confounding factors* (sometimes called confounds). These refer to any factors, *other than your program,* that may account for observed changes on the outcome measure (e.g., an increase or decrease in the problem). Confounding factors bias the measurement of program outcomes. In research design textbooks, these confounding factors are often labeled threats to the internal validity of the experiment.

Biased selection is one common confound of which to be careful. In many criminal justice interventions, especially offender treatment and post-release programs, researchers view reducing recidivism as a primary objective. However, upon close inspection of many interventions, we often find out that many of the clients who were selected to receive the treatment weren't high risk to begin with. If youths in a delinquency prevention program had no observable risk factors at the start—such as previous arrests, truancy, academic failure, or family problems—it is not surprising if such youths, upon graduation from the program, show a low rate of recidivism. Does this mean that the intervention worked? Or does it mean that client selection was so biased that we have no way of knowing whether the program actually works?

When we refer to confounding factors, we are saying that something else (other than the intervention itself) may have caused the observed change in the problem, or something may have disrupted (confounded) the way we measured a change in the problem. Confounding factors introduce bias into our measurement of outcomes. You need to anticipate potential confounds and design your evaluation to minimize them. The evaluation of each and every intervention should address potential confounds. Here are three of the most typical confounds:

1. *Biased selection:* Systematic bias in client selection procedures results in the treatment group not including adequate numbers of clients with demonstrated needs or problems. Sometimes called "creaming," this problem occurs when a program deliberately or unknowingly selects those clients most likely to show a favorable outcome, rather than those clients most in need of the intervention. For example, many private drug treatment programs claim phenomenal rates of success, but we often find that they have limited their client selection to those with the least severe problems. In other words, clients most in need were not selected, and our suspicions are further aroused if there was no control group against which to compare program outcomes. We have no faith whatsoever in such results.

2. *Biased attrition:* Bias is introduced into the outcome measure because subjects dropped out of one comparison group at higher rates than subjects in other comparison groups. For example, it is a common difficulty in drug treatment programs that those with the most severe problems drop out before the end of the program. The observed result is that those who remained in the treatment program had lower rates of relapse than similar subjects in a control group. The result is biased, however, because the treatment program lost those subjects who were most likely to show the highest rates of relapse.

3. *History:* Some unanticipated event, occurring between the beginning and the end of the intervention, introduces bias into the measurement of program objectives. For example, if a major change in a state's law regarding domestic violence occurred during the course of a mandatory arrest experiment, the new law, rather than the intervention, might explain the observed result of increased arrests for spousal abuse.

Example 6–1   Potential Confounds in the Minneapolis Domestic Violence Experiment

The Minneapolis Domestic Violence Experiment (Sherman & Berk, 1984) has been criticized for potential confounding factors. Some suggest that we cannot adequately determine from this experiment whether a mandatory arrest policy works better than mediation or separation. One measure used was a follow-up interview with victims to ask about victimization following the police intervention. Victims were interviewed immediately after the intervention, then every 2 weeks for 24 weeks. Researchers reported a decrease in the problem, as measured by fewer victim reports of repeat abuse. Of couples who received the mandatory arrest intervention, only 19% of victims reported further abuse in the follow-up study, compared to repeat abuse rates of 33% and 37%, respectively, in the separation and mediation interventions.

Continued

Example 6–1   Potential Confounds in the Minneapolis Domestic Violence Experiment—Cont'd

Here is the difficulty: what if women were scared to report further incidents of abuse because they had been threatened or beaten by their spouse following the previous police intervention (arrest, mediation, or separation)? Sherman and Berk reported that a substantial number of victims in their sample dropped out of the study. Initial interviews with victims were completed in only 62% of all cases. Others couldn't be found, or they refused to be interviewed. Biweekly interviews were completed for only 49% of subjects in the original sample. The study may have lost many of those who were victims of repeat abuse following the experiment.

Sherman and Berk reported that of those victims who they actually contacted, there was no "differential" attrition (i.e., the victim dropout rate for the experiment was about the same for each of the three interventions) (Sherman & Berk, 1984). However, we have no way of knowing how many of those not contacted actually experienced further abuse. Critics expressed doubts about the experimental results because of this potential confound (Lempert, 1989). In addition, attempts to replicate the results of the Minneapolis experiment in other jurisdictions have not been very successful (Sherman, 1992).

In summary, it is not entirely clear that the intervention (mandatory arrest) was responsible for the observed results (a decrease in reported incidents of abuse). We cannot completely rule out the possibility that the results were biased due to the attrition (dropping out) of more than half of the original subjects. We are suspicious that those victims who refused to be interviewed in the follow-up study might have been more likely to experience further victimization than those who agreed to be interviewed. The observed reduction in repeated incidents of abuse may be due to the fact that victims who dropped out of the experiment were afraid to report further incidents of abuse to police or interviewers.

Major Techniques for Minimizing Confounding Effects

There are three major techniques for minimizing confounding effects: (1) *random assignment,* (2) *nonequivalent comparison groups,* and (3) *propensity score analysis.* Each involves creating a comparison group: a different group of clients that is equivalent to the treatment group on any factors that might influence the outcome measure, such as recidivism, but doesn't receive the intervention.

Random Assignment

Random assignment means that researchers randomly assign eligible clients to separate treatment and control groups. This is not the same as random selection, which would make absolutely no sense whatsoever. Students often have a hard time keeping these two concepts separate. As a sampling strategy, one might randomly select subjects to participate in a survey or opinion poll. The purpose would be to obtain a representative, random sample of the population. In contrast, nobody would ever randomly select clients for an intervention; they would instead determine who is eligible for the program, and who needs the program. Once the eligible pool of clients is determined, they might then randomly assign subjects to the treatment and control groups. Clients in any intervention are not randomly selected; they are deliberately selected on the basis of need and eligibility. Once selected, they might be randomly assigned to treatment or control groups.

What random assignment does, in theory, is equalize two different groups on unknown differences (e.g., intelligence, previous criminal history, etc.) that might bias the outcome results. With a large enough sample, the chances of equally distributing characteristics of subjects across the treatment and control groups is very good. This is the best method for dealing with confounds, when possible. For ethical and practical reasons, however, random assignment is not always possible. In many social interventions, those most in need of the intervention must be selected, and randomization would be unfair or even unethical (see the example at the end of this chapter).

Nonequivalent Comparison Groups

Often we cannot randomly assign subjects to treatment and control groups, but we can attempt to construct treatment and comparison groups made up of clients with similar characteristics. It is especially important that the two groups are similar in terms of their level of need, and in terms of characteristics that might influence the outcome of interest (e.g., recidivism). We must decide with care exactly which factors might be important to control for. We usually look to previous research to determine important variables. We might then attempt to create matched control groups, so that average client characteristics are distributed relatively equally across the two groups (aggregate matching), or so that every client in the treatment group is matched one-to-one with a similar nonclient in the control group (individual matching). Aggregate matching is much easier than individual matching, unless one is dealing with an extremely large pool of eligible clients. Individual matching is more precise, but we lose a very large number of potential cases as we try to match individuals rather than groups on a large number of variables. For example, we may be measuring recidivism as a program outcome. It would be important to match our treatment and control groups on variables known to influence recidivism, such as previous criminal behavior, age of offender, employment and job skills, and so on.

Propensity Score Analysis

Recent evaluation studies have illustrated that it is possible to identify comparison groups when random assignment is not possible, using methods that control for naturally occurring differences between the treatment and comparison groups. A method known as *propensity scoring* allows researchers to estimate treatment effects by collapsing variables known to be associated with the decision to place individuals into the program into a single score, and controlling for that score (Rosenbaum & Rubin, 1983, 1985; Rubin, 1997). This creates comparison and treatment groups that can be considered comparable on all known covariates that are believed to be related to the outcomes of interest. Propensity score analysis approximates a randomized control trial by matching subjects on a single score that represents all known factors that may have been associated with their being assigned to the program being evaluated.

Specify the Research Design

In this section, we attempt to acquaint readers with a few of the most basic research designs used to evaluate program impacts. In general, such designs specify when and how measures will be collected to assess program impact. Each involves comparisons of certain groups of subjects, and measurement on specific variables, over particular time periods, to evaluate outcome. We will diagram and describe several of the most commonly used research designs.

You might want to think of an example as you go through the diagrams and descriptions of different research designs. Imagine, for example, a 6-week prevention program designed for adolescents at high risk of abusing drugs. The program attempts to raise youths' self-esteem. The program's rationale is that increasing self-esteem is a means of increasing one's ability to make independent decisions without being unduly influenced by one's peers. In order to measure change in self-esteem, a self-report self-esteem instrument such as the Rosenberg Self-Esteem Scale is used (Braga, Pierce, McDevitt, Bond, & Cronin, 2008; Gover, MacDonald, & Alpert, 2003).

The Simple Pretest-Posttest Design

The simple pretest-posttest design (see Figure 6–4) is an easy-to-use design, but it is not a good one. Because there is no comparison or control group, we cannot adequately determine whether the program or some other unmeasured influence (confounding factor) produced the observed change from O_1 to O_2. How do we know, for example, if self-esteem wouldn't have increased (or decreased) even without the intervention? How do these clients compare to a similar group who didn't receive the intervention?

The Pretest-Posttest Design with Control Group

The pretest-posttest design with control group (see Figure 6–5) is a much better design than the simple pretest-posttest design. A control group gives us some means of comparing initial measures with later measures. If the two groups are relatively equivalent on variables likely to influence the outcome measure, we can compare the outcomes observed for the two groups to evaluate program impact. If change in the outcome measure for the treatment group is significantly better than change on the same measure for the comparison group, we have evidence that the program is effective.

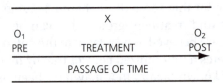

FIGURE 6–4 The simple pretest-posttest design.

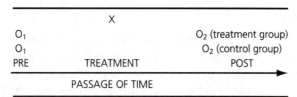

FIGURE 6–5 The pretest-posttest design with control group.

The Pretest-Posttest Design with Multiple Pretests

The pretest-posttest design with multiple pretests (see Figure 6–6) is a slight improvement over the pretest-posttest with control group design. It gives us a better assessment of clients' and nonclients' condition before treatment. This design allows us to obtain a baseline of behavior or attitudes for each group before the intervention begins. A baseline is always preferable to a one-shot (cross-sectional) assessment of pre-intervention characteristics. This is valuable because it gives us a much better indication of how stable or unstable the specific behavior we might be interested in is, and whether treatment or comparison groups differ in their baselines prior to treatment. In Figure 6–6, you can see that the design calls for separate but identical assessments of the outcome measure before treatment begins.

The Longitudinal Design with Treatment and Control Groups

The longitudinal design with treatment and control groups (see Figure 6–7) is the most favorable design, but it tends to be expensive, takes a long time, and is difficult to conduct. It is the most favorable because it gives us a baseline for both the treatment and control groups, both before and after the intervention begins. With this design, we measure the outcome at several points after the treatment has ended in order to be certain that our outcome results are stable.

```
                          X
O₁              O₂              O₃              O₄ (treatment group)
O₁              O₂              O₃              O₄ (control group)
PRE                     TREATMENT                       POST
                                                            ──►
                PASSAGE OF TIME
```

FIGURE 6–6 The pretest-posttest design with multiple pretests.

```
                          X
O₁     O₂     O₃     O₄     O₅     O₆     O₇ (treatment group)
O₁     O₂     O₃     O₄     O₅     O₆     O₇ (control group)
PRE                   TREATMENT                 POST
                                                    ──►
               PASSAGE OF TIME
```

FIGURE 6–7 The longitudinal design with treatment and control groups.

The Cohort Design

When it is difficult to actually assign clients to treatment and control groups, the evaluator may decide to use a cohort design (see Figure 6–8), which uses similar groups of people who go through the same system or experience but at different times. One cohort gets the intervention program; the other cohort (the control group) doesn't. This design is often used for school studies. For example, you've identified the ninth grade in one school as a group particularly vulnerable to experimentation with drugs, but still "reachable." The following steps might be taken to set up a cohort design.

1. Measure self-reported drug use of the ninth-grade class in 2009-2010.
2. At the beginning of the next school year (2010-2011), you start a drug awareness education program in the new ninth grade.
3. At the end of the school year (2010-2011), you measure the level of drug use in this second cohort.
4. You determine whether drug use is lower in the second group (the 2010-2011 cohort) than the first cohort (2009-2010), the one that didn't receive the program. This design assumes that all other conditions in the school (e.g., funding, security measures) have remained relatively constant from one year to the next.

Time Series Analysis

It is often the case in evaluating interventions that entire populations are affected; thus, an alternative evaluation design and statistical analysis are needed. Time series analysis involves analyzing rates of some phenomenon, such as domestic violence arrests, within a population over a long period of time prior to implementation of a policy and then comparing those data to the same rate information for a period of time following implementation. The data points must be separated by precisely the same period of time, such as monthly or quarterly rates (Braga et al., 2008; Gover et al., 2003). In some studies, the same process is conducted with a comparison group, but often the pre-intervention period provides the comparison.

Typically the pre-intervention data exist prior to the study. Gover et al. (2003; see note 18), for example, found that creation of a domestic violence court in Lexington County, South Carolina, significantly reduced rates of recidivism among defendants arrested for

	X	
O_1		O_2 (1997-1998 cohort)
O_1		O_2 (1996-1997 cohort)
PRE	TREATMENT	POST

PASSAGE OF TIME →

FIGURE 6–8 The cohort design.

domestic violence. In this study, they used 60 months of data to construct a time series (similar to a trend line). The domestic violence court was implemented at the end of month 34, thus interrupting the status quo.

It is not sufficient to find a change in the rate months before and after implementation of the court occurred. In time series analysis, statistical models of the time period prior to the policy's implementation are constructed that take into account seasonal variation (thinking that spending more time confined to the house in winter produces more domestic violence than in warmer weather), characteristics of individual defendants, changes in police behavior, and other factors that can be expected to affect changes in the rates of interest. These statistical models are then used to assess whether changes following implementation of the intervention can be attributed to the intervention. Moreover, if other types of violent behavior change in the same manner as domestic violence, then it is likely that forces other than the court are causing these changes. By creating time series based on these alternative forms of violence, it is possible to test other hypotheses about the reason for changes in domestic violence recidivism. The authors of this study were able to conclude that the domestic violence court reduced recidivism among these defendants.

Identify Users and Uses of Evaluation Results

Who will be interested in the results of this evaluation, and how will they use the information? If any evaluation is to be useful, it should serve the information needs of the program or policy and its stakeholders (see Chapter 2). Major stakeholders include the funding agency, but any intervention has multiple stakeholders such as citizens, politicians, criminal justice officials, volunteers, targets, and so on. The time spent previously (at Stages 2 and 3) identifying and communicating with stakeholders should not be wasted. Evaluation is a critical means of demonstrating accountability, and hopefully effectiveness, to stakeholders.

Typical evaluation uses are the expansion and replication of successful programs and policies, elimination of unsuccessful ones, and an investment in developing promising programs. Evaluation results can be used solely to make judgments about programs and policies, or they can become part of a process of continuous improvement. In the latter case, changes are made to the program that are thought to improve chances of better results, and then this revised program design is retested.

The change agent should develop plans and assign responsibility for packaging and communicating evaluation results to different users. It is particularly important to find means of communication that different audiences can understand. Even at academic conferences, for instance, many eyes in the audience glaze over when a presenter puts up overheads cluttered with complicated statistical results. If the results are to be useful, and used, one must create means of communication that intended audiences could understand and react to. Stakeholders must be able to participate in a dialogue with the report writer or presenter.

Discussion Questions

1. What is meant by the term "evaluation"?
2. What are the main differences between performance and impact evaluations?
3. How can an automated information system increase the availability of evaluation data?
4. Define and describe an example of efficiency analysis.
5. What are the three prerequisites for evaluation? Explain.
6. What can we learn from developing a logic model?
7. Define: (a) reliability, and (b) validity.
8. (a) Define confounding factors. (b) Describe the three most common types of confounding factors.
9. Refer back to Example 6–1 (the Minneapolis Domestic Violence Experiment). How were confounding factors illustrated by this example?
10. How does one minimize possible confounding effects in an evaluation? Make sure you discuss the two major techniques.
11. How are intermediate and ultimate outcomes different?
12. Describe each of the following research designs: (a) simple pretest-posttest, (b) pretest-posttest with a control group, (c) pretest-posttest with multiple pretests, (d) longitudinal design with treatment and control groups, (e) cohort design, and (f) time series analysis.

EXERCISE 6–1

Your instructor may ask you to analyze a published evaluation study. One good example is Chicago's Operation Ceasefire, conducted by Skogan, Hartnett, Bump, and Dubois (2009), and available at http://www.ncjrs.gov/pdffiles1/nij/grants/227181.pdf.

Retrieve and read the article and answer the following questions: (a) what were the program's intended outcomes? (b) what confounding factors were addressed by the researchers? (c) what research methods were used? and (d) to what degree, if any, did the program achieve its intended outcome objectives? Give specific examples and evidence from the article to support your answer.

■ ■ ■ ▬▬▬▬▬▬▬▬▬▬▬▬▬▬▬▬▬▬▬▬▬▬▬▬▬▬

Case Study 6–1 Evaluation of an Illegal Immigration Enforcement Policy

Although some research designs are stronger than others, evaluation studies often make use of multiple methods in order to answer different questions or to increase the validity of conclusions drawn from the study. One such study is the evaluation of an illegal immigration enforcement policy that was implemented in Prince William County, Virginia. Prince William County is a wealthy section of Virginia and part of the Washington, DC, metropolitan area. The evaluation involved three research centers and multiple methods to address several questions regarding the impact of a new policy. Between 2000 and 2006, Prince William County experienced a large increase in the number of Hispanic residents. Concerns were raised not only about the possibility that many of these new residents were illegal immigrants, but that crimes associated with this population were also increasing. The County Board soon passed an illegal immigration law requiring police officers to inquire about the status of any person *stopped* for any reason and for whom there was probable cause to suspect their immigration status. It also reduced county services to all persons found to be illegal immigrants. After only *2 months*, the law enforcement part of the policy was revised to target only persons *arrested* for a law violation, thus narrowing the number of potential illegal status checks. This was done to avoid claims of ethnic profiling.

Goals and Outcomes

The illegal immigration policy was designed to reduce the number of illegal immigrants, street crime, and public disorder, and to reduce chances that county revenues were being expended on services to illegal immigrants. At the same time, the County Board wanted to protect the general reputation of the county. Of course, there remained the possibilities that some subjects of the policy would protest their treatment and sue the county for violations of their civil rights and that desired relations with the Hispanic community would deteriorate.

Methods Used

This study focused primarily on the police-related provisions and procedures of the policy. Thus, the researchers measured effects on the police department and effects on the community that resulted from police activity. Obviously, there was no opportunity for use of an experimental design, and use of comparison groups was limited, but efforts were made to compare changes in several types of crime rates in Prince William County with adjacent counties, using UCR data.

The quantitative analysis depended mainly on data reported by the county police department to the FBI's Uniform Crime Reports (UCR) system, UCR data on adjacent counties, crime data from the [Washington] Metropolitan Council of Governments, a two-wave survey of all uniformed police officers in Prince William County, a county-wide community telephone survey, and U.S. Census data, some of which were available in the form of micro-samples.

The qualitative data employed for this study included police officer focus groups, key informant interviews with government agency leaders and community stakeholders, interviews with small samples of Hispanic residents identified through community organizations, and observations of how police officers implemented the policy.

Trend and time series analyses were the primary methods used for analyzing these data. For example, it was possible to examine changes in crime rates over time in both Prince William County and adjacent counties, and then insert implementation of the new policy into the models. Census data also showed immigration trends over time, and whether insertion of the illegal immigration policy changed trajectories of these trends.

The qualitative data were primarily useful for interpreting the quantitative data. They allowed the researchers to test assumptions about implementation of the policy and to examine implementation issues from multiple perspectives (police, other stakeholders, non-Hispanic community members and Hispanic community members).

Conclusions

Police experience with implementation of the policy indicated that there was some damage to relations with the Hispanic community, but through careful training and outreach programs, this damage was minimized and good relationships were restored. Moreover, procedures with U.S. Immigration and Customs Enforcement, soon worked smoothly enough to ensure that initially strained detention services were no longer burdened by a population spurt.

In the end, the evaluators concluded that the policy reduced the illegal immigrant population in the county and leveled off growth in the Hispanic population in the county. Except for aggravated assaults, crime rates were not affected by the new policy, largely because Hispanic residents were relatively small in number and were arrested primarily for public order crimes. In addition, the reduction in aggravated assaults appears to have occurred in reaction to announcement of the policy, not gradually in response to its implementation. We can also see that an established population will often react negatively to a large influx of immigrants. Fear of change, and resentment directed at the newcomers, are expressed as fear for public safety, and demands for government intervention soon follow. How local governments and police departments respond to these reactions can make the difference between a peaceful transition and increased conflict.

Questions

1. Explain how Case Study 6–1 illustrates the following concepts discussed in Chapter 6, providing evidence to support your answer: (a) time series analysis; (b) nonequivalent comparison groups; and (c) confounding factors.
2. Why is it sometimes preferable for an evaluation study to make use of multiple research methods?

(Guterbock et al., 2010)

Case Study 6–2 Evaluating Outcomes of Community-Based Delinquency Prevention

Instructions

Read the case study below, and then answer the question that follows.

The Problem, Program Design, and Goals

To assess concerns of minority overrepresentation in the Pennsylvania juvenile justice system, and to respond to changes in federal guidelines for states participating in the Juvenile Justice and Delinquency Prevention (JJDP) Formula Grant Program, the Minority Confinement Subcommittee of the Pennsylvania Commission on Crime and Delinquency (PCCD) Juvenile Advisory Committee concluded that some action could be taken to slow the entry or reentry of minorities into the juvenile justice system, and they recommended the development and support of community-based intervention activities. Five programs were funded in Dauphin County (Harrisburg) beginning in 1991-1992; those programs concluded their third and final year of PCCD funding early in 1994. It was expected that programs would obtain their own funding after two and a half years of initial funding from PCCD.

All programs stressed the value of supervised activities to keep youths out of trouble. All provided "life skills training," which often included training in problem-solving skills, conflict resolution, and cultural diversity and awareness training. Most provided homework or tutoring assistance, structured recreation and/or field trips, some form of career development or vocational training, and community service. All programs, as requirements of their PCCD funding, had two mandated goals: (1) to reduce future involvement with the juvenile justice system, and (2) to improve school behavior and performance.

Research Design

We were contracted as evaluators quite some time after the programs began operations, and agencies were already utilizing diverse referral sources. Because neither randomization nor matched constructed control groups were possible, our choices for forming comparison groups were limited. We had no control over client selection and referrals, and referrals came from different sources (e.g., self and family, probation, school, and police). Requirements of informed consent also limited research design options. To gain access to inspect agency records (e.g., police, probation, school) for individual program clients, we were required to obtain a release form signed by the client and a parent. As a result, a strict "control" group was not possible (i.e., one that was identical to the intervention group in all respects except that no treatment was delivered). It was not possible to obtain police and school records for nonclients unless they had already granted consent but never subsequently participated in any of the programs.

Comparison groups were constructed on the basis of frequency of client participation in the programs. Numerous studies have suggested that the intensity of treatment (e.g., frequency of contacts; number of contact hours) is one of the most crucial variables influencing the success of intervention, including alcohol and other drug treatment and delinquency prevention (Palmer, 1992). We would expect that if a program works at all, a critical variable affecting client outcome is treatment intensity or degree of exposure to the program. We were aided by the fact that many of the clients referred to the programs signed a release of information form, but they never attended the programs.

To determine the adequacy of these constructed comparison groups for each cohort, we examined the possibility of biased selection (i.e., did the groups differ on critical preselection variables that might affect the outcomes of interest?). While our data allow us to examine group differences on numerous risk factors, the most crucial factors to examine are those most likely to affect the dependent variables. Recidivism, for example, is known to be related to previous delinquent activity and age (older juveniles are at greater risk of arrest and rearrest). Sources of referral could potentially bias comparison groups (e.g., probation referrals may be more likely to have been arrested than other referrals). For analyses of school outcomes, it is advisable to examine possible preselection differences that could influence educational outcomes (suspensions, truancy, and core GPA). We also examined demographic factors that could have influenced selection (e.g., ethnicity, family structure, parental employment).

We report results for two separate client groups in Harrisburg: those who attended programs during the 1992-1993 school year, and those who attended programs during the 1993-1994 school year.

The 1992-1993 sample consisted of 187 clients. Our first comparison group (the "control" group) was made up of 80 clients (43%) who never participated in any program. The second comparison group was made up of 45 clients (24%) who participated occasionally but accumulated less than 30 total program hours over the 1992-1993 school year. Our third comparison group was made up of 62 clients (33%) who accumulated greater than 30 program hours during the 1992-1993 school year. The three groups did not differ significantly in terms of prior arrests, gender, family structure, parental employment, previous truancy, or prior suspensions. However, the comparison groups did differ in terms of age (high attenders were slightly younger); referral source (probation referrals had poorer attendance; self or family referrals had higher rates of attendance); ethnicity (75% of the total sample were African American, but Latino children were slightly overrepresented in the low- and high-attendance groups); whether the student was promoted the previous school year; and academic performance the previous year (nonattenders had slightly lower grades and were less likely to have been promoted). Because randomized assignment of subjects to comparison groups was not possible, we cannot rule out the possibility that comparison groups differed on other, unmeasured pre-intervention variables related to the dependent variables of interest. For analyses of recidivism and educational outcomes, we can be assured that factors of most concern (prior arrests, suspensions, and truancy) do not contaminate the results. All preselection factors that statistically differentiated the comparison groups (e.g., age, referral source, ethnicity, previous school promotions, and grades) were examined in statistical analyses as control variables.

In the 1993-1994 sample, 97 clients were examined. Our first comparison group (the "control" group) was made up of 32 students (33%) who never participated in the programs. The second comparison group was made up of 31 clients (32%) who participated occasionally, but accumulated less than 50 total program hours over the 1993-1994 school year. Our third comparison group was made up of 34 clients (34%) who accumulated greater than 50 program hours during the 1993-1994 school year. To determine the adequacy of these constructed comparison groups, we examined the possibility of biased selection (i.e., did the groups differ on critical preselection variables that might affect the outcomes of interest?). Upon intake, the three comparison groups did not differ significantly in terms of prior arrests, age, gender, ethnicity, family structure, parental employment, academic retention (1992-1993 school year), prior suspensions (1992-1993 school year), or core GPA (1992-1993 school year). The comparison groups did differ in terms of referral source (probation and police referrals had poorer attendance; self or family referrals had higher rates of attendance; referrals from human services had the highest rates of attendance); and truancy the previous school year (nonattenders and low attenders had higher rates of truancy than high attenders). Once again, because randomized assignment of subjects to comparison groups was not possible, we cannot rule out the possibility that comparison groups differed on other, unmeasured preselection variables related to the dependent variables of interest. For analyses of recidivism and educational outcomes, then, critical factors (prior arrests, age, previous suspensions, previous grades) do not contaminate the results. All preselection factors that differentiated the comparison groups (i.e., referral source, truancy) were examined in statistical analyses as control variables.

Results

Recidivism

Results for the 1992-1993 Harrisburg sample suggest that programs had success in reducing recidivism for high-risk clients. The rate of recidivism over a 3-year period for the high-attendance group (25.8%) was impressive, especially considering that nearly half of these clients had previous arrests prior to their referral. In contrast, the control group had a recidivism rate of 53% for the same period.

Recidivism results for the 1993-1994 Harrisburg sample were less positive. The rate of recidivism over a 2-year period for the high-attendance group (23.5%) was satisfactory, but nearly the same proportion (about one-fourth) of these clients had previous arrests prior to their referral. A prior arrest, then, rather than programmatic intervention, was the strongest influence of recidivism. Compared to the previous year (1992-1993), programs in 1993-1994 targeted clients who were much younger and much less likely to have previous arrests.

Academic Performance

Impacts on academic performance were somewhat disappointing, although missing data resulted in smaller samples than desirable for multivariate tests. For both the 1992-1993 and 1993-1994 samples, Harrisburg programs had no significant effects on academic performance. For the 1993-1994 sample, academic performance either remained stable or declined slightly for all comparison groups over a 2-year period, and statistical analyses suggested that programs had no significant effect on grades. The absence of any directional improvement in grades over time suggests that programs have made little progress in impacting upon their clients' educational performance.

Dropout Rates

For the 1992-1993 sample, Harrisburg programs had no significant effects on dropout rates. Only previously poor academic performance significantly explained dropout rates. Although the 1993-1994 sample was young and the follow-up period brief, results did not reveal any statistically significant program effect on dropout rates. However, results for the 1993-1994 sample were in a positive direction (the high program attendance group had a dropout rate of 4.3% compared to 26.9% for the control group).

Truancy

For the 1992-1993 sample, Harrisburg programs had no significant effects on truancy. All comparison groups showed a large increase in truancy from 1991-1992 to 1993-1994. Although the sample was young and the follow-up period brief, results for the 1993-1994 sample were similarly disappointing. However, while no statistically significant programmatic effect on truancy was found, results were in a positive direction (i.e., there was a slight but statistically nonsignificant decrease in truancy from 1993-1994 to 1994-1995). The only significant predictor of post-intervention truancy for the 1993-1994 sample was previous (pre-intervention) truancy.

Implications

Although the results were somewhat disappointing, it is important to recognize that results do not reflect the total success or failure of the programs. For example, findings about recidivism were compromised by the fact that there were so few youths with prior arrests in the 1993-1994 sample. Academic performance, dropout rates, and truancy did not improve significantly, but it may be unrealistic to expect dramatic changes in youths who participated in the programs only sporadically. Further, programs may influence educational outcomes only to a small degree compared to the more pervasive effects exerted by schools and families.

Results may be influenced by various factors, some of which we can account for in our data (e.g., gaps in the delivery of program services, inconsistent patterns of youth participation in programs, insufficient program resources, inadequate measures of client skills and attitudes), and some that lie outside the parameters of our evaluation (e.g., inadequate funding for public schools, poverty, and family trauma). It may also be the case that some programs evaluated individually, rather than as a combined sample, would produce more positive results. Unfortunately, because the number of clients in each program was so small, and there was so much missing data, we could not effectively evaluate outcomes for individual programs.

Another problem is presented by the need for adequate measures of additional objectives that programs attempt to achieve (e.g., improved self-esteem, problem-solving skills, and interpersonal behavior). We vigorously attempted to measure such outcomes using self-report measures and staff ratings of client behavior in the 1994-1995 cohort, but program staff did not have the time or resources to complete the assessment process at required 3-month intervals. Thus, there may be areas of program impact that we were unable to measure adequately.

Concern was raised by the diverse nature of referral sources during the 1993-1994 school year. Rather than selecting clients on the basis of their suitability for each program, intakes during the 1993-1994 school year were marked by a high diversity of client characteristics and needs, perhaps indicating a desperate attempt by the coalition to get referrals from anywhere possible. Program funding, therefore, may not yet have stabilized to the degree necessary for programs to concentrate more intensively on defining their intended target population and strengthening their service delivery to meet specified client needs.

Question

1. Explain how Case Study 6–2 illustrates concepts discussed in Chapter 6, providing evidence to support your answer: (a) reliability and validity; (b) nonequivalent comparison groups; (c) confounding factors; and (d) reassessing the entire program or policy plan.

(Adapted from: Welsh, Jenkins, & Harris, 1997, 1999)

Case Study 6–3 Evaluation of Prison-Based Therapeutic Community Drug Treatment Programs in Pennsylvania (Welsh, 2003)

Instructions

Read the case study below, and then answer the question that follows.

This project was built upon a collaborative research partnership between Temple University and the Pennsylvania Department of Corrections (PA-DOC) that began in 1999. A Steering Committee consisting of senior executive and research and treatment personnel from the Pennsylvania Department of Corrections and researchers from the Center for Public Policy at Temple University in Philadelphia was formed to guide research activity and facilitate the department's overall research agenda. This group continues to meet regularly to provide oversight of the research process and consider the larger organizational and policy issues that the research raises. Steering Committee members participated in the entire oversight of this project. Findings were presented and discussed at Steering Committee meetings, and members provided helpful comments on an earlier version of this report.

An in-prison Therapeutic Community (TC) is an intensive, long-term, highly structured residential treatment modality for hard-core drug users convicted of a criminal offense. TC emphasizes the necessity of the inmate taking responsibility for his or her behavior before, during, and after treatment. Several evaluations of in-prison TC have produced promising results. However, studies have been criticized for small sample sizes, faulty research designs (e.g., selection and attrition biases), and inadequate attention to interactions between inmate characteristics, treatment process, and treatment outcomes. No studies have examined prison-based TC across multiple sites or attempted to include programmatic and contextual variations in analyses of outcome. Numerous questions remain about the potential impacts of unmeasured variations in inmate characteristics, treatment programs, and multiple outcome measures.

In this study, we examined in-treatment measures and multiple post-release outcomes for 2,809 inmates who participated in TC drug treatment programs ($n = 749$) or comparison groups ($n = 2,060$) at five state prisons. Matched comparison groups made up of TC-eligible inmates participating in less intensive forms of treatment (e.g., short-term drug education and outpatient treatment groups) at the same five institutions were constructed based upon known predictors such as drug dependency, need for treatment, and criminal history. Process and outcome measures incorporated a range of institutional, intermediate (e.g., attitudinal and behavioral change, participation in treatment), and post-release measures (e.g., drug relapse, rearrest and reincarceration, employment, levels of parole supervision). At the time of this report, 462 TC inmates and 1,152 Comparison inmates had been released from prison, with follow-up periods extending up to 26 months (mean = 13 months). The two groups did not differ significantly on amount of time at risk since their release from prison. We continue to track releases and recidivism for the entire sample. Below we summarize our major findings, recommendations, and conclusions. Details of analyses and further discussion are provided in the full Final Report for this project.

Major Findings

- Offenders in TC received 15 times the treatment "dose" that the Comparison group received.
- We found positive effects of TC treatment upon reincarceration and rearrest rates, but not drug relapse rates (Table A).
- Post-release employment strongly and significantly reduced the likelihood of drug relapse, rearrest, and reincarceration (Table B).
- Treatment outcomes were generally invariant across institutions, with one important exception. Significantly higher rates of drug relapse were observed for inmates treated at Cresson (44%) and Houtzdale (43%), compared to Waymart (24%), Huntingdon (32%), and Graterford (35%).

Table A Effects of TC versus Comparison Group on Three Measures of Recidivism

	Comparison Group	TC Group
Reincarceration rate	41%	30%*
Rearrest rate	33%	24%*
Drug relapse rate	39%	35%

*$p < 0.05$.

Note: Statistics shown are based on logistic regression results where all control variables including a categorical variable indicating membership in the TC versus Comparison Group were entered into analyses. Results shown thus reflect outcomes controlling for the effects of all other variables (see Section "Results" in full report for further details).

Table B   Effects of Post-Release Employment on Three Measures of Recidivism

	Full-Time	Part-Time	Unemployed and Able to Work	Unemployed and Unable to Work
Reincarceration rate	17%	26%	24%	65%*
Rearrest rate	21%	34%	27%	41%*
Drug relapse rate	30%	39%	38%	44%*

*$p < 0.05$.

Note: Statistics shown are based on logistic regression results where all control variables including a categorical variable indicating membership in the TC versus Comparison Group were entered into analyses. Results shown thus reflect outcomes controlling for the effects of all other variables (see Section "Results" in full report for further details).

- TC inmates evidenced numerous positive improvements in psychosocial functioning and involvement in treatment over the first 6 months of treatment, as indicated by subscales of the TCU Resident Evaluation of Self and Treatment (REST) form, and the TCU Counselor Rating of Client (CRC) form. TC inmates showed significant decreases in depression and risk-taking behavior, and significant increases in self-esteem, therapeutic engagement, personal progress, trust in group, opinions of program staff, and perceptions of counselor competence. The strongest area of consistency across the five TC programs was in the high ratings that inmates gave of counselor rapport and counselor competence.
- Each unit, while implementing the basic TC philosophy, also exhibited some programmatic variations. For example, two of the five TC units were rather large (100+ inmates). Large units make it difficult to implement the TC philosophy properly, which depends heavily upon positive peer interactions. Second, while the overall termination rate for TC (26%) was reasonable, one program (Waymart) was very low (5%), and another (Graterford) was very high (71%).
- Eighteen REST scales and eight CRC scales measuring various dimensions of inmate psychosocial functioning and responses to treatment were then entered into logistic regression analyses as predictors of the three measures of recidivism (controlling for all other variables). Significant predictors of reincarceration included anxiety, hostility, therapeutic engagement, counselor rapport, ratings of program structure, and rapport with other inmates. No additional predictors of rearrest were statistically significant. Significant predictors of drug relapse included self-efficacy, risk taking, and self-confrontation.
- The validity of our findings were bolstered by the fact that we were able to precisely account for total treatment exposure for all inmates in our sample, and we examined the effects of treatment exposure as a control variable. Previous studies have failed to do so.

Limitations

- The major limitation was the brevity of the follow-up periods and associated sample sizes available for multivariate analyses so far. As more inmates are released, and as average time at risk increases, we will revisit the analyses and conclusions formulated in this report.
- Our ability to examine post-release outcomes was limited by the unavailability of automated data regarding participation in aftercare treatment. Aftercare may interact with employment and other observed predictors to influence outcomes. Further research

should examine ways to better integrate prison-based drug treatment with post-release needs and resources.

- It was difficult to determine the degree to which employment was a cause or an effect. To do so, it would be useful to obtain more detailed information on parolees' type of post-release employment, employee performance, income, etc. To disentangle potential causes, research should also determine how other factors (e.g., intelligence, cognitive abilities, education, in-prison and pre-prison work history, job training) might interact with drug treatment to influence post-release outcomes (employment, drug relapse, reincarceration, and rearrest).

- However, none of the control variables examined in this study (e.g., assessed level of need for drug treatment, prior and current offense severity, age) substantially weakened the observed relationship between employment and reduced recidivism, leading us to conclude that the effect of post-release employment is quite robust.

Question

1. Explain how Case Study 6–3 illustrates concepts discussed in Chapter 6, providing evidence to support your answer: (a) reliability and validity; (b) nonequivalent comparison groups; (c) confounding factors; and (d) reassessing the entire program or policy plan.

■ ■ ■

References

Berk, R. A., & Rossi, P. H. (1998). *Thinking about program evaluation* (2nd ed.). Newbury Park, CA: Sage.

Braga, A. A., Pierce, G. L., McDevitt, J., Bond, B. J., & Cronin, S. (2008). Strategic prevention of gun violence among gang-involved offenders. *Justice Quarterly, 25*(1), 132–162.

Forgatch, M., Patterson, G., & DeGarmo, D. (2005). Evaluating fidelity: Predictive validity for a measure of competent adherence to the Oregon model of parent management training. *Behavioral Therapy, 36*, 3–13.

Gaes, G. G., Flanagan, T. J., Motiuk, L. L., & Stewart, L. (1999). Adult correctional treatment. In M. Tonry & J. Petersilia (Eds.), *Prisons: Crime and justice, a review of research.* Vol. 26 (pp. 361–426).

Gendreau, P., & Little, T. (1996). A meta-analysis of the predictors of adult offender recidivism: What works! *Criminology, 34*, 575–608.

Gover, A., MacDonald, J., & Alpert, G. (2003). Combating domestic violence: Findings from an evaluation of a local domestic violence court. *Criminology and Public Policy, 3*, 109–132.

Guevara, M., & Solomon, E. (2009). *Implementing evidence-based policy and practice in community corrections* (2 ed). Washington, DC: National Institute of Corrections.

Guterbock, T. M., Koper, C. S., Vickerman, M., Bruce, T., Walker, K. E., & Carter, T. (2010). *Evaluation of Prince William County's illegal immigration enforcement policy: Final report.* Charlottesville, VA: Center for Survey Research, University of Virginia. The full report is available at http://www .pwcgov.org/docLibrary/PDF/13188.pdf.

Lempert, R. (1989). Humility is a virtue: On the publication of policy-relevant research. *Law and Society Review*, 145–161.

Lipsey, M. W., & Wilson, D. B. (1993). The efficacy of psychological, educational and behavioral treatment: Confirmation from meta-analysis. *American Psychologist, 48*, 1181–1209.

Lipsey, M. W., & Wilson, D. B. (2001). *Practical meta-analysis.* Thousand Oaks, CA: Sage.

Mihalic, S. (2004). The importance of implementation fidelity. *Emotional & Behavioral Disorders in Youth, 4*, 83–86 (99-105).

Palmer, T. (1992). *The re-emergence of correctional intervention.* Newbury Park, CA: Sage.

Patton, M. Q. (1996). *Utilization-focused evaluation: The new century text.* Thousand Oaks, CA: Sage.

Rosenbaum, P. R., & Rubin, D. (1983). The central role of the propensity score in observational studies for causal effects. *Biometrika, 70,* 41–55.

Rosenbaum, P. R., & Rubin, D. (1985). Constructing a control group using multivariate matching methods that incorporate the propensity score. *The American Statistician, 39,* 33–38.

Rosenberg, M. (1965). *Society and the adolescent self-image.* Princeton, NJ: Princeton University Press.

Rossi, P. H., Lipsey, M. W., & Freeman, H. E. (2003). *Evaluation: A systematic approach* (7th ed). Thousand Oaks, CA: Sage.

Rubin, D. B. (1997). Estimating causal effects from large data sets using propensity scores. *Annals of Internal Medicine, 127,* 757–763.

Rutman, L. (1984). *Planning useful evaluations: Evaluability assessment.* Beverly Hills, CA: Sage.

Sherman, L. W. (1992). *Policing domestic violence: Experiments and dilemmas.* New York: Free Press.

Sherman, L. W., & Berk, R. A. (1984). The specific deterrent effects of arrest for domestic assault. *American Sociological Review, 49,* 261–272.

Skogan, W. G., Hartnett, S. M., Bump, N., & Dubois, J. (2009). *Evaluation of CeaseFire-Chicago.* Washington, DC: U.S. Department of Justice. Available at: http://www.ncjrs.gov/pdffiles1/nij/grants/227181.pdf.

Stokey, E., & Zeckhauser, R. (1978). *A primer for policy analyses.* New York: Norton.

Thompson, M. (1980). *Benefit-cost analysis for program evaluation.* Beverly Hills, CA: Sage.

Welsh, W. (2003). *Evaluation of prison-based therapeutic community drug treatment programs in Pennsylvania: Executive summary.* Philadelphia: Department of Criminal Justice, Temple University. Available at: http://www.pccd.state.pa.us/pccd/site/.

Welsh, W. N., Jenkins, P. H., & Harris, P. W. (1997). *Reducing minority over-representation in juvenile justice: Results of community-based intervention in Pennsylvania.* Philadelphia: Temple University, Department of Criminal Justice (1992-95).

Welsh, W. N., Jenkins, P. H., & Harris, P. W. (1999). Reducing minority over-representation in juvenile justice: Results of community-based delinquency prevention in Harrisburg. *Journal of Research in Crime and Delinquency, 36,* 87–110.

Welsh, W. N., & Zajac, G. (2004). A census of prison-based drug treatment programs: Implications for programming, policy and evaluation. *Crime & Delinquency, 50,* 108–133.

Wholey, J. S. (1994). Assessing the feasibility and likely usefulness of evaluation. In J. S. Wholey, H. P. Hatry & K. E. Newcomer (Eds.), *Handbook of practical program evaluation* (pp. 15–39). San Francisco: Jossey-Bass.

Wholey, J. S., Hatry, H. P., & Newcomer, K. E. (Eds.). (1994). *Handbook of practical evaluation.* San Francisco: Jossey-Bass.

7

Reassessment and Review

CHAPTER OUTLINE

- **Planning for failure.** Failure of an intervention can occur for a number of reasons, including (1) conflicting or overly ambitious goals, (2) poor design, (3) poor implementation, or (4) failure to maintain support of key stakeholders.

- **Planning for success.** Ongoing reassessment, learning, and revision are crucial elements of successful interventions. Four tasks increase chances of success: (1) communication with stakeholders, (2) building internal capacities for leading and learning, (3) studying information about program or policy performance, and (4) increasing the fit between needs and characteristics of the environment and capacities of the program or policy.

- **Learning and adapting.** Interventions, their organizations, and surrounding environments change over time, and successful interventions must adapt to change by consciously tailoring the program or policy.

- **A caution about program and policy survival.** Interventions sometimes survive long after they are known to be ineffective. Survival is often dependent on how well the intervention serves the personal goals of key stakeholders.

- **The tasks of implementation.** Plans from Stages 3 to 6 are finally implemented: Initiating the Design (implementing Stage 3 plans); Initiating the Action Plan (implementing Stage 4 plans); Monitoring Program/Policy Implementation (implementing Stage 5 plans); and Evaluating and Providing Feedback to Users and Stakeholders (implementing Stage 6 plans).

At this point, the program or policy is ready to be launched. Ideally, all six stages of planning should be completed prior to the initial start date for the intervention. We recognize, however, that time constraints imposed on the planning process may result in less than optimal program designs and action plans. Nonetheless, at this stage, for the first time, our program or policy takes on life. While planning and reviewing is a continuous process, we now begin doing what we have planned.

We rarely have any control over the environments within which policies and programs are implemented: they have lives of their own, driven by visions and goals that may be independent of our new innovation. Or, they may be wholly driven by political and financial arrangements that may seem irrational and chaotic. Because our program or policy operates in a dynamic organizational or system environment, we need to pay attention to changes that occur in areas such as political climate, fiscal health of funding sources, key policymakers, and policies related to our intervention. Sometimes these changes will occur independently of our intervention, but in other cases our interventions will cause reactions that require adaptation. As we discussed in Chapter 1 in relation to force field analysis, some of the forces that sustain a problem or issue over time are more potent than others. As these potent forces shift in strength, it becomes critical for programs and policies to change. As an example, consider turnover among CEOs of state agencies.

Example 7–1   Turnover at the Top

When a new governor is elected, it is common for him or her to replace senior public agency administrators with persons more valued than those currently holding those positions. These changes at the top produce other changes within state agencies, and new administrators may view your intervention differently. Building relationships with a new administration becomes an important challenge every time major political shifts occur.

We repeat our warning from the Introduction: *planned change improves the likelihood of successful intervention, but it cannot guarantee it.* Good planning increases the odds of success by explicitly considering important factors that might lead to failure or success.

Example 7–2   *Criminal Justice Planning and the Lesson of Jurassic Park*

Our preference for rational planning is a value that guides our writing and research. We are not so naïve, however, to believe that careful planning always produces successful outcomes. Even the most carefully crafted plans can have no effect, make problems worse, or create unintended effects. There are other times when energy and resources are wasted because planning processes are terminated prematurely. In general, subtle facets of the criminal justice system (see Chapter 2) can frustrate good planning. In real life, systems don't always behave the way we want them to.

In *Jurassic Park* (Crichton, 1990), Ian Malcolm, a mathematician (played in the 1993 film by Jeff Goldblum; Universal Films, 1993), warns of the larger, more powerful natural rhythms of nature that can undermine what appear to be great scientific advancements. "My point is that life on earth can take care of itself," he raves. "In the thinking of a human being, a hundred years is a long time. . . . But to the earth, a hundred years is nothing. A million years is nothing. This planet lives and breathes on a much vaster scale. We can't imagine its slow and powerful rhythms, and we haven't got the humility to try. We have been residents here for the blink of an eye. If we are gone tomorrow, the earth will not miss us."

Doleschal (1982) sounded a similar warning, this one directed at criminal justice reform efforts. He argues that forces that continually shape the justice system should be allowed to interact naturally. When reforms are implemented, the results are often the opposite of those intended. For example, many efforts intended to reduce prison populations through the creation of community-based programs have failed to do so. Instead, community programs have often extended supervision and control over less serious offenders. Other examples include policy changes intended to reduce discretion that only moved discretion to other, less visible decision points in the system. For example, mandatory sentencing policies shift discretion from judges to prosecutors, but overall, discretion never disappears. Doleschal likens these reforms to a program conducted in Alaska and Canada to protect herds of caribou from their natural predator, the wolf. By shooting the wolves, environmentalists hoped to increase the caribou population. Instead, old and sick caribou that previously were killed and eaten by the wolves faced death by starvation and disease.

Example 7–2 Criminal Justice Planning and the Lesson of *Jurassic Park*—Cont'd

Rather than give up on planning, we can learn from these experiences. In many cases, failures become the means for discovering the nature and strengths of forces we are trying to change. Sometimes we may decide that our knowledge and resources are inadequate to the task, but in other cases we become better equipped to try again.

In the Introduction, we noted that you may be assessing an existing program rather than planning the launch of a new one. Evaluating the effectiveness of an intervention involves examining the extent to which it has been adopted by organizations and individuals in its operational environment. By examining strategies used to adapt the innovation locally, we can gain a better understanding of the factors that have contributed to its success or failure, popularity or unpopularity, or even its expansion or demise.

Planning for Failure

Failure of any program or policy is related to two broad types of difficulties: (1) insurmountable obstacles within the implementing agency or its environment, and (2) breakdowns or omissions in the planning process.

First of all, it is possible for a program or policy to fail even when its designers have planned thoroughly and carefully. It may be the case that certain obstacles are too big or too powerful to overcome, or inadequate resources are available to do so. As we discussed in Chapter 1, such obstacles may be *physical* (e.g., the physical design of a courthouse precludes more efficient case processing), *social* (e.g., existing barriers related to class, gender, or race are unchanged by the program or policy), *economic* (lack of sufficient funding), *educational* (e.g., special training or education is required to implement an intervention), *legal* (e.g., criminal justice agencies are legally obligated to do certain things and prohibited from doing other things), *political* (e.g., motivations of partisan stakeholders can block a specific change), or *technological* (e.g., problems with managing the information system required to implement a new policy). A criminal justice systems analysis and a force field analysis should help planners anticipate such obstacles and develop strategies to overcome them. Such activities increase the probability of success.

The second set of difficulties concerns planning breakdowns, omissions, or deficits: one or more critical planning tasks have not been properly executed. The examples and case studies presented in Chapters 1 through 6 illustrate some of the most likely deficits in the planning process. We reiterate here common difficulties at each stage (Figure 7–1).

Consider the following example: Wilson and Davis evaluated a prisoner reentry program in New York City, called Project Greenlight, that utilized evidence-based program design components. From the design, we would expect that the program would have been successful, but Project Greenlight was not (Wilson & Davis, 2006). In fact, the Greenlight participants did significantly worse than the control group. The authors reject selection

Stage 1: Analyzing the Problem
- Insufficient information about the problem has been examined. We don't really know how big the problem is, where it is, or who is affected. We may not even have a clear definition of the problem.
- No theory guided the intervention. We don't know how or why the expected change should have occurred.
- Inadequate examination of previous interventions: we may have recreated the wheel, or recycled an old, broken wheel by failing to learn about previous attempts to change the problem.
- Important stakeholders were not identified or included in the planning process.
- Inadequate examination of the larger system or environment was conducted.

Stage 2: Setting Goals and Objectives
- Goals and objectives were not clearly stated.
- Substantial disagreement about goals or objectives persists among stakeholders.
- Incompatible goals or values in the larger system were not identified.
- Exaggerated goals were posed in order to obtain support from key stakeholders.
- Needs for interagency collaboration were not sufficiently addressed.

Stage 3: Designing the Program or Policy
- No specific intervention approach was identified.
- Target populations and selection were not adequately identified.
- Program components or policy provisions and procedures were unclear.
- Responsibilities of program staff or policy authorities were unclear.

Stage 4: Developing an Action Plan
- Required resources have not been properly identified.
- Required resources have not been acquired.
- Responsibilities for implementation have not been clearly assigned.
- Insufficient attention was devoted to maintaining support and anticipating resistance.

Stage 5: Developing a Plan for Monitoring Program/Policy Implementation
- No monitoring of program or policy implementation was attempted.
- Information systems for monitoring were inadequate.
- Monitoring instruments were unreliable.
- Responsibilities for data collection, storage, or analysis were unclear.
- Monitoring data was not used to make necessary adjustments to the program or policy.

Stage 6: Develop a Plan for Evaluating Outcomes
- Prerequisites for evaluation were not adequately met.
- Outcome measures were not reliable or valid.
- The research design was inadequate to determine outcomes.
- Confounding factors were not adequately addressed.
- Users of evaluation results were not adequately identified or consulted.

Stage 7: Initiating the Program or Policy Plan
- Inadequate review of the planning process was undertaken before implementation began.
- Substantial obstacles within the implementing agency or its environment subverted the aims of the program or policy.
- Planning breakdowns, errors, or omissions occurred.
- The change agent failed to learn and adapt during implementation.
- The change agent failed to execute plans properly.

FIGURE 7–1 Common planning deficits at each stage.

bias or program design explanations for this outcome. Instead, they highlight implementation problems such as doubling the number of participants in cognitive skills classes and poor relationships between some case managers and participants, suggesting that some staff were not qualified for the roles they were asked to play. Moreover, the risk-assessment tool originally adopted was dropped, so that some participants were poorly matched to the program. Wilson and Davis observe that poorly implemented programs may not simply fail, but they may actually produce harm.

Implementation failure easily occurs when leaders overstate the goals of a program or policy (Stage 2) in order to garner support from stakeholders in the larger political environment (Stage 1). When innovations are oversold, stakeholders feel deceived and cheated. Clear, Flynn, and Shapiro (1987) observe with humor the range of promises attached to intensive probation services (IPS): "Advocates of IPS programs are not humble in the claims they made for these programs. Commonly, IPS is expected to reduce prison crowding, increase public protection, rehabilitate the offender, demonstrate the value of probation, and save money. Even a skeptic is bound to be impressed" (p. 32). These exaggerated objectives eventually spelled trouble for the evaluation (Stage 6). Petersilia and Turner (1990) found in their evaluation of 14 IPS programs that the primary purposes of intensive supervision were rarely achieved:

- The programs did not alleviate prison crowding and may have increased it in some sites.
- They cost considerably more than is generally realized (Stage 5).
- They were no more effective than routine probation and parole in reducing recidivism.

The best that can be hoped for in the wake of such disappointing outcomes is a careful reassessment of the entire planning process, followed by necessary adjustments (Stage 7), especially a more realistic accounting of goals and objectives (Stage 2).

Planning for Success

The important point to keep in mind at the implementation stage is that the planning process has not yet ended. In fact, it never will. New information pertinent to the program or policy will emerge, some of it through evaluation research, that may suggest modification to the original design. This is what learning is about. The organization's capacity to learn will largely determine the extent to which the goals of the innovation are achieved. There are four tasks that need emphasis at this point in order to increase the chances of success.

1. *Communicate:* Continually communicate to constituents and potential opponents the need for the program or policy. Develop advocates for the program or policy among a wide range of public officials so that the vision of what you are up to is passed on to others who may be asked about the need for it. Publicize widely and frequently information on the program and its performance.

2. *Build internal capacities for leading and learning:* Those persons who are carrying out the activities articulated in the design are your most valuable assets. Their command of the vision, goals, and activities described in the design are critical to the innovation's success. Their ability to lead, support each other, think strategically, adapt, and carry out their assigned tasks are essential to a program's success. Your organization needs to invest in their development.

3. *Study:* The need for information is essential for learning to occur. Data regarding implementation of the program or policy's design, data on performance, and data on changes in the environment need to be tracked and brought into discussions among key stakeholders.

4. *Improve the fit:* Purposefully permit the innovation to take shape as new information about the needs and characteristics of the environment emerge and as the capacities of the program or policy develop. The better it fits the needs and priorities of the political environment, the greater will be the level of acceptance.

These four tasks will become a permanent part of managing an effective program or policy, and can be used to assess the quality of a program's administration.

Learning and Adapting

In the Introduction, we mentioned the concept of *mutual adaptation:* the program (or policy) and the organizational environment in which it operates will both change during the implementation process. Programs change over time. Not only is there continual reshaping of a program design before it is put into action, but programs continue to change following the point at which "the tire meets the road." It is this change in program characteristics that makes components of a program design poor predictors of program success. Then, too, program staff, program clients, and decisionmakers, rather than being passive participants in the implementation process, directly affect how the innovations are used, adapting the innovations to existing organizational structures and norms, and using them to serve their own purposes.

In addition, the same program design can produce drastically different results in different settings, thus supporting the conclusion that context is critical to outcome. You may recall from our discussion in Chapter 1 regarding systems analysis that the private sector has played a critical role in criminal justice for many years. Some local criminal justice systems, however, have had disastrous experiences with private-sector programs. In corrections, for example, the promised fiscal advantages of private corrections have not always materialized (Shichor, 1995).

But it is not only innovations that undergo change during the implementation process; the organization within which the innovation is used also undergoes change. Specifically with regard to a probation program in Texas, Markley (1989) observed that when program management personnel changed, line staff became "demoralized." Their commitment to the program was dependent on the leadership provided by a few individuals.

Other common disruptions include the transfer of personnel to a new program, the hiring of outsiders (new staff) to staff the new program, and the requirement that staff acquire new skills in order to continue doing their jobs.

Implementation of a program or policy in any organizational setting requires both adaptation by individuals and adaptation of the innovation in order for the implementation process to succeed (Castro, Barrera, & Martinez, 2004; Durlak, 2008). This process of mutual adaptation implies that the same innovation can look very different across different settings (Ellickson & Petersilia, 1983). The crucial point to be made is that unless a program or policy is carefully tailored to the setting in which it is to be used, successful implementation is unlikely.

An excellent example of this kind of tailoring of the innovation can be seen in the approach that The Center for Alternative Sentencing and Employment Services (CASES) in New York City has taken to ensure that its clients fit their target population: jail-bound rather than probation-bound offenders. Data on sentencing in New York revealed that sentencing practices differed across the five boroughs. Judges in Queens, for example, require fewer misdemeanor offenses than do those in Manhattan before sentencing an offender to serve significant jail time. In order to prevent use of the CASES Community Service Sentencing Project (CSSP) from being used as a replacement for probation, criteria for accepting offenders into CSSP are adjusted to sentencing patterns at the borough level (Neises, 1993).

Not only does tailoring itself promote effective adaptation, but so do the structural characteristics of organizations. Decentralization of program control, for example, permits different sites to develop a program design at their own pace and allows the program to adapt to the idiosyncrasies of each site in ways that improve chances for successful implementation. It may be that a program is more effective under some conditions than under others, but it may also be the case that different modes of adaptation make it possible for an innovation to adapt to a variety of organizational environments.

Another way in which programs adapt is when a change occurs in the target population or our knowledge about the target population. Both adult and juvenile correctional programs have traditionally been designed for males. Girls make up a small proportion of cases in the juvenile justice system, so programs for delinquent youths of both sexes are typically based on problems and needs derived from studies of boys. The risk factors associated with delinquency among girls, however, are different than those found among boys. Granted, there are strong similarities among adolescents of both sexes, but programs need to be tailored to meet the unique needs of girls. Some of the risk factors found among girls that require program modification are: family conflict; sexual, physical, and emotional abuse; low self-esteem; and substance abuse (Bloom, Owen, Deschenes, & Rosenbaum, 2002). Girls are much more likely than boys to be suffering from post-traumatic stress disorder (PTSD). Several states have engaged researchers and experts to assist them in adapting their correctional programs to the specific needs of girls.

It is critical during implementation to uncover any changes in the intended program or policy design and describe them. These changes are deviations from the original plan and must be understood before a sound evaluation can be conducted.

A Caution about Survival

Mutual adaptation also means that acceptance of and continued support for an innovation may serve the personal goals of decisionmakers. For example, if a program can screen cases and make admission decisions rapidly, life is made easier for referring agents such as probation officers and judges. A policy may be passed that gives prosecutors greater discretion (power). This has been the case in many mandatory sentencing schemes in which it is the charges that determine the sentence. Rothman (1980) refers to these latter motivations as *convenience* in contrast to the benevolent interests (what Rothman calls *conscience)* that may have served to motivate the creators of the innovation.

Unfortunately, even in the face of clear evidence that an innovation is failing, these interests of convenience may be powerful enough to sustain the innovation. Valuable resources can then be wasted that could be put to better use in the service of promising programs and policies. For example, in spite of overwhelming research evidence that the D.A.R.E. program does not work, D.A.R.E. programs continue to exist (Birkeland, Murphy-Graham, & Weiss, 2005; Rosenbaum & Hanson, 1998). Reasons for this phenomenon include (1) the fact that school administrators never expected D.A.R.E. to prevent drug use, but no other program has been proposed, and (2) D.A.R.E. is believed to be useful for generating positive relationships between young students and the police, an outcome unrelated to any of D.A.R.E.'s stated objectives. To counter this problem, evidence of what works and what doesn't should be shared as widely as possible. If evaluation data are not collected and results are not disseminated, or if they are kept confidential to protect the political interests of individuals, we run the risk of "convenience" (self-interest) winning out. As the D.A.R.E. example demonstrates, however, even widely accepted evidence of ineffectiveness may not be sufficient to counter purposes other than achievement of a program's objectives.

The Tasks of Implementing a New Innovation

Implementing the program or policy plan (Stage 7) involves putting into motion the program design (Stage 3) and the action plan (Stage 4), monitoring implementation (Stage 5), and, if appropriate, evaluating outcomes (Stage 6). Once evaluation data are analyzed, feedback is provided to all stakeholders, and the program should be thoroughly reassessed to determine where revisions are necessary. At the end of the process, the change agent asks whether further adjustments are necessary to meet program objectives. What are the strengths and weaknesses of the program? Decisions may have to be made about whether the program should be continued, and whether it should receive further funding. Reassessment and review of the program or policy should occur periodically from this point on.

Initiating the Program/Policy Design

In Chapter 3, we examined how a program or policy is constructed. Every program or policy must have a clearly defined design that includes: targets (e.g., eligibility, numbers to be served, access, screening, intake), program staff or individuals responsible for implementing the program or policy (e.g., selection, training, duties), and program components or policy provisions (e.g., specific goods, services, opportunities, or interventions to be delivered). Initiating the design, then, requires doing everything that was previously specified. Together with the action plan, the design lays out the major tasks for implementation.

Initiating the Action Plan

In Chapter 4, you learned how to develop an action plan that specified the entire sequence of tasks that need to be completed in order to successfully launch or implement the program or policy. These included technical and interpersonal tasks (e.g., identifying and acquiring the necessary resources; locating office space and/or meeting space; hiring and training staff; designing client intake and reporting forms; purchasing equipment and supplies; setting dates and assigning responsibility for the completion of specific tasks). The action plan is, in essence, a "blueprint" explaining how to translate a vision of the program or policy into reality.

Like the director of an orchestra, the change agent must coordinate the program or policy activities of all the different individuals and groups associated with the program or policy. Managers must hire and train their staff; they must build good relations with potential referral sources (e.g., police, schools, probation); they must train staff to use required intake forms and keep client records; they must build good relations with citizens and businesses in the neighborhood; and they must provide regular reports of progress to their funding providers. Remember three guidelines to ensure smooth coordination: (1) maintain consistency between staff job descriptions and actual tasks, (2) maintain clear and frequent communication among staff members, and between staff and supervisors; and (3) keep an eye on the time line: make sure that activities required for successful progression from one step to the next are carried out on time (e.g., make sure that staff are hired and trained by the dates specified in the action plan; make sure that all record-keeping forms are printed and procedures are clearly understood by staff).

Remember that some resistance is inevitable with the start-up of a new program or policy. Resistance may come from any of the participants involved: clients, targets, or even the intervention's own staff (i.e., the action system). Resistance that appears should be dealt with fairly and seriously. Conflict is not something to be avoided at all costs. It may provide the opportunity to identify and resolve misunderstandings, and it may also point out difficulties in implementation that truly deserve attention.

Begin Monitoring Program/Policy Implementation

At Stage 5 (see Chapter 5), you laid out a plan for monitoring program or policy implementation. As program or policy operations begin, it is time to start monitoring. *Implementation* refers to the initiation, management, and administration of the action plan. Once the intervention actually begins, we want to minimize discrepancies between what was planned (i.e., the program or policy on paper) and what is actually done (i.e., the program or policy in action). *Monitoring* attempts to determine whether program/policy implementation is proceeding as planned. Monitoring is a process that attempts to identify any gaps between the program or policy on paper (design) and the program or policy in action (implementation).

For the target population, monitoring data should assess the following questions: What were the characteristics of the actual individuals targeted by the intervention? Were targets selected who were truly in need or at risk? Is the intervention meeting its specified criteria in terms of target eligibility (e.g., age, sex, income, region) and numbers to be served? Were proper recruiting, screening, and intake procedures followed? How were referrals made? For program components, monitoring data should answer the following questions: who did what to whom in what order, how much, and how often? Were there variations in service delivery or activities? Did different staff deliver programming in a different manner? Was there more than one program site or location, and if so, were program activities administered consistently across different sites? Make sure that monitoring data also provide information about service tasks and responsible authorities: Were proper staff or authorities identified? Did they fit the specified roles and job descriptions? Did they understand their duties and perform them as expected?

Begin Evaluating and Providing Feedback to Users and Stakeholders

If any evaluation is to be useful, it should serve the information needs of the intervention and its stakeholders (see Chapter 1). Most notably, the program or policy's major stakeholders include its funding agency, but any intervention has multiple stakeholders such as the community, businesses, politicians, criminal justice agencies, volunteers, clients, and so on. The time spent previously (at Stage 1) identifying stakeholders should not be wasted. Evaluation (Stage 6) is a critical means of demonstrating accountability, and hopefully effectiveness, to stakeholders. The change agent should now assign individual responsibility for packaging and communicating evaluation results to different users. If the results are to be useful, and used, one must create means of communication that intended audiences could understand and react to.

Planning Tasks for an Existing Program or Policy

In reassessing an existing program or policy, we will want to ensure that planning tasks are continuing. After all, our experience with an innovation over time generates valuable information that can be used to improve the innovation or more effectively replicate it elsewhere. In the Introduction, we laid out the core of those planning tasks that are ongoing. First, we need to examine the goals and objectives in terms of whether they were realistic and whether we were able to measure the objectives in a way that is informative. If, for example, a program is attempting to increase employment among participants in a prisoner reentry program, and the objective is 100% employment within six months of admission, it may be that 100% employment is overly ambitious.

Another critical question is whether there is ongoing reassessment, learning, and revision of the program design (this step is less relevant in the case of policy). Evaluations of intermediate and long-term outcomes should be ongoing. After all, client turnover, staff turnover, and changes in the larger system may affect the delivery of program services. We should never assume that because a program was evaluated once, it will be effective forever. Evaluation is also a tool for continuous program development.

Changes in the environment surrounding an intervention may require a program or policy to change—to adapt. If a city that had implemented a community policing strategy is encountering rapid gentrification of an area, the police will need to adapt both to the changing population of that area and to pressures put on areas where poorer citizens are relocating. Expectations of and attitudes toward the police will be quite different in the gentrified area compared to the situation that had existed in the past. In addition, the area to which lower-income residents are being displaced may become less stable, producing higher levels of conflict among neighbors.

Changes to a program design, then, are likely as time passes. Both knowledge development and changes in needs and demands of the local environment make it necessary to revisit the design of a program or policy, consider changes to the action plan, improve monitoring methods, and upgrade evaluation procedures.

Conclusion

Implementation is an ongoing process of adaptation, negotiation, and communication. In order to maximize the mutual fit between a program or policy and the environment within which it is initiated and allowed to develop, both the innovation and the environment must change.

At this point, we hope that you have a good idea of the kind of analyses and kind of questions we need to ask to figure out what works to reduce or prevent any specific problem. We have argued throughout this book that many criminal justice interventions fall short of their goals because of poor planning, poor implementation, and poor evaluation. What we truly need is not *more* programs and policies, or *new* programs and policies, per se: we need *better* programs and policies. We need a better understanding of planned change to improve the effectiveness of criminal justice interventions. Such change is ubiquitous in governmental, community, private, and nonprofit agencies. This book has attempted to provide a systematic, seven-stage framework for analyzing and improving existing interventions, but also for planning new ones so as to maximize chances of success. Major steps of analysis were summarized in Figure 1–1.

Which of the following interventions are effective? How would you know, or how would you find out?

- Prisoner reentry initiatives and programs, including prison-based drug treatment and community aftercare, vocational and basic education, post-release employment assistance, and reentry courts that provide assessment and treatment services in conjunction with traditional criminal sanctions.

- Drug Awareness Resistance Education (D.A.R.E.) for elementary, middle, and high school students.
- Federal "Weed and Seed" program (dual policy of first stamping out drug sales in specific communities, and then "seeding" the communities with protective, economic, and social resources).
- Shelters, counseling, and victim assistance for abused women.
- Mandatory arrest policies for suspected wife abusers.
- Juvenile waiver laws (serious juvenile offenses may be transferred to adult courts, or automatically tried as adult offenses).

We reiterate a few major propositions to conclude this endeavor. First, we need a systematic plan for any change effort. Interventions, both new and old, need to be subjected to thorough scrutiny and analysis. Successful interventions are a product of hard work, careful planning, and a willingness to revise where necessary.

Second, good intentions are rarely sufficient to bring about successful change. Beware of the "activist bias" (Sieber, 1981), by which well-intentioned advocates of change assume that they already know what the problem is and what is needed. Such advocates may insist that we desist all this prolonged planning and simply "get on with it." The perils of unplanned or poorly planned change should by now be obvious: expensive, poorly articulated, poorly implemented, ineffective programs and policies that are unable to successfully compete for scarce funds.

Third, program or policy planning is an interactive and ongoing process. It is crucial to review and modify planning (where needed) at each stage of the analysis. This takes time, but it is time well spent.

Fourth, a rational planning approach provides a framework for developing logical and effective programs and policies. The default (all too commonly) is to use unarticulated and untested assumptions to guide planning. Finally, participation of and communication with all key actors, or stakeholders (e.g., program staff, clients, individuals or agencies whose cooperation is needed, funding sources, citizens affected by the intervention, elected representatives), throughout the change process are keys to success. While careful planning and analysis cannot guarantee success, it will increase the probability of success.

Discussion Questions

1. Why should intervention planning and evaluation occur on a regular basis? Why is it necessary to continually revise and reassess?
2. What can be done to increase the chances that an innovation will succeed? What factors increase the chances of failure?
3. What steps (activities) are involved in "initiating the program or policy plan"?
4. What are some ways that stakeholder or constituent support can be maintained after a program or policy is implemented?

5. Why do programs continue to change even after they are implemented?
6. What is mutual adaptation, and why is it important? Give an example.
7. Why might a program that is known not to work continue to receive support?
8. How can you tell when a program or policy is ready to be evaluated?

■ ■ ■ ━━━

Case Study 7–1 Implementation Woes: Providing Residential Substance Abuse Treatment (RSAT) for Inmates in State Prisons

Instructions

First read the background below, and then read the article that follows. Answer the questions at the end of the case study.

"The best-laid schemes o' mice and men gang aft agley...." Scottish poet Robbie Burns said it well. No matter how carefully "wee timorous beasties" or humans plan for the future, things never work out exactly as planned. Even when planned change is successful, it may not be permanent. Why not, you may ask? People who play critical roles ("stakeholders"), including leadership roles, come and go over time, initial enthusiasm abates, the political environment changes, the priority assigned to a specific public problem shifts, and the actual change that resulted may not have been sufficiently dramatic to maintain or recruit new support. Planned change is dynamic, like the problems it seeks to address. The need for substance abuse treatment among prison inmates is widely accepted. Developing effective methods to address those needs is quite another matter. The following case study summarizes some of the implementation problems that have been faced by a federally sponsored initiative (Harrison & Martin, 2003).

Background

The Residential Substance Abuse Treatment (RSAT) Program was created as part of the Violent Crime Control and Law Enforcement Act of 1994 to meet the needs of state correctional systems for resources to address a growing problem. Through the act, state authorities gained access to funds, technical assistance, and a network of innovators that could help them build their own local treatment programs. Every state took advantage of these funds, and by March of 2001, more than 2,000 RSAT programs were involved in providing services to adult inmates and parolees, as well as juvenile offenders.

With so many programs in place, the need to learn about the effectiveness of different treatment approaches was immense. Consequently, the federal government sponsored a national evaluation program. From a monitoring perspective, large numbers of inmates and parolees were receiving treatment, but to learn about what works takes time. In the meanwhile, information regarding implementation was assembled and became part of the strategy for continued program development. Some of the major implementation difficulties encountered by RSAT programs are summarized below.

Program Difficulties

The most severe problems reported by state officials involved locating or constructing appropriate facilities, recruiting trained treatment staff, and contracting with treatment providers under lengthy or complex bidding and proposal processes. More than half (53%) reported moderate or severe delays related to difficulties in locating facilities for the residential treatment program, and 37% reported delays resulting from the need to construct or physically alter existing structures. About one-fourth of the states (28%) reported encountering difficulties as a result of state regulations, and one-fifth (21%) reported delays due to state bidding or competitive processes. Nearly two-thirds (62%) of the states reported difficulties in obtaining training for treatment staff.

Lack of Aftercare

The National Evaluation's report expressed concern over the lack of aftercare, particularly because the RSAT Request for Proposal (RFP) for states emphasized that in-prison programs with aftercare services should be given preference. Aftercare was not funded, however, and RSAT funds could be used only for the residential treatment component. The National Evaluation found that work release (23%) or halfway houses (20%) were incorporated as aftercare programs in less than half of the RSAT programs. A few others had parole-supervised treatment as part of aftercare, but these numbers were not reported in the National Evaluation. The National Evaluation determined that 86% of RSAT in-prison treatment programs have either specified how graduates may continue treatment in the community or indicated their intention to do so. Continuity of care is an important element in treatment for offenders and is strongly linked to reductions in recidivism and drug use.

Merging of Treatment Components

The National Evaluation also expressed concern over the merging of treatment components. RSAT programs are "intended to develop the inmate's cognitive, behavioral, social, vocational, and other skills," which lends itself to a multifaceted approach. Yet the evaluators pointed out that therapeutic communities, and 12-step programs in particular, are based on different theories and practices. The 12-step programs are spiritually based, which is different from professional therapy. Nevertheless, 12-step programs have worked in conjunction with therapeutic communities for many years. The National Evaluation accurately pointed out that combination treatments have not been fully evaluated and that many combinations may result in watered-down components, leading to less effective treatment.

Other Problems

The National Evaluation showed that 55% of the RSAT programs lacked one or more operational treatment components, and 53% of program directors still considered their programs to be in the "shakedown" phase rather than stabilized at the RSAT midpoint. Programs had difficulty recruiting staff trained in the therapeutic-community and/or cognitive-behavioral methods as suggested in the RSAT RFP. Many states encountered difficulties employing ex-offenders and recovering addicts as counselors in prison therapeutic communities; often, individuals with criminal records were not allowed to enter the institutions to work or visit. Evidence regarding therapeutic community staff effectiveness, however, shows that staff should consist of a mixture of recovered therapeutic-community graduates and other counseling (social work, educational, or mental health) professionals (Wexler, 1997).

Question

1. Using the chart in the Introduction (Table 1–2) as a guide, identify two major steps in the seven-stage model of planned change that could help explain what happened with the RSAT programs nationally. Use specific concepts from the text, and provide evidence from the article to support your answer.

References

Birkeland, S., Murphy-Graham, E., & Weiss, C. (2005). Good reasons for ignoring good evaluation: The case of the drug resistance education (D.A.R.E.) program. *Evaluation and Program Planning, 28*(3), 247–256.

Bloom, B., Owen, B., Deschenes, E. P., & Rosenbaum, J. (2002). Moving toward justice for female juvenile offenders in the new millennium. *Journal of Contemporary Criminal Justice, 18,* 37–56.

Castro, F. G., Barrera, M., & Martinez, C. R. (2004). The cultural adaptation of prevention interventions: resolving tensions between fidelity and fit. *Prevention Science, 5*(1), 41–45.

Clear, T., Flynn, S., & Shapiro, C. (1987). Intensive supervision in probation: A comparison of three projects. In B. McCarthy (Ed.), *Intermediate punishments: Intensive supervision, home confinement, and electronic surveillance* (pp. 31–51). Monsey, NY: Criminal Justice Press.

Crichton, M. (1990). *Jurassic park.* New York: Ballantine.

Doleschal, E. (1982). The dangers of criminal justice reform. *Criminal Justice Abstracts, 14*(1), 133–152 (March).

Durlak, J. A. (2008). Implementation matters: A review of research on the influence of implementation on program outcomes and the factors affecting implementation. *American Journal of Community Psychology, 41*(3–4), 327–350.

Ellickson, P., & Petersilia, J. (1983). *Implementing new ideas in criminal justice.* Santa Monica, CA: RAND.

Harrison, L. D., & Martin, S. S. (2003). *Residential substance abuse treatment for state prisoners: Implementation lessons learned.* Washington, DC: U.S. Department of Justice, Office of Justice Programs, National Institute of Justice. http://www.ncjrs.org/pdffiles1/nij/195738.pdf (NIJ Special Report (NCJ 195738, web-only document)). Accessed March 17, 2011.

Markley, G. (1989). The marriage of mission, management, marketing and measurement. *Research in Corrections, 2,* 49–56.

Neises, E. (1993). *Report: The Center for Alternative Sentencing and Employment Services.* New York: The Center for Alternative Sentencing and Employment Services. http://www.cases.org/programs/abh/ (CASES web site).

Petersilia, J., & Turner, S. (1990). Comparing intensive and regular supervision for high-risk probationers: Early results from an experiment in California. *Crime & Delinquency, 36,* 87–111.

Rosenbaum, D. P., & Hanson, G. (1998). Assessing the effects of school-based drug education: A six-year multilevel analysis of project D.A.R.E. *Journal of Research in Crime and Delinquency, 35*(4), 381–412.

Rothman, D. (1980). *Conscience and convenience: The asylum and its alternatives in progressive America.* Boston: Little, Brown.

Shichor, D. (1995). *Punishment for profit: Private prisons/public concerns.* Thousand Oaks, CA: Sage.

Sieber, S. D. (1981). *Fatal remedies.* New York: Plenum.

Universal Films. (1993). *Jurassic park.* Directed by Steven Spielberg. Produced by K. Kennedy and G.R. Molen. Written by M. Crichton and D. Koepp. Based on the novel by M. Crichton. Photographed by D. Cundey. Edited by M. Kahn. Music by J. Williams.

Wexler, H. K. (1997). Therapeutic communities in American prisons: Prison treatment for substance abusers. In F. Cullen, L. Jones & R. Woodward (Eds.), *Therapeutic communities for offenders* (pp. 161–179). Chichester, NY: John Wiley and Sons.

Wilson, J. A., & Davis, R. C. (2006). Good intentions meet hard realities: An evaluation of the project Greenlight Reentry Program. *Criminology & Public Policy, 2,* 303–338.

Appendix ⣿

A Seven-Stage Checklist for Program/Policy Planning and Analysis

Stage 1. Analyzing the Problem

A. *Document the need for change:* Collect and analyze data to define what the problem is, where it is, how big it is, and who is affected by it. What evidence of the problem exists?

B. *Describe the history of the problem:* How long has the problem existed? How has it changed over time?

C. *Examine potential causes of the problem:* What causes the problem? What theories do we have? The intervention to be chosen must target one or more specific causes supported by research.

D. *Examine previous interventions* that have tried to change this problem. Identify the most promising interventions and choose a preferred intervention approach.

E. *Identify relevant stakeholders:* Do different groups of people have different definitions of the problem? Who is affected by the problem?

F. *Conduct a systems analysis:* Conduct research on the justice system where the problem exists, and determine how the system may create, contribute to, or maintain the problem.

G. *Identify barriers to change and supports for change:* Who is likely to support a certain course of action? Who is likely to resist it?

Stage 2. Setting Goals and Objectives

A. *Write goal statements* specifying the general outcome to be obtained. Consider the goals of criminal sanctions and normative values driving desired outcomes.

B. *Write specific outcome objectives for each goal:* These should include a time frame for measuring impact, a target population, a key result intended, and a specific criterion or measure of impact.

C. *Seek participation* from different individuals and agencies in goal setting. Consider top-down versus bottom-up approaches.

D. *Specify an impact model:* This is a description of how the intervention will act upon a specific cause so as to bring about a change in the problem.

E. *Identify compatible and incompatible goals in the larger system:* Where do values of different stakeholders overlap or conflict?

F. *Identify needs and opportunities for interagency collaboration:* Whose cooperation and participation is needed to achieve the goals of this program or policy?

Stage 3. Designing the Program or Policy

A. *Choose an intervention approach:* Integrate the information collected at previous stages to decide what the substance of an intervention will be. Decide whether a program or policy approach is appropriate.

B. Program design requires four major activities:

(1) *Define the target population:* Who is to be served, or changed?

(2) *Define client selection and intake procedures:* How are clients selected and recruited for the intervention?

(3) *Define program components:* The precise nature, amount, and sequence of services provided must be specified. Who does what to whom, in what order, and how much?

(4) *Write job descriptions* of staff, and *define the skills and training* required.

C. Policy design requires four major activities:

(1) *Define the target population of the policy:* Which persons or groups are included, and which are not?

(2) *Identify the responsible authority:* Who is required to carry out the policy, and what will their responsibilities be?

(3) *Define the provisions of the policy:* A policy should identify the goods, services, opportunities, or interventions that will be delivered, and the conditions that must be met in order for the provisions to be carried out.

(4) *Delineate the procedures that must be followed:* Individuals responsible for implementing a specific set of rules must clearly understand the specific steps and actions to be taken to ensure that the policy is carried out consistently.

Stage 4. Action Planning

A. *Identify resources needed and make cost projections:* How much funding is needed to implement a specific intervention? Identify the kinds of resources needed, estimate costs and make projections, and develop a resource plan.

B. *Plan to acquire or reallocate resources:* How will funding be acquired? Identify resource providers, and be prepared for making adjustments to the resource plan.

C. *Specify dates by which implementation tasks will be accomplished, and assign responsibilities to staff members for carrying out tasks:* A Gantt Chart is particularly useful for this purpose.

D. *Develop mechanisms of self-regulation:* Create mechanisms to monitor staff performance and enhance communication, including procedures for orienting participants, coordinating activities, and managing resistance and conflict.

E. *Specify a plan to build and maintain support:* Anticipate sources of resistance and develop responses.

Stage 5. Program/Policy Implementation and Monitoring

A. *Design a monitoring system* to assess to what degree the program or policy design (see Chapter 4) is being carried out as planned. Is the intended target population being reached? Are program/policy activities or provisions actually being carried out as planned? Are appropriate staff or responsible authorities selected and trained, and are they carrying out their assigned duties?

B. *Design monitoring instruments to collect data* (e.g., observations, surveys, interviews): Collect data to find out what is actually being delivered to clients or targets. The purpose is to identify gaps between the program/policy on paper (design) and the program/policy in action.

C. *Designate responsibility for data collection, storage, and analysis:* Ensure that there is no ambiguity about what information is to be collected, who is responsible for collecting it, or how it is to be collected, stored, and analyzed.

D. *Develop information system capacities:* Information systems may consist of written forms and records that are filed, or fully computerized data entry and storage systems.

E. *Develop mechanisms to provide feedback to staff, clients, and stakeholders:* Depending on the results of monitoring analyses, it may be necessary to make adjustments either to what is being done (the program or policy in action) or to the intended design (the program or policy on paper).

Stage 6. Evaluating Outcomes

A. *Decide which type of evaluation is appropriate, and why:* Do major stakeholders (including those funding the evaluation) want to know whether the program or policy is achieving its objectives (impact), how outcomes change over time (continuous outcomes), or whether it is worth the investment of resources devoted to its implementation (efficiency)?

B. *Determine whether two prerequisites for evaluation have been met:* (1) Are objectives clearly defined and measurable? (2) Has the intervention been sufficiently well designed and well implemented?

C. *Develop outcome measures based on objectives:* Good outcome measures should be valid and reliable.

D. *Identify potential confounding factors* (factors other than the intervention that may have biased observed outcomes): Common confounding factors include biased selection, biased attrition, and history.

E. *Determine which technique for minimizing confounding effects can be used: random assignment or nonequivalent comparison groups:* Each involves creating some kind of comparison or control group.

F. *Specify the appropriate research design to be used:* Examples include: the simple pretest-posttest design; the pretest-posttest design with control group; the pretest-posttest design with multiple pretests; the longitudinal design with treatment and control groups; and the cohort design.

G. *Identify users and uses of evaluation results:* Who is the intended audience, and how can results be effectively and efficiently communicated? How will the results be used?

H. *Reassess the entire program or policy plan:* Review the entire planning process from start to finish, looking for any inconsistencies, contradictions, or inadequacies.

Stage 7. Reassessment and Review

A. *Initiate the program or policy design and the action plan* developed at Stages 3 and 4: Make sure that specific individuals are responsible for coordinating all program or policy activities.

B. *Begin monitoring program/policy implementation* according to plans developed at Stage 5.

C. *Make adjustments* to program or policy design as monitoring detects gaps.

D. *Determine whether the program or policy is ready to be evaluated.*

E. *Implement the research design* developed at Stage 6. Collect and analyze evaluation data.

F. *Provide feedback to stakeholders.*

G. *Reassess the entire program/policy plan and make necessary modifications* to increase fit with the program or policy's environment.

Index

Note: Page numbers followed by *f* indicate figures and *t* indicate tables.

measurable and specific, 82
Minneapolis Domestic Violence
Experiment, 83
process *vs.* objectives, 83
Owen, B., 207

P
Packer, H.L., 80
Palmer, T., 193
Parent, D., 23, 94, 100
Parsimony, normative value, 81
Participants
data, 153
selection of, 106–107
Participation, goal setting, 84–85
Participation in setting, 84–85
Patterson, G., 179
Patton, B., 132*f*
Patton, M.Q., 175
PCL-YV. *See* Psychopathy Checklist-Youth
Version (PCL-YV)
Pealer, J., 162
Performance evaluation (outcome-based
information systems), 176
Petersilia, J., 8, 55*f*, 104–105, 205, 207
Petrosino, A., 7
Philadelphia Drug Treatment Court (program/
policy design), 113
Philadelphia Municipal Court, 113
Pierce, G.L., 97, 186, 188
Piven, F.F., 6–7
Planned change
activist bias, 21–22
change agent, 3
collaborative strategies, 9–10
conflict strategies, 9
definition, 1–2
need for, trends causing
accountability, 7–8
declining resources, 6–7
expansion of knowledge and technology,
8–9
perils of, 9–10
problem-solving model, 10–21

resistance, 9
trends affecting, 6–9
vs. unplanned change, 2–4
Planning deficits, during each stage,
203, 204*f*
Police brutality, conflict strategies, 10
Policy
birth of, 1, 3*f*
definition, 4, 108
designers, 108–112
design of activities for, 16–17
programs distinguished from, 15–16
provisions, 16
Policy and program development and analysis,
4–6
Pontell, H.N., 47, 54
Pope, C.E., 37
Portland (Oregon) Community Court, 68
Pratt, T.C., 8
Pretest-Posttest Design with Control
Group, 186
Pretest-Posttest Design with Multiple
Pretests, 187
Prison-based therapeutic community drug
treatment programs, 19
academic performance, 195
dropout rates, 195
implications, 195–196
problem, program design, and goals,
192–193
research design, 193–194
truancy, 195
Prisoner reentry initiatives, 1, 2*f*, 211
Prisons, privatizations, 87–88
Probation, reparative, 65–66
Problem analysis (stage 1), in seven-stage model
activities, 11–14
boundaries, 33–34
causes of problem
family-oriented theories, 43
levels of, 42–44
organizational theories, 43
social-structural perspectives, 43
sources of information, 44